CULTURE AND HISTORY
1350–1600
Essays on English Communities, Identities and Writing

CULTURE AND HISTORY 1350–1600

Essays on English Communities, Identities and Writing

Edited by
David Aers

WAYNE STATE UNIVERSITY PRESS
DETROIT

U.S. Edition published by
Wayne State University Press
Detroit, Michigan 48202

Typeset in 10/12pt Galliard by
Keyboard Services, Luton

Printed and bound in Great Britain by
BPCC Wheatons Ltd, Exeter

Library of Congress Catalog Card
Number 91–68391

ISBN 0–8143–2415–0 (cloth)
ISBN 0–8143–2416–9 (pbk.)

Contents

Introduction

David Aers

> It may indeed be impossible to recover more than a small
> fraction of the things that Plato, say, was doing in *The Republic*.
> My point is only that the extent to which we can hope to
> understand *The Republic* depends in part on the extent to which
> we can recover them. . . . My first step is thus a generalization
> . . . of Collingwood's dictum to the effect that understanding
> any proposition requires us to identify the question to which
> the proposition may be regarded as an answer. I am claiming,
> that is, that any act of communication always constitutes the
> taking up of some determinate position in relation to some
> pre-existing conversation or argument.[1]

This book explores the making of human identities and agency in
English communities from around 1350 (after the great plague) to
around 1600. It also involves reflections on the processes in which we seek
to understand past cultures and their texts. Absolutely basic to the formation
of any human identity is a fact spelt out by Aristotle and St Thomas Aquinas
but recently articulated by Charles Taylor in the course of his wonderful
study of 'the modern identity':

> one cannot be a self on one's own. I am a self only in relation to certain inter-
> locutors: in one way in relation to those conversation partners who were essential
> to my achieving self-definition; in another in relation to those who are now
> crucial to my continuing grasp of languages and self-understanding – and, of
> course, these classes may overlap. A self exists only within what I call 'webs of
> interlocution'. It is this original situation which gives its sense to our concept of
> 'identity', offering an answer to the question of who I am through a definition of
> where I am speaking from and to whom. The full definition of someone's identity
> thus usually involves not only his stand on moral and spiritual matters but also
> some reference to a defining community.[2]

Or, more often, communities: this, at least, we share in common with the women, men and children of the medieval past we study. The infinitely complex quest is for the 'webs of interlocution' in which medieval identities and their communities were sustained and changed, in which they confronted new circumstances and challenges. This is the quest pursued, in different ways, by these essays: a quest to discover where people spoke from, to whom they spoke, and in response to what questions, difficulties and aspirations. In such a quest nothing could be more mistaken than to abstract the unitary ambitions of certain discourses propagated by social elites and use these prescriptions as adequate descriptions of medieval cultures and communities. As Mervyn James reminded us, pronouncements of 'social wholeness' in late-medieval English towns 'were in historical fact projected by societies which were deeply divided – riven by intense competitiveness: by the struggle for honour and worship, status and precedence, power and wealth'.[3]

Contrary to certain mythologies, medieval societies were never unitary: their communities and the forms of life enabled and cultivated in these different communities formed 'a diversity of intersecting networks of social interaction'. What Michael Mann says of human societies in general applies to those of the Middle Ages: 'The most important of these networks form relatively stably around the four power sources', namely, economic, ideological, political and military, but 'the dynamics of society comes from the myriad social networks that humans set up to pursue their goals'.[4] In Taylor's 'webs of interlocution', in Mann's 'networks of social power', distinct but intersecting medieval communities provided the materials and the forms for different but intersecting and overlapping identities. Some of these, together with continuities and changes between 1350 and 1600, are the subjects of this book.

However various their sources, the contributors to this book share an understanding of languages and human symbols as 'webs of interlocution' which are themselves social actions made by human agents in circumstances that they did not choose but which they nevertheless can, individually and collectively, work to maintain or to challenge, working, of course, within the given material and spiritual resources of specific traditions, communities and social positions. The words, symbols and deeds with which this book is concerned did not take place only in the endless and indefinite referral of signifier to signifier, in a world of gamesome and self-referential textuality. They took place in a world that often proved, as it still does and always will, intractable to many human projects and their textual panoplies, a world that 'can well defy the concepts that are indexed to it', a world in which reference and practical agency puts the systems of sense-making textuality at risk.[5] And such risks could involve not just textual aporia but the risks of individual and collective catastrophe in the real (yes, real) world in which we live and die. Our own century gives us no reason to forget the nature of such risks and their consequences. Perhaps here we should recall, for those besotted with phrases like 'the textuality of all history', what Derrida himself says of a statement in *Of Grammatology* which has become a 'slogan' for some deconstructionists: 'il n'y a pas de hors-texte', he insists, must be understood in a way that 'does not suspend reference – to history, to the world, to reality, to being, and especially to the other'. Furthermore he stresses that there can be no question of accepting all readings of this redefined 'texte' as necessarily of equal legitimacy, no question of dissolving all distinctions between understanding and misunderstanding, while he rejects the familiar alignment of his own deconstruction with relativism and scepticism: 'this definition of deconstruction is *false* (that's right: false, not true) and feeble; it supposes a bad (that's right: bad, not good) and feeble reading of numerous texts, first of all mine'.[6] While the following essays never share the objectivist illusions of pre-critical positivism, long since devastatingly criticised by hermeneutic traditions and by the Frankfurt School, they are equally far removed from those who, under the sign 'Derrida', have denied the very possibility of referentiality to the natural and social worlds, from those who have denied, in principle, any distinction between true and false claims about the worlds human beings inhabit.

Lee Patterson's essay encourages a substantial re-examination of widespread assumptions about the history of self-fashioning and the common assertions about decisive discontinuities in this area between the sixteenth century and the Middle Ages. It invites us to question the strict linearity of the paradigms that shape our thinking about this history. He focuses on the court of Richard II, Sir John Clanvowe's *Book of Cupid* and the way courtly poetry was a social practice inextricably bound up in the self-fashioning of Ricardian courtly males. He shows how such writing was laden with ideological values as a range of pressing political issues was addressed within amatory discourses. Love poetry, we see, became a form in which Ricardian courtiers could interrogate power, patronage and lordship in a 'highly competitive and untrustworthy environment'. Perhaps the situation of Tudor courtiers and poets did not involve the sharp break with medieval culture that it is so often presented as being. The next two essays, by Miri Rubin and Sarah Beckwith, move away from court culture and secular politics, away from the self-fashioning of male identities among the elites. They turn to medieval Christianity, to the most powerful symbol created in medieval culture, a symbol whose great force was known in all medieval communities and experienced in the making of personal and collective identities at all social levels: the eucharist, Corpus Christi. These two essays explore the rich heterogeneity of medieval religion, a heterogeneity disclosed even in its most potent symbol of unity. Whereas for some recent historians the eucharist is a 'social miracle' or the rather passive 'reflection of the social body', here we see the eucharist as a symbol which its users shape in different ways, re-creating and struggling over its meanings in a dynamic and changing web of relationships. In this account we see how theologians and priests always had to negotiate with different voices, different communities and with those whose gender was different from theirs. We see just why and how the eucharist became a polysemous site of contestation, one which contributed, sometimes with terrible violence, to making, excluding and demonising the identity of the Other – Jews, heretics and women. Sarah Beckwith's focus within these eucharistic discourses and practices is on the East Anglian *Croxton Play of the Sacrament*. Her inter-disciplinary reading unpacks the ways this extraordinary play offers us insights into the making of identities and the treatment of major religious anxieties in a region where there were extremely successful mercantile networks, a serious set of conflicts between clerical lordship (the great Benedictine abbey of Bury St Edmunds) and laity, and a marked presence of heretical activity challenging orthodox versions of the Church and orthodox doctrines on the meaning and administration of the eucharist. This essay shows how the play's brilliant and often grotesquely hilarious conversion of dismembered bodies into unity and wholeness in the body of Christ achieves a vision of universal incorporation which nevertheless remains riven with ambiguities which carry the marks of the divided community whose concerns it stages.

Peter Womack's wide-ranging chapter also sets out from the sacred drama of late-medieval towns, but he concentrates on the sixteenth century. He investigates ways in which an officially Protestant culture sought to replace the body of Christ by the imagined community of the English nation. For this, dramatists sought to invent an appropriate symbolic body in the new metropolitan theatres under courtly patronage. His essay analyses the destruction of urban Corpus Christi cycles by political, religious and economic forces in Elizabeth's reign, even as it suggests how the same forces now converged to create a social space in London and a version of the year that offered very different theatrical contexts from those of the Catholic culture they gradually superseded. While Peter Womack discusses John Bale's agitational theatre, his focus is on the commercial theatre of Marlowe and Shakespeare. This was a new institution demanding new ways of representing its constituent communities and their identities: how could the potentially anarchic 'Other', that many-headed monster, be enacted and incorporated within the officially Protestant nation state? Shakespeare's answer, Peter Womack explains, involved the invention of a new communal identity, and the different forms this took are investigated in *King John* and the *Henry VI* plays, an investigation which shows how these works dealt with the social and political tensions and conflicts of the 1590s.

The next chapter considers very different sources and issues. In it Judith Bennett studies accounts of the history of women in English society from the fourteenth to the sixteenth century and in response to these she sets out to analyse continuity and change in women's work in the economy of production. She develops a challenge to the dominant paradigm which has organised most versions of women's history. While these habitually present the medieval period as a relatively 'golden age' from which the seventeenth century is a fall, Judith Bennett suggests on what weak foundations such accounts rest. Her own study of women's work, pay and status in the Middle Ages, together with her study of the inegalitarian distribution of resources within the family and the systematic exclusion of women from the sources of political and ideological power at all levels of both rural and urban communities, offers us a world that cannot be construed as a 'golden' contrast to the fallen early-modern period. Whatever the religious, political and social changes between 1350 and 1600, she argues that these did not transform the experiences of women. Indeed, many features that early modernists treat as innovations, distinguishing their own period of special-isation, she shows to be familiar features of women's lives in English com-munities of the Middle Ages. She finds no good reason to perpetuate a paradigm which is merely an inversion of Burckhardt's.

The book's final chapter also addresses the master narrative Judith Ben-nett challenges, albeit from a very different cluster of materials. This essay is a response to certain tendencies in current writing about 'the history of the subject'. In Britain the most influential proponents of the history in question are critics who may be loosely grouped as Cultural Materialists, while in the USA it frequently appears in the work of various New Historicists. The tendency is to maintain that interiority and the subjectivity to which that belongs emerged in Western culture around the time of Shakespeare. While such a history is by no means the monopoly of radical critics, it turns out to be a very puzzling one. In fact it shows how a powerful, entrenched paradigm can lead critics to pronounce with the greatest confidence broad historical claims which are readily falsifiable. I have tried in this chapter to understand the attractiveness of the history in question to those who propagate and assume it. Here a second meaning of 'the subject' becomes relevant and the book concludes with some brief reflections on the history of that other subject, medieval studies in the formation of modern literary critics.

Notes

1. Q. Skinner, 'A reply to my criticis', in *Meaning and Context: Quentin Skinner and his critics*, ed. J. Tully, Cambridge: Polity Press, 1988, p. 274. Since, as a postgraduate student, I came across his 'Meaning and understanding in the history of ideas', *History and Theory*, **8**, 1969, 3–53 (reprinted in this excellent

collection), I have found Quentin Skinner's unfolding work an unfailingly stimulating reflection on what I take to be basic tasks in seeking to understand the writings and cultures of the past.

2. C. Taylor, *Sources of the Self: The making of modern identity*, Cambridge: Cambridge University Press, 1989, p. 36. In Taylor's text the last two sentences begin a new paragraph. For Aristotle and Aquinas see, respectively, *The Politics*, rev. edn, Harmondsworth: Penguin, 1981, I.2, 1252 b27–1253 a18; *De Regimine Principum*, ed. and trans. A. P. D'Entreves and J. G. Dawson, Oxford: Basil Blackwell, 1965, I.1, *passim* and *ST*, I–II. 72.4 *ibid.*, p. 108.

3. M. James, 'Ritual, drama and social body in the late medieval English towns', *Past and Present*, **98**, 1983, 3–29.

4. The quotations come from M. Mann, *The Sources of Social Power*, Cambridge: Cambridge University Press, 1986, vol. 1, pp. 16 and 19; see similarly p. 506. Medievalists should be especially interested in Chapters 1, 12–14.

5. M. Sahlins, *Islands of History*, Chicago: Chicago University Press, 1985, pp. 145, 149, 156: I have found this book immensely helpful in my own attempts to understand the tasks of historical critics and cultural historians.

6. J. Derrida, 'Afterword: Toward an ethic of discussion', pp. 111–60 in *Limited Inc.*, ed. G. Graff, Evanston IL: Northwestern University Press, 1988; here pp. 136–7, 146. For practices which bear out this line, as opposed to that of so many American literary critical deconstructionists seeking an escape from history and the burdens of referentiality in allegedly joyful and always indeterminate textual play, see 'Racism's last word', *Critical Inquiry*, **12**, 1985, 290–9 and 'But beyond . . .', *Critical Inquiry*, **13**, 1986, 155–70, with its insistence on the 'massively present reality [of apartheid], one which no historian could seriously put in question'. Whether this Derrida is, as he himself maintains, compatible with the Derrida of 'Structure, sign and play' (in *The Languages of Criticism and the Sciences of Man*, ed. R. Macksey and E. Donato, Baltimore MD: Johns Hopkins University Press, 1970) and 'Signature event context', *Glyph*, **1**, 1977, 172–97 (reprinted in *Limited Inc.*, ed. Graff), must be left to Derridologists to debate.

Court Politics and the Invention of Literature: The Case of Sir John Clanvowe

Lee Patterson

> The language of poetry naturally falls in with the language of power. . . . The principle of poetry is a very anti-levelling principle. . . . Poetry is right royal. It puts the individual before the species, the one above the infinite many, might before right.[1]

Hazlitt's disillusioned comments on the politics of poetry – comments prompted by what he feared were the anti-democratic attitudes of his beloved Shakespeare – express a common embarrassment. So many poets are so politically incorrect that to admit one's interest virtually amounts to self-conviction as a reactionary – unless, of course, one chooses to convict the poet instead. For medievalists the situation is if anything worse. Having chosen to immure ourselves in the distant past, does not our wilful irrelevance make us automatically guilty? Indeed, the recent resurfacing of political concerns in medieval studies seems to represent an attempt at political rehabilitation in two senses: not only do we wish to show that the issues that animate other members of the professorate concern us as well, but in finding even medieval literature political we show that we are *hyper*-political ourselves.

The irony in all this, of course, is that the Middle Ages has been, ever since its invention as an object of scholarly study in the seventeenth century, one of the most highly politicised sites of historical knowledge. This was especially the case during the formative period of the nineteenth century:

7

since the Middle Ages was understood to be the time when European
civilisation most became itself, medievalists were responsible for discover-
ing the true political and cultural character of their various national states.
Hence their work was invested with immense political value: a vivid example
is Fustel de Coulanges's claim that the Germans won in 1871 because they
understood the Middle Ages better than the French.[2] Not, of course, that
there was *a* Middle Ages. Always at issue was what Gaston Paris called the
'double manner of understanding the Middle Ages'. Was it the golden age
of the monarchy, the nobility and the Church (as the Ultramontane Léon
Gautier asserted), or the source of 'modern freedoms, municipal independence, and the control of government by the people' (as the liberal Paris
himself preferred to think)?[3] And in literary terms, the argument was
whether the essence of the national literature was martial and pious (i.e.
aristocratic) or realistic and satiric (i.e. bourgeois). Were its origins to be
found among the nobility or lower down the social scale?

The political temperature of English studies has generally been lower
than across the Channel, but these debates have none the less left their mark
on our scholarly enterprise. Even today, and even in America, there are two
Chaucers that roughly correspond to Gaston Paris's two Middle Ages. In a
book published in 1986, Paul Olson presented Chaucer as a courtier-poet
serving 'a royal government in quest of social order', and the *Canterbury
Tales* as a 'poetic commentary on the state of the commonwealth' that
expresses the views of that government.[4] Not surprisingly, Olson's Chaucer
is a didactic allegorist whose poems speak a single, unvarying message of
moral and social governance. On the other hand, Paul Strohm's *Social
Chaucer*, published in 1989, presents a poet socially 'at large within the
turbulent and ill-defined middle ranks of society', 'middle strata' that bespeak
the new social possibilities available in late-fourteenth-century England.
And this location enables what Strohm calls the 'tonal variation' of
Chaucer's poetry, his 'mixture of styles and tones of voice', his ability to
'entertain different perspectives and tolerate a high degree of contradiction
between them', and his exploitation of 'mixed perspectives and open forms',
'abrupt shifts in direction and tone' and 'an urbanely impartial attitude'.[5]

My purpose in this essay is not to adjudicate between these two accounts
but instead to challenge their shared, unspoken assumption. For Olson
Chaucer's ideological commitment to the court entails a poetry of didactic
straightforwardness; for Strohm, since Chaucer's poetry is complex and
subtle he must be located within the 'middle strata' instead of within an ideologically narrow court. For both critics, in other words, the court cannot be
the site of the kind of formally intricate and thematically complex writing
that we now take literature to be. For Olson, Chaucer's location in the court
entails ideological commitment; for Strohm, Chaucer's ideologically un-
committed writing entails a location outside the court. I want to suggest,

however, that while Strohm is right in thinking that Chaucer's poetry is complex, subtle and eschews explicit ideological commitment, Olson is also right in thinking of him as a court poet. In other words, I want to propose that the court is indeed a site where literature is produced, that it is even the most important of such sites in the crucial period of the late fourteenth century, when a vernacular literary tradition was in the process of self-conscious formation. For I believe that Hazlitt was right when he said that 'the language of poetry naturally falls in with the language of power'. But it is also a language whose final allegiances can never be predicted.

The focus of my argument, however, is not upon Chaucer himself. Although Chaucer's way of writing was formed from within the court and largely reflected its interests, he also regarded it as a historical origin to be transcended. In the *House of Fame*, for example, he presents a trenchant commentary on both the vagaries of service in the prince's court and its effect on literary ambition; and the *Legend of Good Women*, both in its Prologue and in the individual Legends, groans under the harsh demands of an insensitive monarch and the burden of both political and cultural authority. Under the influence of the Italian humanists, and especially Dante, Chaucer aspired to a view of the poet as speaking not to local but universal values: this is the meaning, for example, of the passage at the end of *Troilus and Criseyde*, derived from *Inferno* 4, where he instructs his poem to kiss the footsteps of Homer, Virgil, Ovid, Lucan and Statius. As A. C. Spearing has said, Chaucer was 'the father of English poetry in the sense that before him there was no such thing as an *idea* of English poetry', an idea derived in large part from *trecento* Italy.[6] In other words, he shares with the humanist tradition – the tradition in which Strohm writes – the belief that historical contingencies such as the court preclude the production of literature.

Such ambitions were not visible, however, in the writing of the fully-fledged courtier-poet Sir John Clanvowe. Clanvowe was a chamber knight in the household of Richard II, one of the so-called 'Lollard knights', and a member of what has come to be called Chaucer's circle.[7] Almost exactly the same age as Chaucer (both were born in the early 1340s), he was both a friend and literary colleague.[8] Two works have been ascribed to him: a religious treatise called *The Two Ways* and a poem, until the end of the nineteenth century thought to have been written by Chaucer and known as *The Cuckoo and the Nightingale*, but now accurately entitled *The Boke of Cupide* and correctly, I believe, ascribed to Clanvowe. This poem must have been written in the late 1380s or early 1390s: it alludes to the *Knight's Tale* and the Prologue to the *Legend of Good Women*, both written in the late '80s, and Clanvowe died in 1391. The poem is a dream vision that recounts a debate between a cuckoo and a nightingale about the nature of love. The nightingale naturally promotes unswerving amorous devotion, the cuckoo a blunt scepticism, and although the cuckoo seems to win the debate – at least he leaves the nightingale speechless – the confrontation ends inconclusively: the cuckoo is driven off, but when the nightingale asks the other birds for reparation they refuse to act, deciding instead to hold a parliament the following St Valentine's Day to consider the case. The poem as a whole itself then ends with the nightingale singing a lyric – we are given only the first line, 'Terme of lyve, love hath withholde me' – that awakens the narrator.[9]

The poem used to be much admired – Milton imitated it and Wordsworth translated it – although now that it has fallen out of the Chaucer canon it is apparently little read, or at least little written about.[10] Gervase Mathew called it 'clearly a court poem' – a poem specifically 'of the court' rather than a 'courtly' poem expressing aristocratic values in general.[11] It is an elegant and witty instance of court *makyng*, a poem that argues about love in order to provoke amorous conversation among the knights and ladies of the court. Hence recent critics have called the poem 'a courtier's frippery', a poem composed to provide 'intellectual and social diversion and amorous dalliance among a minuscule elite group', in the words of Rossell Hope Robbins, and therefore bearing 'little relation to reality'.[12] But of course the court is as real as anything else, and in the late fourteenth century it had itself become, as we shall see, a major political issue. Moreover, the self-designation of court poetry as mere entertainment, far from precluding relevance, may well enable it: triviality can be used to represent reality as well as escape from it.

The lyric line that concludes the poem provides an instance: 'Terme of lyve, love hath withholde me' (289). Read as a courtly dictum, this line means simply that the nightingale has wholly committed herself to love. But it also bears a topical political sense. In Middle English to 'withhold' someone means to retain them: it is the term used in the indentures of retaining that began to be written in English just after this time.[13] Hence the line should be translated, 'I have been retained for life by love'. Now it can hardly be a coincidence that it was at just this time – beginning, that is, in 1389 – that Richard began to indulge, systematically and extensively, in life retaining.[14] The nightingale's service to the God of Love is thus not merely metaphoric but defined by a specific form of indenture, and the poem is asking questions about lordship and service that seem to have a topical relevance.

In fact, the poem can be read as a kind of political allegory. It opens by citing Chaucer's *Knight's Tale*, where Theseus comments on Cupid's power – 'The god of love, a! benedicite, / How myghty and how grete a lorde is he!' (1–2) – power that Clanvowe represents as utterly unrestricted: 'al that euere he wol he may, / Ayenst him ther dar no wight say nay' (16–17).[15] Moreover, the nightingale is not only 'loves seruaunt' (148, 159) in a conventional sense but a creature whose very being derives from Cupid. He provides the terms in which her identity is defined, the conditions of her existence, the structure of value by which she understands the world: 'in that beleve I wol bothe lyve and dye' (162). Service to this God requires not merely one's loyalty but one's selfhood: 'He that truly loues seruaunt ys,/Were lother to be schamed than to dye' (159–60). And to be the servant of this lord precludes any alternative: 'For who that wol the god of love not serve,/I dar wel say he is worthy for to sterve' (133–4).

But this conception of love's power, defined by the narrator and promoted by the nightingale, is challenged and finally subverted in the course of the poem. For one thing, the opening citation from the *Knight's Tale* contains a hidden critique, since Theseus's words were in their original context ironic: he was mocking the ferocity with which the young lovers Arcite and Palamon fight over a lady who is unaware of their very existence, much less their love.[16] Second, and more important, throughout the debate the cuckoo attacks the legitimacy of Cupid's authority. For him Cupid is nothing but a tyrant – 'love hath no reason but his wille' (197) – and his court is correspondingly capricious: 'In this court ful selde trouthe avayleth,/So dyuerse and so wilful ys he' (204–5). This critique invokes the standard medieval definition – prominent throughout the Middle Ages – of the tyrant as a figure of angry self-indulgence, a ruler who abrogates the rule of law in favour of the 'illegal power of his will', to cite one of the articles of Richard's deposition.[17] And when the nightingale defends Love as a lord who rewards the man 'whom him likes' (195), for the cuckoo, as for medieval political thought in general, this is not only no defence at all but a profound indictment. This is also an indictment that speaks to the condition of Ricardian kingship, and in a language familiar in contemporary poetry. For if, as is generally accepted, Alceste's cautionary injunctions to the God of Love in the Prologue to the *Legend of Good Women* comment on Richard's tendency to what Chaucer calls 'wilfulhed and tyrannye' (G, 355); and if John Gower's revision of the *Confessio amantis* bespeaks his awareness that Richard is less the benevolent Cupid who presides over his parliament of lovers in Book 8 of the *Confessio* than the tyrant whom he was to excoriate in the *Chronica tripertita*; then surely Clanvowe's wilful Cupid is another commentary on Ricardian kingship.

Oddly enough, however, the poem presents its dictatorial Cupid as strangely ineffective, as an impotent tyrant. In part Clanvowe again makes his point by means of Chaucerian allusion. It is on 'the thirde nyght of May' (55) that his narrator goes forth to perform his love service, the same date on which Palamon escaped from prison (I, 1463) and met Arcite in the grove where he too was performing love service. And again there is a battle: after the nightingale is reduced to tears, she begs the God of Love to come to her aid and is rescued by the narrator himself, who drives the cuckoo off by throwing stones at him, thus reducing the heroic combat of the *Knight's Tale* to comic contretemps. Not only does Cupid decline to help his loyal servant, but when the nightingale asks the other birds to 'do me ryght/Of that foule, fals, vnkynde bridde' (270), they also demur by insisting upon holding a parliament at which the cuckoo can defend himself, and to which must be summoned the eagle 'our lorde' and the 'other perys that ben of recorde' (276–7). Only at this parliament, to be held on St Valentine's Day at Woodstock before the Queen's chamber window, 'shall be yeven the iugement,/Or elles we shul make summe acorde' (279–80). In effect, then, Cupid disappears from the poem as a figure of authority, replaced by a parliament constituted by carefully prescribed procedures and uncertain in its outcome, and held, moreover, before the Queen but with neither her authority nor participation – a gesture that not only excludes the King but limits the role of royalty per se in parliamentary deliberations. Clanvowe's Cupid, then, is less the all-seeing sun god before whom Chaucer quakes in the Prologue to the *Legend of Good Women* than a *deus absconditus* whose servants must rely upon a stone-throwing buffoon for defence and turn to an independent and uncertain parliament for justice. This ineffectiveness gives special point, then, to the nightingale's concluding song: 'Terme of lyve, love hath withholde me' (289). A life retainer, she has learned in the course of the poem a bitter lesson about the unreliability of her lord. Clanvowe is thus saying two, not entirely consistent things: on the one hand, the God of Love's tyranny is rightly castigated by sceptics and wisely restrained by parliament; but on the other, he is unable to protect those upon whom his authority rests and who most nearly feel the pressure of his ambition. His power is both excessive and inadequate, his aspirations at once illegitimate and disappointingly ineffective.

It is tempting to explain this contradiction in terms of Clanvowe's biography. Clanvowe first entered royal service in 1373 as a knight of the household of Edward III, and he was inherited by Richard upon his accession to the throne in 1377. Later Richard included him among the 'new group of chamber knights, clearly men of the king's own choice', who were installed in 1381.[18] Throughout his career in the royal household he participated in military campaigns, including Richard's Scottish expedition in 1385, and he performed the usual diplomatic and administrative services typical of his rank. But probably because he was a generation older than the king he never became one of his favourites, and in 1388, although he was dismissed from the household by the Lords Appellant, he avoided more severe punishment.[19] The following year he returned to the household upon Richard's reassumption of power, but in 1390 he and his friend William Neville apparently obtained permission to join the Duke of Bourbon's crusade against Tunis. Then in 1391 they both died in Constantinople, probably while on pilgrimage. Walsingham included Clanvowe as one of the so-called Lollard knights in the royal household, and it seems clear that he and the men with whom he associated shared the purist, biblicist piety that was widespread in the late fourteenth century and that the Lollards developed into a full-blown, theologically sophisticated heresy.[20] This was not, however, a religious style much favoured by the king, who was drawn to more established forms of piety: even the anti-royalist Walsingham praised Richard for his defence of the faith, and the king's religious preferences are perhaps best shown by his patronage of Carthusian monasticism.[21]

Given this history, it is not unreasonable to see Clanvowe as being in a complex, even conflicted relation to the court, both at its centre but also somewhat detached. He had witnessed Richard's incipient tyranny in the period 1382–6 and its chastening by the Lords Appellant working through Parliament in 1386 and 1388. And while he did not himself suffer greatly in 1388, many of his colleagues did. His enlistment in the crusade of 1390, and then in the pilgrimage of 1391, perhaps bespeaks a desire to distance himself from a court in which he had lost faith. If we are to read the *Boke of Cupide* at the level of conscious intention and topical relevance, then, it is perhaps best to see it as at once a critique of Richard's tyranny and a lament for Clanvowe's stalled career, as at once satire and complaint.

But topical decoding can hardly encompass the full political meaning of Clanvowe's poem. Court poetry, after all, is not merely a kind of writing but also a social practice, and one laden with ideological value. Literary historians have rightly insisted on the instrumental, pragmatic nature of court poetry, its role as part of the 'courtly conversation' with which the court entertained itself.[22] But if this writing entertained court servants, it also trained them: it provided what *la belle dame sans merci* called a 'school' of 'fayr langage', teaching its students, in Christine de Pizan's wonderful phrase, to 'parler mignot'.[23] From the time of its medieval beginnings in the eleventh century, courtliness had always made verbal facility a central value: *facetus* is virtually a synonym for *curialis*, and it means both 'elegant' and 'clever', both 'refined' and 'witty'.[24] According to another medieval definition, a man who is *facetus* is one who can get what he wants out of words, whether it be a subtle meaning or a desired effect.[25] And if to be courtly is to be adroit with words, the riddles, acrostics, *jeux partis* and *demandes d'amour* that are preserved, either intact or in allusion, are evidence of the assiduity with which this talent was practised and displayed.[26] According to Thomas Usk, a sergeant-of-arms in Richard's court, Love teaches her servants 'to endyten letters of rethorike in queynt understondinges'.[27]

As Usk's phrasing suggests, a correlative courtly talent is the capacity to interpret, to read with understanding the elegantly metaphoric and topically allusive language of the court poem. In the *Prison amoureuse*, for example,

Froissart explains that a courtly poem is 'a gloss of something which cannot or must not be openly stated'.[28] In the *Livre messire Ode*, written by Oton de Grandson while at the Ricardian court in the 1370s and '80s, the narrator overhears a lover grieving for the loss of his sparrowhawk but fails to understand that he is speaking 'par poetrie' and really means his lady.[29] And in the *Book of the Duchess* Chaucer had already used the same device but had laid bare the social meaning it contains: his narrator's inability to understand the Black Knight's metaphor of the chess game is a function of his lower social status. It is this interpretive alertness, even suspicion, that led Puttenham in the sixteenth century to call the trope of allegory – 'which is when we speake one thing and thinke another' – 'the Courtly figure', one known not only to 'euery common Courtier, but also [to] the grauest Counsellour'.[30]

As literary historians have shown, court writing was in no sense the preserve of a special group of professional poets.[31] The demise of the minstrel in the late fourteenth century represents not merely the shift from one kind of taste to another but the *de*professionalisation of writing per se. No longer was literary activity confined to a particular group of specially trained men but became instead the preserve of the court as a whole. Hence the fact that not only does none of the large number of documents that record Chaucer's career refer to him as a writer, but that his career was probably not advanced by his literary activity.[32] To have acknowledged that Chaucer could do something special that other members of the court could not would have been to undermine the socially legitimising function of courtly *makyng*. According to Deschamps's *Art de dictier*, there are two kinds of music: a 'musique artificiele' played on instruments by 'le plus rude homme du mond', and a 'musique naturele', the harmony of verse ('une musique de bouche en proferant paroules metrifiées') inspired by the 'amorous desire to praise ladies' that inhabits gentle hearts.[33] In fact, a great many courtiers did write poetry: we have the names and some of the poems of over a dozen noble *makers* from late-medieval England, as well as the rather bizarre fact that Richard II wanted his epitaph to compare him to Homer.[34] Indeed, one of the tasks of the professional poet (if the title be admitted at all) was to collaborate with the patron in the production of the courtly text. Froissart's *Prison amoureuse*, for instance, records the way in which the poet instructed his patron, Wenceslas of Brabant, in the art of making, and both this text and the later *Méliador* contain poems by both authors.[35] The same is true of Machaut's *Fonteinne amoureuse*, which describes the departure of Jean, Duc de Berri into exile and incorporates several of the Duc's laments. Indeed, it is not impossible that in Chaucer's *Book of the Duchess* the rather inept lyrics ascribed to the grieving Black Knight were really written by John of Gaunt, to whom the poem was dedicated.

This expansion of literariness to include the court as a whole also helps to account for a pronounced generic shift in the literary system of fourteenth-century England. Romances and histories, almost entirely in prose, continued to be copied and read, as library lists and manuscript survivals demonstrate. But the literature of fashion produced within the court – excluding, that is, works of instruction – was almost exclusively lyric. This category includes not only lyrics per se, the many 'compleyntis, baladis, roundelis, virelais' that Lydgate ascribed to Chaucer and that must have been written by other courtly versifiers in the hundreds, but also the new genre of the *dits amoureux* produced by Machaut and Froissart.[36] For all their apparently narrative form, these works are in fact sets of lyric performances enclosed within a narrative frame: they provide lyrics with a context that is, in their usual, free-standing state, only implied. The *Book of the Duchess*, largely derived from the *dits amoureux*, is the first poem to transfer this form into English; and while there are no Chaucerian poems that fully replicate the French paradigm, we can recognise in the roundel of the *Parliament of Fowls*, in the complaint of *Anelida and Arcite*, in the balade of the Prologue to the *Legend of Good Women*, and above all in the many lyric moments, both celebratory and lamenting, of *Troilus and Criseyde*, the overwhelming pressure of the lyric impulse.[37] We also recognise it in the *Boke of Cupide*, in the nightingale's lyric outburst in defence of love (149–62), a song appreciated even by the cuckoo: 'thou spekest wonder faire' (166), he admits.

This privileging of lyricism not only encourages the production of the small-scale, intricately wrought verse that best displays the verbal talents courtliness admires, but also reminds us that court poetry is part of the aestheticisation of life to which late-medieval court culture as a whole was dedicated. Just as cuisine transforms food into art, just as haute couture transforms the body into a visual display, so court poetry transforms language and feeling into the elegant artifice of lyric. The court poet must balance, in the words of Daniel Poirion, 'le désordre de la passion et l'ordre de la parole'.[38] On the one hand he languishes in sorrow, fearful of madness ('ʒe haue broken þe balance / Of my resoun', says one poet) and brought by 'cruell peyne' to the point of death: 'I dee! I dee! so thrillith me that thorne!' Yet he is also the artist who crafts these feelings into a beautiful artefact: these lines are spoken by a female narrator in a poem that is in fact written by a man, and written in order 'to Obey [the] hie commaundement' of an unnamed princess: in the epilogue the poem is revealed to be a precious offering.[39] As French literary historians especially have insisted, court poetry is a 'jeu des formes', aspiring to pure aestheticism and seeking to create a cultural *hortus conclusus* where the aristocratic 'culte égocentrique' can find a fulfilment impossible in the difficult historical world of the late Middle Ages.[40]

But it is also more than this. For we must never forget that court poetry is also part of that world, a social practice designed to construct the courtier.

The court is what Brian Stock has called a 'textual community', a 'micro-society organized around the common understanding of a script'.[41] The court lyric provides a paradigm not merely for behaviour but for an internalised ethics: it allows specific structures of feeling to be experienced as rational and appropriate. Certainly lyricism is privileged because it is the literary form that best allows for the theatricalisation of the courtly self. But perhaps more important, it also provides a way to discipline as well as to construct the aspiring courtier. It creates 'rhetorical man' from the inside as well as from without.[42]

The notion of the courtier as a self-made man, constructed by social practices specific to the court, has particular force in Ricardian England. Already in the latter years of Edward III, the business of government had become increasingly concentrated in the king's household, and especially in the *camera regis* into which the doting monarch withdrew.[43] The court also became less itinerant, confining its movement to a small area around London. In 1376 Parliament responded by banishing from court not only the hated Alice Perrers but those courtiers who, in the words of Peter de la Mare, the Speaker of the Commons, 'scoff and mock, and work for their own profit', an appropriate description of men well practised in courtly *facetiae*.[44] Many of these men, moreover, came from very humble backgrounds, and included a group of merchants whom the peers would certainly not have considered to be of gentle status.[45] But this housecleaning could not solve the problem in the long term. When the young Richard came into authority in the early 1380s, he also surrounded himself with *familiarissimi* and allowed the household to function not as 'the focus of the aristocratic community' as a whole but as his *privata familia*.[46] Moreover, Richard's development of the court as an exclusive society wholly dedicated to the fulfilment of the wishes of the king was not simply a matter of personal style. It was also part of a political programme aimed at dispossessing the traditional ruling class of England and replacing it with a courtier nobility created by Richard and located largely in the household.[47]

Not surprisingly, then, throughout the 1380s attacks continued to be made upon the court: in 1380, in 1381 (when Parliament complained about both evil counsellors and the 'outrageouses nombre des Familiers esteantz en l'hostiel'), in 1386–7, and finally, and with bloody consequences, in 1388.[48] At issue were questions of policy, of course, and especially the war with France, which Richard sought to resolve but which most of the nobility were eager to continue. But more important was the king's attitude towards both the nobility, the peerage that he excluded from his councils, and towards the very idea of nobility itself. It was bad enough that Richard banished from his councils those who thought it their right to be there, replacing them with men – and mostly very young men – whom he found personally congenial: John Beauchamp, Simon Burley, Michael de la

Pole, and, above all, Robert de Vere (as the nightingale says of the God of Love, he rewards 'whom him likes' [195]). But what was worse was Richard's degradation of the very idea of nobility. For he persistently violated the traditional link between land and status upon which noble identity had traditionally rested. When the Earl of Buckingham was created Duke of Gloucester in 1385 he was given not the land needed to support his dignity but simply an annuity; and when John Beauchamp was created Baron Kidderminster the title was conferred as a personal honour, that is, without a barony – an event unprecedented in English history. Richard's creation of a courtier nobility thus offended a central principle of aristocratic identity: he defined it according to the ideology of courtliness rather than the economic and political realities the nobility held dear. When in 1385 he created de la Pole Earl of Suffolk, he said in the patent of creation that 'we believe that the more we bestow honours on wise and honourable men, the more our crown is adorned with gems and precious stones'. As Anthony Tuck comments,

> The aristocracy, in Richard's view, existed to shed lustre on the crown, and the practical implication of this view is that the titled nobility do not need any independent territorial standing or any great wealth or military reputation to justify their ennoblement: title depended upon royal favour, and upon the particular noble's relationship with the crown.[49]

For Richard the nobility was not an independent body with its own political rights but simply an embodiment of the king's magnificence, its titles dependent on his will.

By concentrating the power of government in the court, Richard was able to give free play to his absolutist impulses. Much has been written about Richard's sense of his own supremacy: he not only entitled himself 'entier emperour de son roiaulme' but also sought to become Holy Roman Emperor, an enterprise in which the Wilton Diptych, with its startling analogy between the court of Heaven and Richard's earthly court, perhaps played a role.[50] The elaborate public ceremonies and devices of which he was fond seem to have had a counterpart in a highly developed court ritual.[51] Richard had a keen sense of the honour due the king, and the magnificence of the court – both its physical environment, on which Richard lavished huge sums of money, and its elaborate ceremonial – played a major role in promoting his sovereignty.[52] This fact was not lost on contemporaries. In 1395 Roger Dymmok's attack on the Lollards, dedicated to Richard, included a detailed defence of the *magnificentia* of the royal court against its critics: he addressed the king as Royal Magnificence and argued that sumptuous display was an appropriate demonstration of power.[53] As Patricia Eberle has said, Richard was 'the first English king to cultivate magnificence in the style of his court, self-consciously and on principle, as a means of enforcing his autocratic rule'.[54] Not just his famous and much-hated white hart livery, but court fashion per se, indeed fashionableness itself, became an expression of Richard's political programme.

Richard's fetishising of the court was a way of not merely promoting himself to others but reaffirming to himself his sense of his unbridled authority. In the royal household, as in noble households generally, the authority of the *paterfamilias* was unquestioned.[55] For Richard, the absolute dominion he exerted over the court was no doubt a model for the kind of governance he wished to impose upon the nation as a whole. We have, in fact, a striking account of Richard's manner of holding court. On feast days

> he leet ordeyne and make in his chambir a trone, wherynne he was wont to sitte fro aftir mete vnto euensong tyme, spekynge to no man, but ouerlokying alle menn; and yf he loked on eny mann, what astat or degre that evir he were of, he moste knele.[56]

The chronicle source of this passage dates this behaviour in 1398, at the very end of Richard's reign; but in the F-Prologue to the *Legend of Good Women*, written a decade earlier, Chaucer's account of the angry gaze of the sunlike God of Love implies a characteristic Ricardian style: 'his face shoon so bryghte/That wel unnethes myght I hym beholde', says the poet, while Love himself 'sternely on me . . . gan beholde,/So that his loking dooth myn herte colde' (232–3, 239–40). Richard's anger and imperious bearing were much commented upon by contemporaries, and historians have seen them as psychological analogues, if not causes, of his political programme.[57]

For the nobility, the aristocratic lifestyle was above all martial and chivalric, a conservative self-understanding that had been reinforced by the years of war with France.[58] Now the king wanted to end that war, and was simul-taneously promoting a lifestyle that celebrated elegance of dress, subtlety of speech, and sophisticated and perhaps indelicate forms of recreation, innova-tions that were by no means fully consistent with more traditional con-ceptions of chivalric virtue. This was a lifestyle, moreover, that was above all dedicated to the idea of *fashion*, which privileged a self-chosen elite of new men who were naturally more concerned with surfaces and manners – the 'newe gyse' – than with a substance they themselves lacked.[59] If, as Norbert Elias has argued, the civilising process is marked by the transformation of a warrior into a courtier nobility, then late-fourteenth-century England pro-vided a particularly intense, if short-lived moment of struggle.[60]

Not surprisingly, then, the Ricardian court and its values were burn-ing issues among contemporaries: as Eberle has rightly argued, the late fourteenth century saw a politics of courtly style. Of course Richard's courtiers were attacked for their elaborate clothing, a target that was only a metonymy for larger concerns. But there was also a continual criticism of the courtly style of speech. One thinks here of Walsingham's famous attack on Richard's courtiers as 'knights of Venus rather than knights of Bellona, more valiant in the bedchamber than on the field, *armed with words rather than weapons, prompt in speaking but slow in performing the acts of war*'.[61] There are recurring complaints that Richard surrounded himself with young men who misled him with what one chronicler called their *laciuiis verbis*.[62] Gower inveighed against 'the bland words of the cunning' men who were misleading Richard, clever courtiers who were so young as not to realise how culpable were their *facetiae*: 'To boys, it is not wrongdoing but joking, not dishonor but glorious sport.'[63] According to another poet, court games are in fact conspiratorial plots: 'Whan falshed lawheþ, he forgeþ gyle;/Half in malice is his play'.[64] And in the blunt words of yet another poet, 'Falshede is called a *sotilte*/And such a nome hit haþ hent': the word *sotilte* seems here to refer to court games and theatricals.[65]

The problem of truth-telling at court is an habitual topic of discussion in court texts. The court is a dangerous place – in the words of one poem, 'Thow wenyst he be thy frend; he is thy foo certeyne' – so 'Whate euer thow sey,/A-vyse the well'.[66] Even the lover's song must be carefully guarded: 'whan thou . . . criest like a nightingale', advises another poem, 'Be ware to whom thou tellest thy tale'.[67] Given these anxieties, courteous speech is on occasion defined not as periphrastic or ornamental but as succinct: let your language be 'curteis et brief', advises one Anglo-Norman poem, two terms that are usually antithetical.[68] There is much advice in court literature on sage speaking, with attacks on obscure or ambiguous speech, on mocking and joking, on the *facetiae* that in other contexts are the courtier's stock in trade: here the ideal seems to be the discourse of Chaucer's Clerk, 'short and quyk and ful of hy sentence' (I, 306).[69] And there is also praise for the man who will risk the wrath of the prince to tell the truth directly.[70] For truth-telling at court is a dangerous activity – 'who say soth he shal be shent' becomes a proverbial phrase in the late fourteenth century. 'I kan & kan nauȝt of court speke moore,' says Langland nervously.[71]

Moreover, the truth-teller cannot get a hearing in such a world, for his true words will not even be understood. For the author of *Mum and the Soothsegger*, the crafty Mum is 'right worldly wise of wordes', while the Soothsegger 'can not speke in termes ne in tyme nother,/But bablith fourth bustusely ass barn vn-y-lerid'.[72] Unable to speak the discourse of the court, the Soothsegger can find no audience for his 'trewe tales'.[73] And his exclusion is graphically illustrated in the alliterative style of the poem itself, with its distinctly unmetropolitan, non-royal provenance. The same understanding is present in another alliterative poem, *Sir Gawain and the Green Knight*, which is structured by the relationship between a royal and provincial courts. It may even be that the representation of the 'childgered' Arthur, 'bisied [by] his ȝonge blod and his brayn wylde', and presiding over an elegantly gamesome court, is meant to reflect Richard. But whether the poem has this topical relevance or not, it is clear that its central social opposition is between monarch and nobleman, metropolis and hinterland.[74] Also clear is the direction of the critique: far from being in need of instruction in courtesy, Bertilak's court reveals an effortless command of the intricacies of court behaviour, especially the 'luf-talkyng' of which Gawain, 'þat fyne fader of nurture', is supposed to be the master. Indeed, not only does the lady battle Gawain to a standstill in their 'dalyaunce of . . . derne wordez' (1012), but she becomes the agent who reveals the superficiality of Gawain's understanding of the meaning of games, and specifically of the 'Crystemas gomen' (283) with the Green Knight to which he has committed himself. From this perspective, the poem's message is not only that the provincial court is as well versed in fashionable behaviour as the Arthurian court, and not only that it maintains a warrior ethos (visible in Bertilak's hunting) that the Arthurian court has evidently lost, but that it actually understands the meaning of court practices more profoundly than the royal court that thinks itself to be the centre of fashion. For the poem reveals both the connection between games and 'trawþe' and the full meaning of 'cortaysye', a term that is here, as in *Pearl* and *Cleanness*, expanded to incorporate large ethical and spiritual meanings.[75] Finally, this kind of poem fits well with its origins in the Cheshire–Shropshire region of northwest England. For this was an area that had very close relations with the crown – Cheshire was a palatinate county with which Richard had a special relation at least as early as 1385 – and yet that remained fiercely independent and enthusiastically in support of a war that Richard sought to end, an enthusiasm that actually generated several armed uprisings in the 1390s.[76]

The point is that *Mum and the Soothsegger* and *Sir Gawain and the Green Knight*, poems that are at once well informed and yet critical of court values, focus much of their attention on the verbal practices current in the court. Because the Soothsegger cannot speak in 'termes' his advice is not heeded; and while Gawain knows 'the teccheles termes of talkyng noble' (917), not only is his proficiency less absolute than he assumes but he does not even know what the terms really mean. Both poems present the court as a place where people have a special way with words, perhaps even speak a special dialect (one courtesy book calls it 'cointise').[77] But while this facility may confirm their sense of social superiority, it alienates them both from the nation as a whole and from deeper, more permanent values.

The relevance of this context to the *Boke of Cupide* is twofold. For one thing, the poem explores with particular acuity the practice of courtly self-fabrication, the way in which courtier identity is socially constructed rather than, as aristocratic ideology requires, naturally given. This topic is staged in the role assigned to Clanvowe's narrator. He is on the one hand a typical instance of the long-suffering lover, catching a love sickness in May – 'Bothe hote and colde, an accesse every day' (39) – and assiduously performing his love service. Yet he is also 'olde and vnlusty', a dissonance that should be read neither biographically nor comically but socially, as a statement about the stresses of self-fashioning. For his devotions are performed in a way that is unmistakably mechanical. He says he cannot sleep because of the 'feueres white' that assail him, yet adds that 'hit is vnlyke to me / That eny herte shulde slepy be, / In whom that love his firy dart wol smyte' (41–5): he is awake because he knows it would be inappropriate for a true lover to sleep.[78] So too, his love service is to go into the woods to hear the nightingale before the cuckoo: he does this because he has heard the 'comvn tale' (48) that this signals good fortune. His behaviour, in other words, is that which is required of one who would be known as a lover.

A sense of the theatricality of his performance, its quality as learned rather than instinctive behaviour, is also implied by two Chaucerian echoes. The initial action of the poem is organised according to the pattern established by Chaucer's narrator in the F-Prologue to the *Legend of Good Women*. As in the F-Prologue, the narrator of the *Boke of Cupide* starts by entering a green meadow 'poudred with daysye': 'Al grene and whit, was no thing elles sene'.[79] And he too hears a harmonious birdsong, a 'foules ermonye' sung by birds who have chosen mates 'vponn seynt Valentynes day' (83, 80): in the F-Prologue the birds sing 'alle of oon acord' in honour of 'Seynt Valentyne' (130–70).[80] But in the F-Prologue the narrator's love service – his passionate worship of the daisy – is both 'constreyned' by 'gledy desir' (105), a 'fir' he continues to feel even while writing the poem (106), and is set in opposition not only to the books he abandons every May but to a court that ritualises such passion into the cult of flower and leaf. In the course of the poem the intensity of the narrator's feelings is subdued to the demands of court poetry, demands that are made explicit in the subsequent dream and that the poem as a whole, with its repeated legends of sub-ordination and constraint, enacts. But in the *Boke of Cupide* this dialectic is reversed: it is the waking love service that confirms the authority of cultic forms of behaviour, while the dream, much to the narrator's consternation, puts this authority into question. What we have, then, is not the disciplining of a potentially rebellious court servant, as in the F-Prologue, but the reluctant recognition by a court servant that he has laboriously rendered service to a lord much less powerful than he had first thought.[81]

The other Chaucerian allusion that can help us understand Clanvowe's narrator has a similar effect. It is when he has fallen into 'a slombre and a swowe, / Not al on slepe, ne fully wakynge' (87–8), that Clanvowe's narrator hears, to his dismay, not the nightingale but 'that sory bridde, the lewede cukkowe' (90). This narrative configuration derives from Book 2 of *Troilus and Criseyde*: 'on Mayes day the thrydde' (56) – the same day on which Clanvowe's poem is set – Pandarus suffers from 'a teene/In love' (61–2) and takes to his bed; and the next morning, 'half in a slomberynge', he hears the song of the swallow Procne, who 'with a sorowful lay/. . . gan make hire waymentyng' (64–5). And just as a disparaging precursor precedes the appearance of the nightingale in Clanvowe's poem, so too here: at nightfall on this same day Criseyde hears a nightingale outside her window singing 'a lay/Of love' (921–2). There are no doubt many reasons why Clanvowe has rewritten a tragic Chaucerian pattern into comedy, but the most obvious effect is to associate his narrator with Pandarus. We might think that the relation is one of likeness, an affinity between Pandarus the ineffective lover and Clanvowe's 'old and vnlusty' (37) narrator. But such a reading depends upon misconceiving Pandarus as simply a comic character; on the contrary, as Gervase Mathew has said, 'he is an experienced English courtier of the late fourteenth century, . . . a man of cultivated sensibility, facilely expressed emotions and quick stratagems – all qualities then prized'.[82] Pandarus has mastered not only the 'chere of court' – when he visits Criseyde and her ladies, 'of this and that they pleide' with 'many wordes glade,/And frendly tales' (2, 148–50) – but also the sophisticated innuendo that constitutes court dialect, what he (and others) called 'wordes white' (3, 901, 1567).[83] In a poem in which the relation of words to meaning is always at issue, Janus-like Pandarus is the presiding spirit.

Clanvowe's narrator, on the other hand, is a flat-footed, wooden version of the labile courtier: he mechanically acts out a ritual of love service and defends his lord by throwing stones at a bird. In fact, the cuckoo's parting shot – 'Farewel, farewel, papyngay!' – provides a shrewd critique. A parrot is a quintessential courtly bird, as the context in which it typically appears in medieval poetry attests: Gawain has parrots embroidered on his helmet covering (611), in the *Romaunt of the Rose* the God of Love's garment is similarly embroidered 'with popynjay, with nyghtyngale' (1913), Langland's Imaginatyf uses them as an emblem of the 'riht ryche men þat reygne here on erthe' (C, 14, 172), and in *Susannah* the elegant garden is inhabited with parrots and nightingales (75).[84] There is even a French romance devoted to the *Chevalier du Papegau*.[85] In fact, in *Mum and the Soothsegger* the word is used to designate a courtier to whom the commons, represented as magpies, once fruitlessly complained: 'piez with a papegeay parlid of oones,/And were y-plumed and y-pullid and put into a caige'.[86] But the parrot also has characteristics that allow it to function as an emblem not just for the courtier but for the courtly over-achiever: its gaudy plumage, its status as the plaything of the rich, and its ability to rehearse, with mindless enthusiasm, the phrases it has been laboriously taught – these rendered it an apt symbol of the fawning, too-perfect courtier.[87] In other words, the cuckoo's mockery is directed not simply at the narrator's alliance with the nightingale but at a certain excess, a zealousness to follow courtly pre-scription – whether it be in the performance of his own love service or in throwing stones to protect Love's servant, the nightingale – that witnesses to effort, application, toil. What the narrator lacks is the quintessential courtly value that Castiglione was to call *sprezzatura*, a virtue that court texts had promoted since the eleventh century. It is the effortlessness that implies natural superiority, the 'calculated underplaying of talents' that bespeaks an excess of talent, the grace possessed by the true aristocrat that assumes 'the natural or given status of one's social identity and [denies] any earned character, any labor or arrival from a social elsewhere'.[88] But the fabricated nature of courtier identity is all too visible in Clanvowe's narrator, a truth to which the 'unkind' cuckoo draws attention with his parting epithet.

The other way in which the *Boke of Cupide* interrogates the social practices of the court is in its focus on the question of verbal decorum. For the nightingale the cuckoo's song is 'elynge' (115) or tedious. But the cuckoo retorts that 'my songe is bothe trewe and pleyn' (118) so that '*euery wight* may vnderstonde me' (121); and he criticises the nightingale for not only 'breke[ing]' the song 'in [her] throte' (119–20) – which evidently refers to a fashionable mode of singing – but for singing in French: 'I haue herd the seye "ocy! ocy!"' says the cuckoo, 'Who myght wene what that shulde be?' (124–5).[89] This is a complaint that reflects contemporary discussion about the politics of language. On the one hand is the elitist dialect of the night-ingale, a discourse that requires an armature of special knowledge and specific ideological commitments to be understood: 'ocy' is not only the traditional literary representation of the nightingale's song, and is not only in French, but encapsulates in a single word the absolutist ideology that is at the centre of courtliness. As the nightingale says, 'who that wol the god of love not serve,/I dar wel say he is worthy for to sterve' (133–4).[90] The alternative to this coded discourse is the cuckoo's truth-telling, which is not only understood by 'euery wight' (121, cf. 150) but possesses a self-evident validity: 'What nedith hit ayens trweth to strive?' (145).

By giving the cuckoo the discourse of truth, the poem validates his position: he is the courageous soothsegger so rarely found at court. And the fact that he is here driven off by a narrator eager to prove his loyalty to a tyrant would seem simply to confirm his virtue, and to ratify the oppositional valence of Clanvowe's poem. For all his 'cherles herte' (147), the cuckoo's political independence allows him to see truths that are closed to the ideologically bound nightingale. He is kin to other marginal figures who destabilise the official views of medieval culture: Marcolf, the cynical peasant who mocks Solomon's sublime wisdom; the many unauthorised voices that impede the progress of *Piers Plowman*, beginning with the

importunate 'lunatik' who interrupts the establishment of the king's governance with a riddling blessing (B, Prologue, 123–7); the 'foules smale' in the
Parliament of Fowls, who demand that the cultic rituals of the gentle birds not
be allowed to thwart their mating habits; and the Miller of the *Canterbury
Tales*, who refuses to accept Harry Bailly's deferentially conservative management of the tale-telling game.[91]

But as these analogies also suggest, it is finally impossible to assume that
the poem simply ratifies opposition. In fact the *Boke of Cupide* asks a deeper,
more troubling question: does the intrusion of marginal values represent a
genuine challenge to authority? Even assuming that the cuckoo possesses
the 'trweth', do the complexities of court discourse automatically foreclose
its declaration? Is it possible to be at once inside and outside the court, to
challenge its assumptions in a language it can understand? For what is
striking about the fate of the cuckoo's voice in the poem is less its final,
inevitable exclusion than the way in which it is gradually absorbed into
court discourse. In the course of the poem the cuckoo is transformed from
the independent truth-teller into the stock figure of court satire, able to rehearse only his own narrow, over-determined message. And he expresses it,
strikingly enough, in the same periphrastic, allusive style that we associate
with court discourse.

At the beginning the cuckoo's challenge was, as we have seen, abrasively
explicit: far from being a lord worthy of service, the God of Love is a wilful
tyrant who at once abuses and neglects his servants. But in the next stage of
the debate he returns to his traditional role as the harbinger of adultery: 'Yf
thou be fer or longe fro thi make,/Thou shalt be as other that be forsake,/
And then shalt thou hoten as do I' (183–5). The effect of this shift is to
reduce the cuckoo from political truth-teller to agent and presiding spirit of
cuckoldry: he becomes simply the conventional 'cukkow ever unkynde'
(358) of the *Parliament of Fowls*, the 'fol kokkow' who speaks of 'myn owene
autorite' (505–6) and cares only for his own interests (603–9). Second, the
cuckoo's attack is phrased in a language of periphrasis and metaphor that
demands careful interpretation. This is partly true of the lines just cited, but
even more so of those that precede them:

> What! louyng is an office of dispaire,
> And oon thing is ther in that ys not faire;
> For who that geteth of love a lytil blysse,
> But if he be alway ther by ywysse,
> He may ful sone of age haue his eire.
>
> (176–80)

Skeat provides a persuasive gloss for these difficult lines, but the point is less
their specific meaning than the difficulty itself: this is hardly the speech

'bothe trewe and pleyn' (118) of which the cuckoo has earlier boasted.[92] Far from speaking in opposition to court dialect, the cuckoo has now been absorbed within it: he has become the other by which the court defines and ratifies its own practices. Just as Chaucer's cuckoo joins in the fashionable roundel with which the *Parliament of Fowls* concludes (it is sung to a tune composed in France), so by the end of Clanvowe's poem the cuckoo no longer poses a threat to courtly social practices. Hence the poem projects as its own sequel a highly traditional and fully courtly parliament-of-birds poem.

To explain this dynamic of cancellation as simply an effect of Clanvowe's personal history is of course reductive. But the little we know of his situation, and of his response to it, does provide a biographical context that is worth our attention. I have already suggested that Clanvowe's relation to the inner circle of the household was complicated, that he may have found the Ricardian court a not entirely congenial environment. Yet what was his alternative? To turn to the Appellant opposition would not only have been an act of betrayal but would have required him to assume an attitude towards the war, and towards chivalric heroism generally, that would have been antipathetic. For despite his military career, he also seems to have been detached from the more conventional chivalric attitudes associated with the anti-court party. There are two pieces of evidence to support this claim. One is a well-known passage in *The Two Ways*, in which Clanvowe attacks those who are 'greete werryours and fiȝteres and þat destroyen and wynnen manye loondis, . . . and of swyche folke men maken bookes and soonges and reeden and syngen of hem'; and he contrasts them to those 'þat wolden lyuen meekeliche in þis world and ben out offe swich forseid riot, noise, and stryf, and lyuen symplely. . . . Swiche folke þe world scoorneth and hooldeþ hem lolleris and loselis, foolis and schameful wrecches.'[93]

The other evidence is Clanvowe's truculent testimony in the famous dispute between Sir Richard Scrope and Sir Robert Grosvenor over a coat of arms. Like the other witnesses, Clanvowe was asked what he knew of the arms in dispute, and replied that he knew them to belong to Scrope. When asked to expatiate, however, he declined to offer a survey of the campaigns on which he had served with Scrope such as had been provided by the other witnesses. On the contrary, he brusquely refused to discuss the matter at all:

> He said that if a man asked him all the questions in the world he would always answer in the same way, that all the times he had fought in the king's campaigns he had never seen any other man carry these arms nor use them except the Scropes, and before this dispute he had never heard of Grosvenor nor of his family.[94]

The irritated comment of Sir Nicholas Harris Nicolas, the document's nineteenth-century editor, nicely captures the tone of this testimony: 'the deposition is chiefly remarkable for the petulance which [Clanvowe] displayed at being interrogated' (2.438). Alone among the 250 witnesses, Clanvowe declined to discuss his military career.

What is also striking about this testimony for our purposes is just this declination: rather than debate, Clanvowe retreats into silence. We see much the same strategy at work throughout *The Two Ways*. Searchers after Clanvowe's heterodox religious opinions have been disappointed in the treatise: for Anne Hudson, it is 'an insipidity' and 'an anthology of puritan pious sentiment', and even K. B. McFarlane found it 'a farrago of pulpit commonplace'.[95] But McFarlane also understood where its heterodoxy was to be found:

> The only trace of Lollardy is in the silences. Clanvow [*sic*] says nothing in favour of confession, pilgrimage, the veneration of the saints, the effectiveness of the sacraments, nothing at all about the priesthood. He ignores the Church as an institution altogether. He was a lay preacher and has assumed to himself at least as much of the clergy's functions. That was what aroused the Church's resentment against the lay party.[96]

It is by not speaking that Clanvowe expresses his resistance to established religion, just as a similar silence serves to criticise the honour code that drove Scrope and Grosvenor to a six-year struggle over a coat of arms. This is also the silence into which the cuckoo is banished. The *Boke of Cupide* demonstrates that the court cannot be spoken to in any language but its own, a language able to accommodate and neutralise all criticism. To speak 'trewe and pleyne' is finally impossible: within the court all discourse becomes nuanced, multivalent, facile. The *Boke of Cupide* cannot help but be a courtier's frippery. But silence has its own force, the eloquence of taciturnity. 'Learne to say wele, say litel, or say noȝt,' advises one court text, a progressive diminishment of voice that matches the cuckoo's gradual exclusion.[97] It is perhaps in a similar silence that Clanvowe's deepest thoughts on the politics of poetry at the Ricardian court are to be found.

Let us now return to our original question. Is court poetry by definition so narrow in its interests, so local in its focus, so bound in its ideology, that it stands in opposition to the form of writing we have come to call literature – a writing that aspires to a more fully inclusive vision of human experience? Or is it not the case that the 'double voicing' characteristic of court poetry, and the very inevitability of its return to its historical context, is itself productive of literary discourse?

The coding of the political in terms of the amorous that we have observed in the *Boke of Cupide* is in no sense unusual. The plaintive tone of so much court poetry, its staging, over and over again, of the single scene of (in Derek Pearsall's words) 'the lover and his mistress for ever frozen into ritual gestures of beseeching and disdain', articulates what was called, as early as the twelfth century, the *miseriae curialium*.[98] Peter of Blois's description of the anguish of courtiers awaiting advancement replicates the lexicon in which lovers will lament throughout succeeding centuries: 'They delight in ardors; what is heavy grows light, what is bitter turns sweet, and our martyrs, though they are weak, do not feel their toil.'[99] Whether the service be compelled by lady or by lord it is service none the less, and in both cases the courtier is a helpless suppliant for the grace of an omnipotent figure far beyond him, a passive petitioner who can do little to affect his own future.[100] In this sense the quintessential courtly form is the complaint: it is at once wholly disinterested, an act undertaken on the assumption of the uselessness of lament – 'What shall I say, to whom shall I complayn? / I wot not who wyll on my sorus rewe' – and yet profoundly pragmatic: only a lover so devoted as to pursue a hopeless suit is deserving of grace.[101] The troubadour Elias Careil made the point explicitly: 'I'm not singing to gain sexual pleasure / but for honor and profit.'[102] Of course we hear this admission only rarely, since part of what makes a courtier worthy of reward is his ability to represent unpalatable truths with nuance and discretion.

But court poetry is in no sense restricted to a single, pragmatic function. In fact, much court poetry is much less a naked bid for advancement than a meditation on the conditions of court life considered in their widest relevance. Many court poems reflect, for example, upon the painful self-discipline that aspiration requires: 'throughe gouernance growethe grace', as one poet ambiguously says.[103] But they also stage a specifically courtly alienation, the courtier's desire to escape from a highly competitive and untrustworthy environment and yet his yearning to perform, to dazzle. These are intensely private poems designed to be overheard: 'Vnto my-selffe a-lone / Thus do I make my mowne', says the lover – lines that begin an elaborately turned virelai.[104] They stage moments of aloneness – 'My selfe and I, me thought we wer Inow', says the lover in *La belle dame sans merci* (86) – but then people them with either personified abstractions or representative examples of the courtly population. And these poems speak as well to the disappointments of the noble life per se. Oton de Grandson's *Livre messire Ode* is an almost unrelieved litany of lament that bears a close relationship to the exiled and disinherited Oton's miserable personal history; Charles d'Orleans's poems return over and over to the issue of troth, not surprising for a man trapped by sharply conflicting loyalties; and the lyrics ascribed to William de la Pole, Duke of Suffolk, express a pattern of constraint and aspiration that takes on a particularly telling valence when correlated with his unhappy life.[105] And we should also remember that these are poems that in many instances mean exactly what they say: they are written by men living in the overwhelmingly male (and masculine) world of the court and, given the medieval requirement of hypergamy, competing for a very few women, all of them above their station.[106] In the court lyric, in other words, a lady is sometimes just a lady.

But above all these are poems about complexity, specifically the complexity of personality and manner entailed by courtliness per se. Their energy derives from the opposition between an absolutist idealism – the monolithic claims of love, the unalloyed intensity of desire, the singularity of erotic selfhood, the unconditional joy capable of satisfying all needs – and the complex world of difference that frustrates its realisation. On the one hand is the lover burdened with a self-possessive, self-possessed desire; on the other the impediments to love – the impassive lady, the faithless man, the mockers who scorn love's law, the very conditions of a social life that precludes absolutes – against which the poet can only pose the impossible voicing of a desire that can never be fully expressed. Every courtly poem is in effect a debate, whether it be between a nightingale and a cuckoo or, as is more commonly the case, between feeling and form, love and the language of love. Over and over again court poets lament the insufficiency of speech. 'Of þis swete nek if I more say, / Me þink my body breke yn tway, / for sorow I may no lenger speke': the palpability of the female body both generates and stands as an analogue to an overwhelming and inarticulate male desire.[107] In another poem the lover decides to 'vn–bynde' his care by writing a letter which 'A-boute my hede I woll . . . wynde, / Tyll sche her-selfe hit wyll vnbynde': the lover becomes an icon of love, the bearer of a message that can be expressed only by silent witnessing.[108] Or the lover seeks 'to tell you Myn entent', but is foiled by both his incapacity ('y haue nothere gamyn ne gle') and the circumstances ('We may not speke but we be schent'), a failure of expression that his unfocused and so all the more powerfully eloquent poem at once intensifies and ameliorates.[109] In a variant of the same dynamic, and one with special relevance to the *Boke of Cupide*, a lover tells his lady that his words will 'be bothe true & playn', a promise that the smoothly artful poem in which it is embedded subverts.[110] And so on: writing is at once the means of communication and the barrier that impedes it, a gesture towards the intensity and singularity of feeling that generates it but which it can never finally encompass. In the words again of Christine de Pizan, the lover may desire to speak 'a voix simplette' but he always ends up talking 'mignot'.[111]

In its most general terms, then, the court poem explores the vicissitudes of simplicity in a world of complexity. Driven by a desire for the absolute but caught within the world of the contingent, the nightingale song of the courtier is constantly accompanied by the raucous tones of a cuckoo. This is a counterpoint that captures a doubleness at the very heart of courtliness. On the one hand, the court is ostensibly composed of 'euery wight that gentil ys of kynde', in the words of Clanvowe's nightingale (150), men and women whose easy elegance bespeaks breeding. And these courtiers exist not only to serve the prince but, in the elegance of their dress and speech, as in the artful shaping of their personalities, to embody his magnificence. Yet the subtlety and nuance this symbolism entails subverts the absolutism to which it is in service, just as the courtier's fabrication requires a discipline that ill sorts with the claim of instinctive superiority. So too, to know and bow to the will of the prince requires a psychological penetration, and an alertness to the complexity of human intention, that is hardly consistent with the ideal of instinctive love and service courtly idealism promotes. Lydgate describes how the prince's 'frowne' causes the courtiers to whisper among themselves – they 'priuely wol rowne/Whan a prynce doth vp-on hem frowne' – but with each arriving at his own meaning: 'Everych conclude[s] lich his fantasye'.[112] Far from creating a court unified by the unquestioning desire to reflect his own image, the monarch instead generates an interpretive insecurity that alienates his courtiers from himself and each other. Instead of the uniformity of will and the simplicity of desire to which it aspires, and which its literature means to celebrate, the court knows itself to be in fact heterogeneous and self-conflicted, a complexity its writing inevitably if uneasily acknowledges.[113]

The dialectical discourse of court writing, mediating between absolutism and difference, uniformity and heterogeneity, self-identity and dispersion, has, as we have seen, both an evident topical meaning for the politics of the Ricardian court and relevance to the ideological formation of courtliness in general. But it also performs cultural work of another sort: it generates a mode of writing that comes to constitute, for much of English literary history, literature itself. Court poetry incorporates a set of irresolvable antinomies: interest and disinterest, work and play, the desire to transcend the social context and yet an unavoidable need to recuperate and refigure it. It posits a twofold audience – one engaged in mere dalliance, another capable of reading ironically – just as it generates an author who does and does not mean what he says. It thus entails a mobile, disunified self capable of assuming a variety of incommensurate subject positions. And it deploys a language not only laden with rhetorical tropes and topoi but capable of understanding its own rhetoricity – a language located, in Paul de Man's phrase, 'in the void of . . . difference'.[114]

These are the characteristics that were used in succeeding centuries to qualify a certain kind of writing as aesthetic, distinguishing it from other, non-literary writing. This is a distinction that is itself not ontological but historical: we now realise that literature is less a specific kind of writing than a writing that is taken, for a variety of reasons, to be literature. But the historical effect of the distinction is beyond dispute. The court provided, in other words, a site not just for the production of specific literary works but for the development of literary discourse per se. To be sure, it was hardly the only site in which this discourse was produced in late-medieval England;[115] and it must also be stressed that a *sine qua non* for the emergence of the *idea* of literature was the importing from Italy of the humanist ideology of a transhistorical writing. But it was in the court that the language of power became the language of poetry. And because of the shape of subsequent literary history – the overwhelming dominance of Chaucer's court poetry in the fifteenth century, and the location of Skelton, Wyatt and Surrey in the Tudor court – this event proved to be decisive. We should not be surprised, then, that the first court poet in English was also the Father of English Poetry, nor that the courtier John Clanvowe produced a poem that Milton and Wordsworth found worthy of imitation. Whether he knew it or not, he was making literature.

Notes

1. P. P. Howe, ed., *Complete Works of William Hazlitt*, London: Dent, 1930, vol. 4, pp. 214–15.
2. Janine Dakyns, *The Middle Ages in French Literature, 1851–1900*, Oxford: Oxford University Press, 1973, p. 196. Gaston Paris founded *Romania* in 1871 and the Société des anciens textes français in 1873 explicitly in order to counter German domination of medieval studies.
3. These citations are from Paris's annual report to the Société des anciens textes français printed in its *Bulletin*, 3, 1877, 57.
4. Paul A. Olson, *The* Canterbury Tales *and the Good Society*, Princeton NJ: Princeton University Press, 1986, pp. 3, 15.
5. Paul Strohm, *Social Chaucer*, Cambridge MA: Harvard University Press, 1989, pp. 55, 63, 75, 80, 82. The claim that the development of Middle English literature is to be explained by the rise of a 'middle class' is pursued in detail by Janet Coleman, *Medieval Readers and Writers 1350–1400*, New York NY: Columbia University Press, 1981; see also, for a much more nuanced account, Anne Middleton, 'Chaucer's "new men" and the good of literature in the *Canterbury Tales*', in Edward Said, ed., *Literature and Society, Selected Papers from the English Institute, 1978*, Baltimore MD: Johns Hopkins University Press, 1980, pp. 15–56.
6. A. C. Spearing, *Medieval to Renaissance in English Poetry*, Cambridge: Cambridge University Press, 1985, p. 34. For the importance of Dante, see also Elizabeth Salter, *Fourteenth-Century English Poetry: Contexts and readings*, Oxford: Clarendon Press, 1983, p. 123; and David Wallace, 'Chaucer's continental inheritance: The early poems and *Troilus and Criseyde*', in Piero Boitani and Jill Mann, eds, *The Cambridge Chaucer Companion*, Cambridge: Cambridge University Press, 1986, pp. 21–2, 29–30.
7. Clanvowe's career, and religious commitments, are treated most fully by K. B. McFarlane, *Lancastrian Kings and Lollard Knights*, Oxford: Clarendon Press, 1972.

8. His only appearance in the *Life-Records* is when he, along with his friends and fellow chamber knights, William Neville and William Beauchamp (also chamberlain of the king's household), and two prominent London merchants, witnessed Cecily Champaigne's writ releasing Chaucer from the charge of rape: Martin M. Crow and Clair C. Olson, eds, *Chaucer Life-Records*, Austin TX: University of Texas Press, 1966, p. 343. For the literary relation to Chaucer, see R. T. Lenaghan, 'Chaucer's circle of gentlemen and clerks', *Chaucer Review*, **18**, 1983–4, 155–60; Paul Strohm, 'Chaucer's audience', *Literature and History*, **5**, 1977, 26–41; Derek Pearsall, 'The *Troilus* frontispiece and Chaucer's audience', *Yearbook of English Studies*, 7, 1977, 68–74.

9. All citations are from V. J. Scattergood, ed., *The Works of Sir John Clanvowe*, Cambridge: D. S. Brewer, 1975; I have also benefited from Erich Vollmer, ed., *Das Mittelenglische Gedicht 'The Boke of Cupide'*, Berliner Beiträge zur germanischen und romanischen Philologie 17, Germanische Abteilung 8, Berlin: Ebering, 1898. Scattergood discusses the poem's authorship in the Introduction to his edition and more fully in 'The authorship of *The Boke of Cupide*', *Anglia*, **82**, 1964, 37–49.

10. For a history of the criticism, see Russell A. Peck, *Chaucer's Romaunt of the Rose and Boece, Treatise on the Astrolabe, Equatorie of the Planets, Lost Works, and Chaucerian Apocrypha: An annotated bibliography, 1900–1985*, Toronto: University of Toronto Press, 1988, pp. 309–12. The most recent discussion may be found in Strohm, *Social Chaucer*, pp. 78–82.

11. Gervase Mathew, *The Court of Richard II*, London: John Murray, 1968, p. 30. The distinction between poetry of the court and courtly poetry is drawn, in somewhat different terms, by Derek Pearsall, *Old English and Middle English Poetry*, London: Routledge & Kegan Paul, 1977, p. 212.

12. The first phrase is from R. N. Swanson, *Church and Society in Late Medieval England*, Oxford: Basil Blackwell, 1989, p. 337; the others from Rossell Hope Robbins, 'The structure of longer Middle English court poems', in Edward Vasta and Zacharias P. Thundy, eds, *Chaucerian Problems and Perspectives: Essays presented to Paul E. Beichner*, Notre Dame IN: University of Notre Dame Press, 1979, p. 245. See also Robbins's 'The Middle English court love lyric', in W. T. H. Jackson, ed., *The Interpretation of Medieval Lyric*, New York NY: Columbia University Press, 1980, pp. 205–32.

13. According to J. M. W. Bean, *From Lord to Patron: Lordship in late medieval England*, Philadelphia PA: University of Pennsylvania Press, 1989, 'When indentures in the vernacular appear in the fifteenth century, the language is generally "beleft and witholden". In the late thirteenth and fourteenth centuries indentures of retinue were almost always in French, the words used being *demore et retenu* or similar language' (p. 33, n. 1; for examples, see pp. 111, 113–14). This is also a Chaucerian usage: Melibee comments on the 'chesynge and . . . withholdynge of my conseillours' (VII, 1233), and in the *General Prologue* we are told that the Parson has not 'been withholde' (I, 511) by a guild as its chaplain; for an instance perhaps even closer to Clanvowe's, in the F-Prologue to the *Legend of Good Women*, when speaking of the companies of the flower and the leaf, Chaucer says that 'I nam withholden yit with never nother' (F, 192); see also *Melibee* (VII, 2202).

14. Chris Given-Wilson, *The Royal Household and the King's Affinity: Service, politics and finance in England 1360–1413*, New Haven CT: Yale University Press, 1986, p. 243.
15. For the relevant portions of Theseus's speech, see the *Knight's Tale* I, 1785–90, 1799–1805. All citations from Chaucer's poetry are from Larry D. Benson, gen. ed., *The Riverside Chaucer*, Boston MA: Houghton Mifflin, 1987.
16. As Strohm points out, 'The irony is double in that it places two contradictory propositions before us: love *is* great, but great in its capacity to make fools of its servants' (*Social Chaucer*, p. 79).
17. See Margaret Schlauch, 'Chaucer's doctrine of kings and tyrants', *Speculum*, 20, 1945, 155; and J. D. Burnley, *Chaucer's Language and the Philosopher's Tradition*, Cambridge: D. S. Brewer, 1979, pp. 11–43.
18. Given-Wilson, *Royal Household*, p. 162.
19. For his dismissal, see Chris Given-Wilson, 'The king and gentry in fourteenth-century England', *Transactions of the Royal Historical Society*, 5th ser., 37, 1987, 91, n. 18.
20. According to McFarlane, 'The contemporary spirit in religion was puritan, biblical, evangelical, anarchic, anti-sacerdotal, hostile to the established order in the Church. Hence there was widespread sympathy with at least the moral content of the Lollard teaching. And it is doubtful how far the knights accepted or even grasped the theological implications of their views. Theirs was a moral revolt by the laity against the visible Church, a rejection of sacerdotalism in favour of the personal, immediate contact between believer and his Creator' (*Lancastrian Kings*, p. 225).
21. Anthony J. Tuck, 'Carthusian monks and Lollard knights: Religious attitudes at the court of Richard II', in Paul Strohm and Thomas J. Heffernan, eds, *Studies in the Age of Chaucer Proceedings 1, 1984: Reconstructing Chaucer*, Knoxville TN: New Chaucer Society, 1985, pp. 149–61.
22. See especially John Stevens, *Music and Poetry in the Early Tudor Court*, London: Methuen, 1961; Robbins, 'Middle English court love lyric', pp. 205–32; and Glending Olson, 'Toward a poetics of the late medieval court lyric', in Lois Ebin, ed., *Vernacular Poetics in the Middle Ages*, Kalamazoo MI: Medieval Institute Publications, 1984, pp. 227–48.
23. For the first two phrases, see 'La belle dame sans merci', in Walter W. Skeat, ed., *Chaucerian and Other Pieces*, Supplement to the *Complete Works of Geoffrey Chaucer*, vol. 7, Oxford: Oxford University Press, 1897, lines 328–9, p. 309; for 'parler mignot', see Christine de Pizan, *Cent ballades d'amant et de dame*, ed. Jacqueline Cerquiglini, Paris: Union Générale d'Editions, 1982, poem 8, line 11, p. 39.
24. See C. Stephen Jaeger, *The Origins of Courtliness: Civilizing trends and the formation of courtly ideals 939–1210*, Philadelphia PA: University of Pennsylvania Press, 1985, pp. 162–8; on the meaning of *facetus*, see Alison Goddard Elliott's introduction to her translation of 'The *Facetus*: or, The art of courtly living', *Allegorica*, 2 (1977), 27–57. Jaeger's book provides a powerful critique of the too-common assumption that the courtly personality is a phenomenon of the Renaissance.
25. This definition is given by Donatus in his commentary on Terence's *Eunuchus*,

cited by Laura Kendrick, *The Game of Love: Troubadour wordplay*, Berkeley CA: University of California Press, 1988, p. 53.

26. Stevens, *Music and Poetry*, p. 163; Part I of the *Knight's Tale* itself provides the occasion for a *demande d'amour*, as do the *Franklin's Tale* and the debate among the noble suitors in the *Parliament of Fowls*. Apparently *demandes* were not always as high-minded as these instances: for a collection of *demandes* that turn on racy *doubles entendres* and so require fast-paced verbal banter rather than lofty eloquence, see Eustache Deschamps, *Oeuvres complètes*, ed. Gaston Raynaud, Société des anciens textes français, t. 8, Paris: Firmin-Didot, 1893, pp. 112–25. For examples of linguistically playful poems in English, see Rossell Hope Robbins, ed., *Secular Lyrics of the XIVth and XVth Centuries*, 2nd edn, Oxford: Clarendon Press, 1955, poems numbers 172, 173 and 177.

27. Thomas Usk, *Testament of Love*, in Skeat, ed., *Chaucerian and Other Pieces*, p. 12.

28. William W. Kibler, 'Poet and patron: Froissart's *Prison amoureuse*', *L'Esprit Créateur*, **18**, 1972, 38.

29. *Le livre messire Ode*, in Arthur Piaget, *Oton de Grandson, sa vie et ses poésies*, Mémoires et documents publiés par la Société d'Histoire de la Suisse Romande, 3ième série, tome 1, Lausanne: Librairie Payot, 1941, line 1478, p. 439.

30. George Puttenham, *The Arte of English Poesie*, London: Richard Field, 1589; printed in facsimile: London: Scolar Press, 1968, p. 155.

31. See especially Richard Firth Green, *Poets and Princepleasers: Literature and the English court in the late Middle Ages*, Toronto: University of Toronto Press, 1980, pp. 101–34.

32. Many years ago, in *Chaucer's Official Career*, Menasha WI: George Banta, 1912, James R. Hulbert showed that Chaucer's career as a king's esquire was exactly analogous, in functions as in rewards, to those of his cohort who were not poets; for the official documents that record the poet's career, see Crow and Olson, *Chaucer Life-Records*.

33. Mathew, *Court of Richard II*, p. 30; Green, *Poets and Princepleasers*, p. 107; Glending Olson, 'Deschamps' *Art de dictier* and Chaucer's literary environment', *Speculum*, **48**, 1973, 714–23.

34. A list of English aristocratic poets of the late fourteenth and fifteenth centuries (compiled largely from Green's discussion) includes John Montagu, Earl of Salisbury; Edward Plantagenet, second Duke of York; Richard Beauchamp, Earl of Warwick; William de la Pole, Duke of Suffolk; John Tiptoft, Earl of Worcester; Anthony Woodville, Earl Rivers; Sir Richard Roos; and of course Sir John Clanvowe. Non-English noble *littérateurs* include Marshall Boucicault and his friends, like the Duc de Berri, who composed the *Livre de cents ballades*; James I of Scotland; René of Anjou and his son, Jean, Duc de Calabre; Wenceslas de Brabant; Charles d'Orléans; and Jean II, Duc de Bourbon. As K. B. McFarlane has said, 'In what other century has the peerage been so active in literature?' (*The Nobility of Later Medieval England*, Oxford: Clarendon Press, 1973, p. 242).

35. See Kibler, 'Poet and patron', 32–46, and Peter F. Dembowski, *Jean Froissart and His Méliador: Context, craft, and sense*, Lexington KY: French Forum, 1983.

36. According to Robbins, 'The Middle English court love lyric', there survive perhaps 300 love lyrics and thirty 'love aunters', by which he means poems such as Lydgate's *Temple of Glass*, *The Flour and the Leaf*, and *The Court of Love* (p. 207).

37. The influence of the *dits amoureux* on Chaucer has been most vigorously argued by Rossell Hope Robbins, 'Geoffroi Chaucier, poète français, father of English poetry', *Chaucer Review*, **13**, 1978–9, 106; see also Robbins's 'Chaucer and the lyric tradition', *Poetica*, **15/16**, 1983, 107–27, and 'The vintner's son: French wine in English bottles', in William W. Kibler, ed., *Eleanor of Aquitaine: Patron and politician*, Austin TX: University of Texas Press, 1976, pp. 147–72; and by James I. Wimsatt, *Chaucer and the French Love Poets*, Chapel Hill NC: University of North Carolina Press, 1968. For the lyric presence in the *Troilus*, see Wimsatt, 'The French lyric element in *Troilus and Criseyde*', *Yearbook of English Studies*, **15**, 1985, 18–32. For an argument that Chaucer's poetry develops out of these lyric moments, see W. A. Davenport, *Chaucer: Complaint and narrative*, Chaucer Studies 14, Cambridge: D. S. Brewer, 1988.

38. Daniel Poirion, *Le poète et le prince: l'évolution du lyrisme courtois de Guillaume de Machaut à Charles d'Orleans*, Paris: Presses Universitaires de France, 1965, p. 77.

39. The poem is the fifteenth-century *Lay of Sorrow*, in Kenneth G. Wilson, 'The *Lay of Sorrow* and *The Lufaris Complaynt*: An edition', *Speculum*, **29**, 1954, 708–27. In MS Bodley Tanner 346, the *Boke of Cupide* is followed by four rhyme royal stanzas dedicating it to an unnamed lady; the same four stanzas also appear in MS Fairfax 16, here appended to the *Book of the Duchess*; see Vollmer, ed., *Das Mittelenglische Gedicht*, pp. 46–7.

40. For 'jeu des formes', see Robert Guiette, 'D'une poésie formelle en France en Moyen Age', *Romanica Gandensia*, **8**, 1960, 17; for the *hortus conclusus* and 'culte égocentrique', see Paul Zumthor, *Essai de poétique médiévale*, Paris: Seuil, 1972, pp. 243, 267. See also Roger Dragonetti, *La technique poétique des trouvères dans la chanson courtoise*, Bruges: De Tempel, 1960; according to Poirion, courtly verse represents 'une évasion, une fuite devant les responsabilités sociales'; 'ces gens attendaient sans doute de la poésie un apaisement, une sérénité que leur destin leur refusait' (*Le poète et le prince*, pp. 23, 25). As he says, 'Cultiver la beauté, ce sera désormais renoncer à l'action morale' (p. 95). In speaking of twelfth-century troubadour poetry, Erich Köhler points out that it is a way for aspirants to 'dissimuler leur impuissance à maîtriser dans la vie les réalités qui répondent à ces notions' 'Observations historiques et sociologiques sur la poésie des troubadours', *Cahiers de civilisation médiévale*, 7, 1964, 34. Much the same point is made about the Italian sonnet sequences of the *quattrocento* by Lauro Martines, *Power and Imagination: City-states in Renaissance Italy*, New York NY: Knopf, 1979, p. 325.

41. Brian Stock, *Listening for the Text: On the uses of the past*, Baltimore MD: Johns Hopkins University Press, 1990, p. 23. See also Stock's *The Implications of Literacy*, Princeton, NJ: Princeton University Press, 1983.

42. For 'rhetorical man', see Richard Lanham, *The Motives of Eloquence*, New Haven C: Yale University Press, 1976, p. 4. Historians of English Renaissance literature have assumed, largely under the influence of Burckhardt, that both a

sophisticated court culture and the self-fashioning it entailed are specifically Renaissance phenomena, and that together they constitute an essential element of modernity. As the evidence presented in this essay suggests, neither of these assumptions is true. For well-informed accounts of medieval court culture, see Jaeger, *The Origins of Courtliness* (n. 24 above), and Joachim Bumke, *Courtly Culture: Literature and society in the high Middle Ages*, trans. Thomas Dunlap, Berkeley CA: University of California Press, 1991.

43. For the account offered in the next two paragraphs, see Anthony Tuck, *Richard II and the English Nobility*, New York NY: St Martin's Press, 1974, and Given-Wilson, *Royal Household*. I have also been much aided by Patricia Eberle's splendid article, 'The politics of courtly style at the court of Richard II', in Glyn S. Burgess and Robert A. Taylor, eds, *The Spirit of the Court: Selected proceedings of the fourth congress of the International Courtly Literature Society*, Cambridge: D. S. Brewer, 1985, pp. 168–78.

44. Cited Given-Wilson, *Royal Household*, pp. 146–7.

45. These low-born men included Richard Stury, a chamber knight who was later to be associated with Chaucer; Richard Lyons and John Peche, London merchants; Adam Burt, a London skinner; and Hugh Fastolf and William Ellis, members of the Great Yarmouth merchant oligarchy (Given-Wilson, *Royal Household*, pp. 148–51).

46. The cited phrase is from D. A. L. Morgan, 'The house of policy: The political role of the late Plantagenet household', in David Starkey, ed., *The English Court: From the Wars of the Roses to the Civil War*, London: Longmans, 1987, p. 37. Morgan argues – wrongly, I believe – that the long-term shift from retinue to court did not occur until the 1430s and '40s, at which time 'the style of the household as a war-band' was supplanted by that of the court. It may be true that the mid-fifteenth century was the time at which this shift became permanent, but it certainly was in effect during the latter years of Edward III's reign and throughout Richard II's; and it may be that we should understand the policy of Henry IV and especially Henry V as a conservative return to an earlier mode of household organisation. The *camera regis* is described by R. F. Green as 'an inner sanctum . . . in which the king and his most intimate companions spent the majority of their time and where the most important business of the *familia* was conducted', 'a kind of household within the household' (*Poets and Princepleasers*, pp. 35, 37). For the relative absence of the nobility at court, see Chris Given-Wilson, *The English Nobility in the Late Middle Ages*, London: Routledge & Kegan Paul, 1987, pp. 175–8.

47. For this interpretation of Richard's court, see Tuck, *Richard II*, and Richard H. Jones, *The Royal Policy of Richard II: Absolutism in the later Middle Ages*, Oxford: Basil Blackwell, 1968.

48. The citation, from the *Rotuli Parliamentorum*, is derived from Tuck, *Richard II*, p. 55.

49. Tuck, *Richard II*, p. 84.

50. For the citation, see Mathew, *Court*, p. 17; for the much-discussed Wilton diptych, see for example J. J. N. Palmer, *England, France and Christendom, 1377–99*, London: Routledge & Kegan Paul, 1972, pp. 242–4.

51. In 1386 he tourneyed at Smithfield wearing red armour and a red gown

embroidered with golden suns; at the tournament of October 1390, itself preceded by an elaborate procession, his team wore the device of the white hart; and in 1392 he ratified the readmission of London to royal favour with a procession that amazed observers. For the Smithfield tournaments, see Juliet R. V. Barker, *The Tournament in England, 1100– 1400*, Woodbridge: Boydell, 1986, pp. 100, 185; Sheila Lindenbaum, 'The Smithfield tournament of 1390', *Journal of Medieval and Renaissance Studies*, **20**, 1990, 1–20; Richard of Maidstone's account of the 1392 procession is translated by Edith Rickert, *Chaucer's World*, New York NY: Columbia University Press, 1948, pp. 35–9.

52. See Mathew, *Court, passim*, and Green, *Poets and Princepleasers*, pp. 17–52. For this as a European phenomenon, see Bernard Guenée, *States and Rulers in Later Medieval Europe*, trans. Juliet Vale, Oxford: Basil Blackwell, 1985, pp. 66–80. Richard's ambitions for his court have often been seen as emulating the Valois court: see Mathew, *Court*, p. 21, and Ralph A. Griffiths, 'The crown and the royal family in later Medieval England', in Ralph A. Griffiths and James Sherborne, eds, *Kings and Nobles in the Later Middle Ages*, New York NY: St Martin's Press, 1986, who describes Richard as having 'a mind that was fascinated with heraldry and kingly dignity, and besotted with things French' (p. 19). For Richard's expenditures on ostentatious luxuries, see George B. Stow, 'Chronicles versus records: The character of Richard II', in J. S. Hamilton and Patricia J. Bradley, eds, *Documenting the Past: Essays in medieval history presented to George Peddy Cuttino*, Woodbridge: Boydell, 1989, pp. 155–76.

53. Eberle, 'Politics of courtly style', pp. 174–5.

54. *Ibid.*, p. 178.

55. See Kate Mertes, *The English Noble Household, 1300–1600*, Oxford: Basil Blackwell, 1987; and Green, *Poets and Princepleasers*, p. 19.

56. John Silvester Davies, ed., *An English Chronicle*, Camden Series 64, London: Nichols, 1856, p. 12.

57. For Richard's anger, with many citations, see Stow, 'Chronicles versus records'.

58. For the centrality of chivalry, i.e. warfare, to aristocratic identity, see Given-Wilson, *Nobility*, p. 2; Nigel Saul, *Scenes from Provincial Life: Knightly families in Sussex 1280–1400*, Oxford: Clarendon Press, 1986, p. 163; Maurice Keen, *Chivalry*, New Haven CT: Yale University Press, 1985.

59. On the fashionableness of the Ricardian court, see Mathew, *Court*, p. 1; and on the idea of fashion generally, Sima Godfrey, 'Haute couture and haute culture', in Denis Hollier, ed., *A New History of French Literature*, Cambridge MA: Harvard University Press, 1989, pp. 761–9.

60. Norbert Elias, *The Civilizing Process*, vol. 1: *The History of Manners*, and vol. 2: *Power and Civility*, trans. Edward Jephcott, New York NY: Pantheon Books, 1982 (1939); unfortunately, Elias assumes this to be a post-medieval phenomenon. For Henry IV's return to a more militaristic household, see Given-Wilson, *Household*, p. 196.

61. H. T. Riley, ed., *Historia anglicana*, 2 vols, Rolls Series, London: Longmans, 1863–4, 2, p. 156; cited and translated by Eberle, 'Politics', p. 69. For the political interests that controlled Walsingham's changing accounts of Richard, see George B. Stow, 'Richard II in Thomas Walsingham's chronicles', *Speculum*, **59**, 1984, 68–102.

62. Thomas Favent, *Historia sive Narracio de Modo et forma Mirabilis Parliamenti apud Westmonasterium*, ed. May McKisack, *Camden Miscellany*, vol. 14, 3rd ser., 37, 1926, 3; Favent is citing one of the charges laid by the Appellants in 1388.
63. John Gower, *Vox clamantis*, in Eric Stockton, trans., *The Major Latin Works of John Gower*, Seattle WA: University of Washington Press, 1962, pp. 232–3.
64. Josef Kail, ed., *Twenty-Six Political and Other Poems*, Early English Text Society, Original Series 124, London: Kegan Paul, Trench, Trübner, 1904, pp. 14–22.
65. Carleton Brown, ed., *Religious Lyrics of the Fourteenth Century*, 2nd edn, rev. G. V. Smithers, Oxford: Clarendon Press, 1957, number 103, pp. 93–4. The fear that courtly conversation is motivated by malevolent self-interest is also implied in Alceste's warning to the God of Love in the F-Prologue to the *Legend of Good Women*: 'in youre court ys many a losengeour,/And many a queynte totelere accusour,/That tabouren in youre eres many a sown,/Ryght after hire ymagynacioun,/To have youre daliance, and for envie' (352–6).
66. F. J. Furnivall, ed., *Early English Meals and Manners*, Early English Text Society, Original Series 32, London: Kegan Paul, Trench, Trübner, 1868, pp. 244–6. This poem is also printed in Carleton Brown, ed., *Religious Lyrics of the XVth Century*, Oxford: Clarendon Press, 1939, pp. 280–2. See also, from a fifteenth-century *Boke of Curtayse* also printed by Furnivall, the warning that 'In swete wordis þe nedder was closet,/Disseyuaunt euer and mysloset' (183). In the twelfth-century *Facetus* the courtier is advised to 'consider it a sin always to tell the truth' (Elliott, ed., *Facetus*, 33), and reminded that 'in the world there is no such thing as a really faithful friend, for every man is shrewd at deception' (51).
67. E. K. Chambers and F. Sidgwick, eds, *Early English Lyrics: Amorous, Divine, Moral and Trivial*, London: Sidgwick & Jackson, 1921, p. 192.
68. H. Rosamund Parsons, 'Anglo-Norman books of courtesy and nurture', *PMLA*, 44, 1929, 409.
69. See, for example, Albertanus of Brescia, *Tractatus de arte loquendi et tacendi*, in Thor Sundby, ed., *Brunetto Latinos Levnet og Skrifter*, Copenhagen: Lunds, 1869, Appendix, lxxxiv–cxix; and *The Babees Book*, in Furnivall, ed., *Early English Meals*, p. 252.
70. See V. J. Scattergood, 'The Manciple's manner of speaking', *Essays in Criticism*, 24, 1974, 124–46, and n. 82.
71. George Kane and E. Talbot Donaldson, eds, *Piers Plowman: The B-version*, London: Athlone Press, 1975, p. 233 (Prologue, 111).
72. Mabel Day and Robert Steele, eds, *Mum and the Soothsegger*, Early English Text Society, Original Series 199, London: Oxford University Press, 1936, Fragment M, 265, pp. 49–50.
73. See Andrew Wawn, 'Truth-telling and the tradition of *Mum and the Sothsegger*', *Yearbook of English Studies*, 13, 1983, 270–87.
74. For an instance of the topical argument, see John H. Fisher, 'Wyclif, Langland, Gower, and the *Pearl* poet on the subject of the aristocracy', in MacEdward Leach, ed., *Studies in Medieval Literature in Honor of Professor Albert Croll Baugh*, Philadelphia PA: University of Pennsylvania Press, 1961, p. 151.
75. In *Cleanness*, when the poet has God say that he himself established courtship, he uses language that invokes the kind of dalliance in which Gawain and the

lady engage: 'þe play of paramoreȝ I portrayed myseluen' (ed. J. J. Anderson, Manchester: Manchester University Press, 1977, line 700).

76. See Michael J. Bennett, *Community, Class and Careerism: Cheshire and Lancashire society in the age of* Sir Gawain and the Green Knight, Cambridge: Cambridge University Press, 1983, pp. 163–8, 208, 233–4. Bennett even suggests (p. 246) that the poem was written by one of Richard's household clerks, a suggestion that, given both its social meaning and the lack of royal interest in alliterative poetry, seems highly unlikely.

77. See H. Rosamund Parsons, 'Anglo-Norman books of courtesy and nurture', *PMLA*, **44**, 1929, 410.

78. Compare the F-Prologue to the *Legend of Good Women*, where Alceste commands the poet to write the legends by saying, 'And thogh the lyk nat a lovere bee,/Speke wel of love' (490–1).

79. In the F-Prologue, the green and white of the landscape is embodied in Alceste, 'Crowned with white and clothed al in grene' (242; cf. 214, 223, 227, 303, 341). At the end of the *Boke of Cupide*, the nightingale tells the narrator that his lovesickness will be ameliorated if he will 'Euery day this May . . ./Goo loke vpon the fresshe flour daysye' (242–3), the same love service as the narrator performs in the F-Prologue.

80. For Clanvowe St Valentine's Day comes in March (80); for the courtly cult of Valentine's Day initiated in the *Parliament of Fowls* and the various possibilities for the date and patron saint, see Jack B. Oruch, 'St. Valentine, Chaucer, and spring in February', *Speculum*, **56**, 1981, 534–65, and Henry Ansgar Kelly, *Chaucer and the Cult of Saint Valentine*, Davis Medieval Texts and Studies, 5, Leiden: Brill, 1986.

81. There is a further analogy between the *Boke of Cupide* and the Prologue to the *Legend of Good Women* that may cast light on the logic of Chaucer's revisions. As he begins to dream, Clanvowe's narrator tells us 'a wonder thinge' (106), that 'Me thoght I wist al that the briddes ment,/And what they seyde, and what was her entent,/And of her speche I had good knovynge' (108–10); in the G-Prologue to the *Legend of Good Women*, the narrator comments that 'to herken [the birdsong] I dide al myn entente,/For-why I mette I wiste what they mente' (G, 139–40). On this allusion, see Vollmer, *Das mittelenglische Gedicht*, p. 50, and for a contrary opinion, J. L. Lowes, 'The Prologue to the *Legend of Good Women* considered in its chronological relations', *PMLA*, **20**, 1905, 754–6, n. 2. The G-Prologue is revised so as to incorporate the discipline that the F-Prologue seeks to impose: in other words, it is a poem that has responded to the authoritarian demands the God of Love makes in the F-Prologue. The lines at issue are an expression of the elitist attitude both poems stage, as we can see from another Chaucerian allusion to them: in the *Squire's Tale*, Canacee's ring is described as 'a wonder thyng' (V, 248) because of which she 'wiste what [the birds] mente/Right by hir song, and knewe al hire entente' (V, 399–400).

82. Mathew, *Court of Richard II*, p. 68.

83. In the fifteenth century a courtier poet included Pandarus's warnings about the dangers of unbridled speech (3, 302–22) in a poem on the dangers of truth-telling and the burdens of service at court: see Frederick J. Furnivall, ed.,

Odd Texts of Chaucer's Minor Poems, Chaucer Society, 1st series, no. 23, 60, London: Trübner, 1868–80, pp. xi–xii.

84. For the *Romaunt*, see *The Riverside Chaucer*, p. 696; Derek Pearsall, ed., *Piers Plowman: An edition of the C-text*, Berkeley CA: University of California Press, 1978, p. 243; Alice Miskimin, ed., *Susannah: An alliterative poem of the fourteenth century*, New Haven CT: Yale University Press, 1969, p. 111.

85. Thomas E. Vesce, trans., *The Knight of the Parrot (Le Chevalier du Papegau)*, Garland Library of Medieval Literature 55B, New York NY: Garland Press, 1986.

86. Day and Steele, eds, Fragment M, 152–5; the editors gloss the passage, 'Once some of the commons discussed their grievances with some one of higher rank, and consequently suffered fines and imprisonments. Now they dare not speak, except privately among themselves' (p. 108).

87. The use of the term 'popinjay' to signal these characteristics seems to have become common only in the sixteenth century, but here it seems to make an early, as yet unrecorded appearance. Clanvowe's usage does not appear in the *MED* entry; the first date at which the *OED* records the meaning 'vain courtier' for 'popinjay' is 1528.

88. The first citation is from Jaeger, *Origins of Courtliness*, p. 40, who shows that what Castiglione was describing was a widely recognised value as early as the eleventh century; the second is from Frank Whigham, *Ambition and Privilege: The social tropes of Elizabethan courtesy theory*, Berkeley CA: University of California Press, 1984, p. 33.

89. 'Breaking' seems to refer to a mannered form of singing; complaining about its presence in church, a contemporary Wycliffite referred to the 'smale brekynge þat stiriþ veyn men to daunsynge more þan to mornynge' (see Kenneth Sisam, ed., *Fourteenth-Century Verse and Prose*, Oxford: Clarendon Press, 1921, p. 123). In the *Miller's Tale* the spurious courtier Absolon sings 'brokkyng as a nyghtyngale' (I, 3377), which seems to refer to the same thing (see J. A. W. Bennett, *Chaucer at Oxford and Cambridge*, Toronto: University of Toronto Press, 1974, pp. 44–5).

90. It may well be that Clanvowe is here commenting on the use of French not just as a literary but as a spoken language in the royal court. That it was spoken is suggested by the court poetry of Froissart (1361–9), Jean de la Mote (*c.* 1360s), and Oton Grandson (*c.* 1369–87, 1392–6): if their poems served as the occasion for amorous dalliance, then French must have been not only read but widely spoken in the court. Similarly, Gower addressed the *Cinquante balades* to Henry IV 'pro desporter vo noble Court roial', although they were probably written earlier for a non-court audience (see John H. Fisher, *John Gower: Moral philosopher and friend of Chaucer*, New York NY: New York University Press, 1964, pp. 72–5). Of course Chaucer's English court poetry shows that English was not only spoken at court but used for dalliance. Some scholars are certain that the language of the court in the 1350s and '60s was French: see James I. Wimsatt, *Chaucer and the Poems of 'CH' in University of Pennsylvania MS French 15*, Cambridge: D. S. Brewer, 1982 and Rossell Hope Robbins, 'Geoffroi Chaucier, poète français'. But this is less certain in the later years of Richard's reign, and if the royal court did speak French as a daily vernacular (as

well as reading it, or using it for games), it was almost certainly the only social circle in England that did. For a well-informed survey of this often-discussed matter, see Rolf Berndt, 'The period of the final decline of French in medieval England (fourteenth and early fifteenth centuries)', *Zeitschrift für Anglistik und Amerikanistik*, **20**, 1972, 341–69. The ambiguity of the situation is well illustrated by the fact that Richard II had two tutors, one English (Simon Burley) and one French (Guichard d'Angle). Linguistic nationalism, while widespread throughout the country in the later fourteenth century, became royal policy only with Henry V: see V. H. Galbraith, 'Nationality and language in medieval England', *Transactions of the Royal Historical Society*, 4th ser., **23**, 1941, 113–28.

91. On Marcolf, see Francis Lee Utley, 'Dialogues, debates, and catechisms', in Albert E. Hartung, gen. ed., *A Manual of the Writings in Middle English, 1050–1500*, vol. 3, New Haven CT: Connecticut Academy of Arts and Sciences, 1972, pp. 737–8 (VII, 68e).

92. 'The sense is – "For he who gets a little bliss of love may very soon find that his heir has come of age, unless he is always devoted to it." This is a mild joke, signifying that he will soon find himself insecure, like one whose heir or successor has come of age, and whose inheritance is threatened' (Skeat, ed., *Chaucerian and Other Pieces*, p. 528; cited [slightly inaccurately] by Scattergood in *Works*, p. 84).

93. Scattergood, ed., *Works*, 69–70.

94. Here is the original in its entirety, as printed in Nicholas Harris Nicolas, ed., *The Controversy between Sir Richard Scrope and Sir Robert Grosvenor*, 2 vols, London: Samuel Bentley, 1832, 1.184–5:

> Mon[sieur] John Clanvowe del age de xxxv. ans armeez p[ar] xx ans & plus p[ro]duct p[ar] la p[ar]tie de mon[sieur] Richard Lescrop[e] jurez & examinez demandez si lez armez dazure ove une bende dor app[ar]teignent/ & deyvent app[ar]teigner du droit & de heritage au dit mon[sieur] Richard. dist q[ue] oil qar il ne oiast unq[eu]s dire la contrairie. demandez p[ar] q[uoi] il sciet. dis q[ue] si un ho[m]me luy demande touz les int[er]roga- toirs du mond il luy respondera a un foitz p[a]r tout & dist c[er]teignement q[ue] p[ar] touz lez foitz ou il ad este armez en lez guerrez du Roy il ne vist unq[ue]s ho[m]me porter lez ditz armez ne lez armer ne user ne lez continuer mes ceux de no[u]n de Lescrop[e] ne ne ad oye p[ar]ler devant ceste debate riens dez Grovenors ne de lour auncestrie.

95. Anne Hudson, *The Premature Reformation: Wycliffite texts and Lollard history*, Oxford: Clarendon Press, 1988, pp. 7, 387; McFarlane, *Lancastrian Kings*, p. 204.

96. *Ibid.*, p. 205.

97. Kail, ed., *Twenty-Six Political and Other Poems*, p. 14 (see above, n. 73).

98. Derek Pearsall, *John Lydgate*, London: Routledge & Kegan Paul, 1970, pp. 92–3.

99. Cited from *Patrologia Latina* 207:45A by Jaeger, *Origins of Courtliness*, p. 59.

100. For 'les rapports entre la terminologie féodale et la poésie courtoise', with bibliography, see Köhler, 'Observations historiques', 34, n. 21.

101. The citation is from a poem ascribed to William de la Pole, Duke of Suffolk, in MacCracken, 'An English Friend', 166.

102. Cited by E. Jane Burns, 'The man behind the lady in troubadour lyric', *Romance Notes*, **25**, 1985, 261.

103. Robbins, ed., *Secular Lyrics*, number 129, lines 37–40.

104. *Ibid.*, number 106, lines 3–4, 107–8.

105. See Piaget, *Oton de Grandson*; Diane R. Marks, 'Poems from prison: James I of Scotland and Charles d'Orleans', *Fifteenth-Century Studies*, **15**, 1989, 245–58; and MacCracken, 'An English Friend'.

106. Köhler, 'Observations historiques'; and Herbert F. Moller, 'The social cause of the courtly love complex', *Comparative Studies of Society and History*, **1**, 1958, 137–59, and 'The meaning of courtly love', *Journal of American Folklore*, **73**, 1960, 39–52. Mertes, *Noble Household*, emphasises how small were the number of women present in the noble households of late-medieval England (pp. 6, 43, 57–9), although of course within the *camera regis* where this poetry was most likely read the ratio of men to women would have been more equal.

107. Robbins, ed., *Secular Lyrics*, number 127, lines 40–2.

108. *Ibid.*, number 134, lines 50–3.

109. *Ibid.*, number 162.

110. *Ibid.*, number 169.

111. For 'voix simplette', see Cerquiglini, ed., *Cent ballades*, number 79, line 12 (p. 110); for 'mignot', see above, n. 23.

112. Axel Erdmann, ed., *Lydgate's Siege of Thebes*, Early English Text Society, Extra Series 108, London: Kegan Paul, Trench, Trübner, 1911, lines 253–4, 257.

113. Thus I would disagree with Louise Fradenburg's claim, in 'The manciple's servant tongue: Politics and poetry in *The Canterbury Tales*', *English Literary History*, **52**, 1985, that the courtier 'becomes a signifier in the totalized discourse of the sovereign. The servant ceases to be an individual and becomes a symbol in the service of his master's meaning' (89). This is, of course, what the sovereign desires, but the evidence of court writing, and of court politics, shows that this Foucauldian control cannot be achieved.

114. Paul de Man, 'The rhetoric of temporality', in *Blindness and Insight: Essays in the rhetoric of contemporary criticism*, 2nd edn, Minneapolis MN: University of Minnesota Press, 1983, p. 207.

115. Another major site for the production of literary discourse was the 'local society' of rural gentry from which emerged the Middle English romance and to which *Piers Plowman* spoke with particular force: see P. R. Coss, 'Aspects of cultural diffusion in medieval England: The early romances, local society and Robin Hood', *Past and Present*, **108**, 1985, 35–79, and especially Anne Middleton, 'The audience and public of "Piers Plowman"', in David Lawton, ed., *Middle English Alliterative Poetry and Its Literary Background*, Cambridge: D. S. Brewer, 1982, pp. 101–23, 147–54. But of course both the romances and Langland's poem play only a fitful role in post-medieval literary history.

The Eucharist and the Construction of Medieval Identities

Miri Rubin

Inasmuch as medieval culture, like any culture, provided the means for communication in the individual and the collective, the private and the public domains, we may see the religious culture of the Middle Ages as a *language* of religion. This language was a symbolic system which both defined and expressed the contours of experience, that which is material and tangible, as well as the inchoate, the imaginary. Medieval religious culture possessed all the nuances usually associated with language, those of register and accent, of dialect and slang, of the normative and the aberrant, of acquiescence as well as subversion, of inclusion and exclusion. To appreciate the variety of communicative possibilities inherent in the medieval language of religion one must recognise it as a set of symbols related by rules, whose use was shaped in a constant encounter between normative and recommended combinations, and readings which conflicted, questioned or extrapolated from them. This language of religion was alive, it was used, appropriated, applied, tested against competing symbolic systems, for its utility and *congruence* with other symbolic claims. To emphasise the openness and indeterminacy of this system may seem at odds with the power and prevalence of the medieval Church in promoting certain symbols and their interpretations. But I do not think this need be so. Into the analysis of culture as language we must try to insert the modes of power, the working of difference, the dynamics of contestation. The very interest of the eucharist is thus as a site for assertion and encounter, and thus of the articulation of identities, even when these are private, sectional, fleeting or covert. This essay will explore the emergence of this language and its capacities. I shall also attempt to demonstrate that neither a single

43

descriptive categorical opposition such as elite/popular, literate/illiterate, formal/informal, nor a single analytical category such as gender or class can adequately explain or encompass the interpretations and meanings which were created by individuals within the language. Rather, I believe, that language which provides means for communicating diverse experiences and their claims transcends such single categories, inasmuch as it is formulated from a variety of positions of individual subjects and groups. The language of religion is thus always in dynamic process, bounded by its expressive possibilities and enacted in the various claims articulated through its use. The resonances of authoritative pronouncements will no doubt echo loud and clear in the medieval language of religion, but so will the many voices of its users, consumers.

So language is not only a grid for communication; around it are structured notions of self and identity. The salient categories of identity, gender and community can be observed in their use of the eucharist. The *gendered* nature of sacerdotal efficacy is powerfully constructed in the exclusive sacerdotality of the male priest; *community* identity as whole and orthodox was reinforced through an emphasis through the eucharist on difference from heretics and Jews; *power* and status in the community was further exercised and represented through relations with the eucharist. Through consideration of writing about the eucharist and ultimately of our own writing about it, this piece will finally be drawn into this volume's theme: gender, community, writing.

I would like to suggest not only that Christianity became the overarching language of medieval society, but also that in the High Middle Ages we witness the internal reorganisation of this system, through the emergence of a central symbol related to a central ritual, the eucharist. I shall trace the ways in which the rise of an old/new authoritative symbol in the twelfth and thirteenth centuries prompted the incorporation of the symbol into the life-worlds and identities around it. I shall explore some interpretive variations which seem to have characterised the understandings of the eucharist, and shall consider some of the life-worlds which underpinned them in the late-medieval world.

Let us begin with an exploration of the emergence of a symbol – the design of the eucharist. Basic reformulations of ideas on work, authority, hierarchy, conscience, law and sexuality occupied the minds of intellectuals in the twelfth century as an effect and a cause in the process of social and intellectual refiguration, sometimes called the Renaissance of the twelfth century. The intensification of all types of cultural production, the more wide-ranging and ambitious intellectual project under way, was taking place in a European world which, for at least a century, had been undergoing some dramatic changes. This reorientation was experienced in towns which were the products of a period of demographic and economic growth, in a world which had come into close contact with other religions and cultures, where mobility and differentiation of occupation and of social roles were leaving indelible marks. In this society all, and especially the professional thinkers, writers and teachers, were hard at work, identifying and formulating categories, boundaries, classifications, rules of conduct, an ideology for an increasingly complex arena. Village communities, towns, monasteries, merchants, kingdoms, the papacy, the Empire, were engaged in a process of self-understanding and in the negotiations for privileges and power which followed from it. In this setting especially hard pressed were those institutions which made universal claims, like Empire and the Church. So from the eleventh century we witness an engagement with the question of papal authority and, more generally, with the roles of the Church and its universal claims. The nature of these claims and their related practices, privileges and rituals were carefully investigated, and their implications considered in the century that followed. As this took place notions that were burdensome and awkward were discarded, that which needed change was rethought and reformulated, and where necessary, new terms were forged. The eucharist was constructed by the convergence of these processes.

The first stirrings in the medieval discussion of the eucharist appear in the works of two mid-ninth-century monks of the monastery of Corbie, Ratramnus and Paschasius Radbert.[1] The Augustinian legacy left open many important interpretations in the eucharist. Like all sacraments, to Augustine the eucharist had a physical dimension, *res*, but even more significantly, it had a symbolic value in faith, in being the community of believers, its charity and faith (*sacramentum et res*). In the eucharist the members of Christ's body, individual believers, were bound. The workings of this affinity, and of the nature of sacramental efficacy, were not further specified.[2] So the monastic exchange was the first discussion of the nature of the eucharist as a sacrament, rather than as a devotional, communal ritual. Paschasius stressed the physical nature of the sacrament as the very body of Christ conjured at the altar by the officiating priest and supported this view with patristic arguments and some clinching miracle tales. His younger fellow monk, Ratramnus, argued against this physical interpretation of Christ's presence and suggested a figurative interpretation. In this ninth-century monastic milieu the nature of the eucharist was an interesting off-shoot to liturgical practice, but the discussion which took place within the walls of Corbie had few immediate repercussions in contemporary theological discussion. It provided, however, the initial orientations and lines of argument for future realignment when eucharistic-sacramental issues became topical.[3]

They did, some two centuries later, when Berengar the canon of Tours, master of the liberal arts and exponent of the Bible, took the issue up while teaching at Tours in the 1040s. This secular scholar, who was trained at

Chartres, the foremost episcopal school of the eleventh century, started, at the apex of his career, to explore the nature of the sacrament through an engagement with the scriptural text which lay at its foundation. For Berengar the eucharist did not summon a physical Christ; as for Ratramnus before him, it was a powerful symbol. In fact, Berengar was wrestling with the implications of Aristotelian logic, studied in his days through the *Logica vetus* of Boethius. This had led him to ask whether the verb to be (*esse*), used by Christ in the Last Supper, could signify a relation of figuration rather than of identity. Could a material object indeed become a great invisible spiritual truth?

By the mid-eleventh century these views were so pregnant with danger for the sacramental-sacerdotal system that the papacy finally intervened in the debate which developed around Berengar's views and in 1059 forced upon him an oath which stressed the physical nature of the eucharist. In it Pope Nicholas II went far beyond the conservative scholarly anti-Berengarian view, as mounted by the main anti-Berengarian polemicist Lanfranc, a view based on patristic authorities. The papacy's formulation emphasised the physical nature of the sacramental body of Christ, claiming 'that the bread and wine which are laid on the altar are after the consecration not only a sacrament but also the true body of . . . Jesus Christ, and they are physically taken up and broken in the hands of the priest and crushed by the teeth of the faithful, not only sacramentally, but in truth'.[4] This was so strong a statement that already in the 1070s, and even more so in the next century, theologians had begun to reformulate it with subtler versions and meanings. The nature of the sacramental transformation experienced by the bread and wine and articulated in Aristotelian language became sufficiently clear to produce by the mid-twelfth century the term transubstantiation, claiming that the bread and wine were wholly transformed into the flesh and blood of the historic Christ. And this symbol of the essence and promise of a sacramental world-view came to be placed at the very centre of a system of power and meaning. This ultimate symbol was placed at the heart of a universal ideology for a Christian world.

The eucharist was, of course, already an established ritual with related practices, but in earlier centuries universal claims resided only in an embryonic form.[5] But in the High Middle Ages, indeed from Berengar's day on, it was becoming increasingly clear that as the Church was adapting to a differentiating and changing world, through strong universal claims, such unclarity could not be tolerated. The Church came to occupy a central role by offering a language for this complex *societas christiana*. It achieved this by insisting on the exclusive right of the clergy to mediate the grace of redemption, the shared Creator and Saviour, to dispense of supernatural power through rituals performed by its clergy alone. The quintessence of this claim now lay in the most powerful ritual of mediation, the eucharist, emerging as it was as a re-enactment, not merely memorial, of the central act of sacrifice which had been foretold in the Last Supper, and suffered in the Passion. To sustain this claim to a unifying power, and to provide the symbols underpinning such a claim, was the burning issue at the heart of the hegemonic intellectual project of the day.[6]

The eucharist: ritual and clerical identity

By the mid-twelfth century and in the University of Paris this project was producing some authoritative and confident statements about the eucharist. Within the emerging group of seven sacraments, defined and explicated by Peter Lombard in his *Sentences*, the eucharist was accorded particular attention. Whereas in the early Middle Ages it was often assimilated into relic worship (like relics it was placed under altars for their consecration, and like them it was shown to work miracles), the eucharist was now being increasingly distanced from relics and their cult.[7] As it was rethought and strong claims were made about it, the eucharist drew more and more attention in theological discussions of the sacraments, and came to soar above the other six rituals. The host could be handled and the eucharist celebrated only by a priest, whereas baptism, marriage and extreme unction could sometimes be celebrated by lay people *in extremis*. It was withdrawn from unguarded exposure and was removed from the bases of altars. In all the sacrament came to symbolise the essence of sacerdotal office, particularly after the implications of the doctrine of transubstantiation were realised. The eucharist was emerging as the most frequently celebrated and attended sacrament, and one which made the most outrageous of claims. Thus the ritual and the idea which underpinned it had to be made to reinforce each other. The mass was thus designed by theologians and liturgists to do just that: to sustain the claim that the little white disc over which the Latin consecration was said was thus transformed into the body of Christ which could occasionally be received into the human body through communion. And if indeed the consecrated host was Christ's very flesh and blood, the historic suffering crucified body, then the implications were many: it was of the utmost importance that it be handled, contained, addressed, cared for and consumed as befitted this divine nature. Guidebooks proliferated from the twelfth century and meticulously considered every garment, gesture, sound, utterance and word in the ritual, stressing their compatibility with the sacramental claim.[8] The concerted attempt to design the mass required consideration not only of appearances, but of contingency, of the accidents and mishaps which might befall the practitioner and the materials in the ritual space and time of the mass. It meant that inclement weather, rickety altars, decrepit clergy, dishonest communicants, shaking hands, dripping roofs, mice around the altar, poor illumination on winter mornings, all the elements which might detract from, impede or confound the ritual experience, were anticipated by canonists and theologians who provided precautions, dignified remedies and deterrent penalties for abuse. Questions about the handling of the eucharist increasingly entered the rubrics of confession and the penance that followed in the growing genre of *Libri poenitentiales* and in synodal decrees. These discussed the penance due for spilling consecrated wine or dropping the host, and laid down procedures for appropriate removal and disposal of the maltreated elements, as well as for due penance by the negligent priest.

But besides the procedures and the appearances, theologians were wrestling with the emerging implications from the claim of transubstantiation, even before this became a belief required *de fide*.[9] These implications were many, and with dialectical rhythm they were addressed, answered, challenged, corrected or resolved. The eleventh-century debate had been enacted before the full implications of the categories of accidents and substances were realised; in the next century little space for evasion was available, a fact which created a constant tension between the theological claim and its philosophical setting. When difficulties were encountered in the schools between opposing positions, consensus usually settled on formulations conducive to the over-arching pastoral project at hand: to provide a system of ideas and practices for the life of a *societas christiana*. This world-view was being formally produced by intellectuals but inasmuch as they intended to provide a viable, resilient, predictable and all-encompassing cultural system for application in all areas of life, and for the use of men and women everywhere, debates were steered away from subtleties and open-ended refinements and towards univocal and unequivocal statements.

The awareness exhibited by the agents of this vast project of eucharistic design of the pastoral end guiding them, is everywhere to be found, not only in the intensity of theological and canonistic work, but in the institutional developments which followed. The twelfth and thirteenth centuries see the emergence of a bureaucracy of priests who were better trained and better equipped for their now more extensive tasks. What is most striking in this period is the increasing concentration on the nature of clerical office, consideration of its scope, provision for its needs and a clearer demarcation of its duties and privileges. If the Gregorian reform first established the Church's claims to be the prime cultural agent in the Christian world, this power could only be justified and utilised by an appropriately trained and groomed clergy, and thus efforts were made to transform the clergy into instruments worthy of the *libertas ecclesia*, in the greater enforcement of celibacy, in insistence on residence and provision of adequate vicarages, in foundation of diocesan schools for the clergy, and the development of a system of Church law which could reach everywhere through a network of diocesan mediation. But most importantly, the sacerdotal claim was empowered through the production of a multitude of uniform, orthodox, easily available and user-friendly reference books which taught and guided in the rudiments of pastoral care and sacramental action.[10] A fuller obligation to teach and preach and a basic curriculum for lay instruction was laid down in the canons of the fourth Lateran Council and in the diocesan legislation which followed throughout the century, to produce a variety of aids, manuals, indices, collections of preaching and teaching material which, often written by the leading thinkers of the day, spelt out the implications of the learning in the schools, after these had been put through the mill of pastoral utility, vernacular translation and idiomatic formulation, to the clergy of rural and urban parishes. These guidebooks instructed the clergy not only in the rudiments of instruction, on the commandments, the articles of faith, the creed, the vices and virtues, but also in their duties as performers of rituals which enacted the hegemonic symbolic system. Thus synodal statutes, mass manuals and rubrics guided priests through their newly designed all-important mass: about lighting, ringing of bells, the meaning of its words and gestures, with the double aim of making the performance uniform and dignified, and providing ready interpretations of it for the performer and for his audience.

Through the creation of tools for the dissemination of orthodoxy and the deciphering of ritual practices the message of the eucharist was more widely and frequently expounded, and at its centre was the claim that the holiest of holies was summoned by the words of the priest. To sustain the claim a whole set of practices was created. The material and form of the host, the image at the centre of the mass, was fashioned to be white, thin, round, and made of pure wheat since, as put by James of Vitry, 'only that which is wheaten will be transubstantiated'.[11] The process of host preparation, from the selection of grains through milling and baking, was increasingly ritualised. The vessels which contained the consecrated host were to be made of precious metals, the cloths and the drapery of particular sizes, colour, number and quality.[12] A bulwark of artefacts and practices was created to sustain the claim of sacramental efficacy and to heighten the ritual effect.

The moment in the mass most laden with symbolic meaning was the consecration, when the transformation of matter into God was said to take place, and it was extremely important to pinpoint that dramatic moment. This was by no means simple. Now bread, now God – the white disc showed little change, and yet a *total* change was taking place in it. Theologians spent the last decades of the twelfth century over the question of the moment of the consecration: was it after the first blessing of the bread, or only after the two blessings, and if the former, in what sense could the body exist without the as yet unconsecrated blood?[13] Despite the variety of views

argued in the University of Paris, consensus settled by the end of the century
on a solution which compromised the spirit of the scripture, but one which
was more manageable in practice: that the body and blood bound through
concomitance were there together already after the first consecration. Once
settled, this climax of the mass was securely marked by an elevation of the
host.[14] The now present Christ was raised in the hands of the priest for all to
see, a focus for prayer, address, exchange, the culmination of sacramental
promise. The moment of the elevation was marked by special illumination,
incense and the ringing of bells; all attention was directed at the little white
shape in which salvation resided.

The eucharist – participation and personal identity

The elevation was a useful provision of a climax to a lengthy and largely
Latin ritual, a moment when people might run into the church from
outside, and one which encouraged the concentration of minds through
flights of imagination upon God, source of salvation and health. It grew in
importance while communion itself became a rare and awesome practice, as
teachings about the proper spiritual and physical conditions of communion
and on the enormity of undeserving reception were explicitly and frequently
expounded.[15] In the carefully designed audio-visual event which the mass
had become, with lights, sounds, props and smells, the elevation was the
climax to this ritual, one which invited participation, while attempting to
anticipate and mould the contours of the experience. The elevation offered
release and ecstasy, a space for the expression of fears, hopes and anxieties.
Guidebooks to the laity instructed them to expect benefits to accrue from
the moment and to express themselves through recommended images
invoking the virgin birth and the Passion.[16] Evidence for the contents and
meanings of these addresses can be found not only in the Latin prayers in
Books of Hours, but more significantly and abundantly in vernacular books,
in collections of carols, scribbled on to flyleaves of formal prayer books,
commonplace books, copied into talismans, inscribed for teaching by parish
priests.[17] Through and beyond the imagery of the Birth and Passion of the
now present Christ the moment offered a site for the imaginary, for the
expression of hopes for health, and of yearnings for protection from evil, sin
and ill-fortune. Through tokens of self-debasement a sort of exchange was
struck between the person who was taking Christ on His own terms,
addressing Him as a real presence ('Welcome, lord, in form of bread') and
who was seeking help and protection as the implicit return. Here the
language of religion provided the devices, the occasion, the space for the
expression of utmost fear, hope, adhesion or transgression.

But there were, of course, other manners of relation to the claims – transubstantiation, sacerdotal sacramental mediation – such as rejection. Lollards in the later Middle Ages challenged both tenets repeatedly and fundamentally. The two are bound in an argument which derides the idea of Christ's physical presence in the eucharistic bread, an idea perpetuated through clerical deception:

A Lord! what wurship don þise new heretikes unto þis sacrament, whenne þei seie þat [it] is not brede, but accident wiþoute subiecte or now3te? And if þer be any accident wiþout subiecte as þei seyne, it is wars in kynde þenne is any lumpe of cleye, as clerkes knowen wele. His semeþ wele bi here dedis þott þei conspiren a3enes Cristis gospel and his pore lyuyng for to maynten here owne pride.[18]

The thrust of intellectual and pastoral activity was to provide arguments which countered such dissent, strengthened orthodox claims through ritual and image, and which integrated the eucharistic view into people's lives, routines, aspirations and hopes.

The eucharist provided not only a doctrine, but also useful procedures and practices. The vigorous discussion which surrounded it exhibits the dynamics of all symbolic systems. Confident definitions of the twelfth century received encyclopaedic treatment in the vast *Summae* of the thirteenth, and by the fourteenth century these were greatly extended and stretched to accommodate further questions, objections and contradictions which were arising in the scholastic discourses as well as in other milieus through the constant use and testing of the symbol. At a point in the thirteenth century the pastoral and intellectual processes intersected to create a feast of the eucharist, a public event designed to summarise, explore and demonstrate the hegemonic sacramental world-view. Corpus Christi provide the site *par excellence* for the meeting of the prescriptive and the creative, the taught and the interpreted, for the presentation or misrepresentation of power through the eucharistic procession.

Inasmuch as it was disseminated by the institution of the Church, the sacramental world-view reached everywhere and everyone, through preaching, through the observation of ritual, in the messages of wall paintings. The Church attempted to provide constant support for its claims through an integration of stimuli and through the anticipation and refutation of contradictions and difficulties inherent in them. Yet, the very ubiquity, the success of the teaching, its many and complex implications for life practices, exposed the symbolic system to ongoing interpretation, to uses, to attempt at its appropriation. And this is in the very nature of any symbolic system, that it is destined, even if not intended, to communicate a variety of differing meanings. And how much more so when the central symbol is also a source of power and experience in its own physical dimension. It is then that those who are meant merely to consume its signifying potential, and who in any case would do so in many individual and unexpected ways, become intent on gaining control over it. This is the problem inherent in a sacramental world-view: that it imbues matter with efficacy. And if this is believed then the very body of Christ was entering one's own body at communion, providing a field for personal experience, fantasies, meanings, suggesting uses and practices which far transcended the hegemonic eucharistic code. The eucharist became a pivot for mystical flights, it served in healing and magic, it elicited fantasies of transgression, and provided hierarchical systems with a focus of power. It is the simplicity and naïveté of the eucharistic symbol, white, round, fragile, which left so ample a space for inscription and superimposition on to this dangerous and seemingly clean slate.

But the problem with the eucharist was not only the tension between the simplicity of the symbol and the power it signified, it was the very nature of the claim which related the two. Some were outraged and others merely bemused by the contradiction between the eucharist and some observed and workaday truths about the natural world. Objections to eucharistic claims were made sometimes by heretics, and other times by joking villagers, or in the privacy of confession, raising some common-sense questions: how large must Christ's body be if indeed it is eaten at thousands of altars every day, or has it perhaps already been eaten up?[19] It was by the application of the common-sensical, the terms with which the world was apprehended in the spheres of work and play, forged from experience, reflecting in differing and interesting ways accepted scientific paradigms, that criticism of the eucharist was articulated. Critiques of this language of religion also developed through analogies between the eucharistic claims and those of other experiences, through extrapolations of the very sacramental world-view, through the confrontation of discourses which made the eucharist not only a thing good to receive annually at Easter, but good to put on the forehead of a sick child.

The dissemination of the sacramental language of religion was accompanied by ongoing attempts to establish its hegemonic status through an appeal to what was taken to be the 'popular mind', to the world-views of *simplices*, *illiterati* and *minores*.[20] Doctrinal formulations were packaged in what were deemed to be appropriate wrappings for the multitude of lay recipients. So hand in hand with the writing of manuals for the edification of the clergy, a literature of practical teaching developed which was aimed at persuasion through elucidation and illustration in tales, *exempla* which were assembled in Latin as well as vernacular collections. The genre had an early history in monastic collections of tales for the edification of novices, such as Caesarius of Heisterbach's classic *Dialogue of Miracles* of *c.*1224, of which there were many copies in England.[21] It received additional impetus with the activities of the friars from the early thirteenth century.[22] And this was an exercise in self-conscious popularisation inasmuch as the tales were designed to correct and elucidate the most difficult points in the normative edifice, and to rectify the most frequent errors through an appeal to what preachers considered to be 'the popular mind' and the difficulties of belief and adherence most frequently encountered by it. The genre operated with what writers believed its audience to *be* in order to turn it into what it *ought* to be. Collections such as the extremely useful *Handlyng Synne* of *c*.1303, a combination of exposition and tale, treated alleged common errors and abuses and attempted to counter them with instruction and with the fortifying power of well-placed miraculous interventions.[23] As such they provide us with a possible channel into an ethnography of eucharistic uses. Read within the discourse which produced these exemplary texts, the language of religion can be revealed as spoken, rather than from the grammar books. Similarly, the disapproving bishop in court, or the correcting archdeacon at a visitation will be constructing narratives related to utterances which they may attempt to correct, and may also thoroughly misunderstand, but which still can be read against other texts to offer an entry into the sacramental symbolic world 'at work'. The eucharistic utterances of individuals reveal areas of experience, and we shall see that these do not adhere to, nor can be captured under, any neat and exclusive categories of explanation such as class, gender, age, occupation. In the reading of experience through opaque and sometimes intractable texts we will attempt to identify clusters of meaning as they were thrown up in social contexts and as they evolved historically.

The eucharist – construction of the Other: Jews, children, women

So a closer look at the *exempla* as correlated with other types of evidence will allow us to examine the struggle between attempts to teach and impart a world-view and its reception (*Rezeption*) which made the creation of a single meaning ultimately unachievable. The *exemplum* usually told of some danger befalling the eucharist; this could be innocent or malevolent doubt about Christ's presence, its use in magic, reception by a sinner, all types of breaches of the eucharistic code. A miraculous occurrence then took place, proved the doubted point, dispelled uncertainty, or punished an evil-doer. It usually ended with the persuasion of the doubter and, through shame and penance, witnessed his or her return to the fold of faith.

Through projection of doubt and abuse on to those who were different and inferior a certain relief was effected, since through the telling of the tale they were voiced and discussed publicly. But the discussion was controlled and ended in the manipulation *a fortiori* which was supposed to shame people into belief as well as strengthen their trust through the direct divine miraculous intervention. The stories involving Others allow the description of the details of abuse while maintaining the boundaries of ultimate interpretation through the manipulation of the very guilt which they brought to the surface.

From the early Middle Ages Jews were used in this genre as perpetrators of abuses or eternal doubters of the eucharistic presence, who were transformed into witnesses of the faith through experiencing a miracle. Such tales have a 'happy end': the Jew converts following a miraculous intervention. But by the late thirteenth century Jews came to be associated, both in *exempla* and in chronicles, with violent attacks on the eucharist, using knives and axes and fire. These were accusations of host desecration: that a Jew or a small group of Jews procured the eucharist from a sinful Christian (usually a woman), abused it violently, and was/were ultimately caught, arrested, tortured and executed.[24] Hundreds of representations in the whole variety of medieval expressive media developed, based on an original case, the Miracle of Paris of 1290 which provided the basic narrative and the authority of a 'real' event.[25] These tales represented the Jews as knowing perpetrators of premeditated crimes, crimes against the eucharist, breaking every rule of access and address. The gory description of the bleeding hosts as these miraculously rebelled against Jewish abuse was violent and bloody, as were the scenes of punishment.[26] These were tales which reinforced ideas about eucharistic power, and about the danger posed by those who threatened the eucharist. So in the eucharistic tales told about Jews from around the thirteenth century Jews were not eventually converted in proof of the faith, the easy solution of earlier centuries; rather they were tortured and executed, often in groups. This attitude falls in with the growing view of the Jews as knowing killers of Christ within mendicant theological circles, the circles which fed the *exempla* genre.[27] In reality, the conditioned response which these tales created meant that mere rumour of a eucharistic crime could be developed along the story-line of an *exemplum* and cost the lives of both individual Jews and of groups or communities. Ronnie Hsia's analysis of the development of ritual murder accusations as exercises in 'communal narration' shows the degree to which the didactic discourse influenced and penetrated the realm of political action, and we will see below how 'real' events were in turn reabsorbed in exemplary form within the repertoire of exemplary tale.[28]

Looking more closely at the most widespread tale in which Jews and eucharist were juxtaposed, the story of the Jewish Boy, we discover another area of sensitivity around the eucharist.[29] It tells of a Jewish boy who went to church with his Christian friends at Christmas, and who received communion with them. He then went home and told his parents that he had communicated, and in some versions he is said to have seen a child in the host.[30] The Jewish parents were appalled and the enraged father threw his son into a burning furnace. Meanwhile some Christians had heard his cries and come to the rescue, to hear from the miraculously unscathed youngster that he had been shielded in the fire under the garment of a lovely lady.[31] This was a very busy day for the Jewish boy: first he was said to have seen a child in the host, he received communion, then he went home to be thrown into the fire, and finally he was saved by that child's own mother. The story first appears in the sixth century and resurfaces in twelfth-century collections, whence it gains in popularity and detail, and finally sent the angry father to death, together with other members of the Jewish community. Within this dramatic and violent scene of cruelty and sacrifice, the gentle appearance of the Virgin in the furnace and the eucharistic vision gain strength, emboldened by the opposition to pathos and disorder.

This tale employs a recurrent motif in eucharistic tales, that of the privileged vision of Christ in the host, a vision granted to someone pious, or pure, and even to the misguided in order to prove eucharistic truth beyond doubt. Here, the Jewish boy's purity allows him to achieve special vision *anagnorisis*, to recognise inherent truths obscured from his adult blind and misguided Jewish parents.[32] Thus children were often used as hypersensitive witnesses to the reality of eucharistic presence in the stories playing on their generic purity. This is related in tales like the one about the child who ran out of church during communion, having seen a baby eaten at the altar. Similarly, a child who had heard talk of 'eating the son of God' took flight to the forest to live with hermits there, lest the same fate befall him.[33]

But more than as pure and privileged seers innocently attesting the truth, children appear in the eucharistic tales as victims, bloodied, wounded, torn limb from limb during communion. We have found this in the words of the fearful boys who saw such child-abuse perpetrated at the altar and feared for themselves. The child in a sacrificial setting was a disturbing and ambivalent image, it produced pathos and built on a stock of biblical tales which often exposed children, like the Massacre of the Innocents, the Sacrifice of Isaac, even the scenes of Presentation and Circumcision which juxtaposed child, offering and altar.[34] The juxtaposition of Christmas–Incarnation images with those of eucharist–sacrifice lies at the very heart of the eucharistic world-view; the mass is the re-enactment of an original act of incarnation and sacrifice. Here was exposed the purest and the most vulnerable – a mere child – as the victim of any eucharistic abuse. This powerful use of a strong evocative image also played on the ambiguities felt towards children within the culture, and created an area for fantasy and transgression in which children were mutilated, immolated, chewed. A child was powerfully seen, immolated, cut up, and received into the mouths of communicants in a miniature illustration to an *exemplum* in a compilation prepared in the late thirteenth century for Lady Joan Tateshal of Lincolnshire.[35] The artist interestingly censored the tale in his illuminations: he represents the child's appearance in the eucharist in one scene (figure 11) and then shows the scene of reception of bloody chunks of his body by communicants (figure 12), omitting the imaging of dissection. In other similar tales the child is seen in the eucharist, elevated in the sacrifice, adored, and then restored.[36] This is nowhere more apparent than in those tales which imputed to Jews the enormity of child-abuse, the ritual murder accusation, in analogy to their role as desecrators of hosts, and above all as tormentors and murderers of Christ. The eucharistic tale besides the ritual murder accusation mutually supported an edifice of orthodoxy, the beliefs which Jews obviously did not cherish, and bolstered it through the makings of a moment of transgression of taboo and in fantastic elaboration of the abuse of children provided in the hearing, telling and ultimate imagining of these eucharistic tales.

We witness thus the creation of a dense world of tale and example, a thick forest of narratives which gave meaning to and gained meaning by the eucharist. The primary identity of Christian orthodoxy was powerfully drawn as opposite to the stances, behaviour, utterances of a series of Others who forsook or denied the host, bringing upon themselves destruction. Gender too was constructed through and around the symbol. The eucharist was loaded with inscriptions of law, order, hierarchy, authority, in face of which women could only exist in obedience, as object, or in total rejection, as enemy or victim. Women are portrayed frequently in stories about the eucharist: obedient and committed adherent, or mistaken, misguided, and sometimes knowing, abuser.

A typical *exemplum* about women and the eucharist was told by Caesarius of Heisterbach and later by Thomas of Cantimpré, about a woman who decided to put the eucharist to good use. She received the host at communion, kept it on her tongue and sprinkled it over her beehive to fructify her bees. When she came back to check on the results she heard a sound of chanting and when she looked in she saw that the bees had erected a little church, an *ecclesiula* in some versions, and an altar within it on which the host was placed and venerated by the hovering, or should one say buzzing, bees.[37] Now the woman obviously believed in the power of the eucharist, but she was misguided in attempting to handle and manipulate it; so the revelation came from the confrontation with simple beings, mere bees, who provided the example of proper veneration and respect of the eucharist. The woman repented and was forgiven, and the audience was meant to learn from her example. A variant on the animal-adoration tale recounts the story of a thief who had stolen the host with some other church ornaments and buried it in his field, only to find that whenever he approached with his team of ploughing beasts, they refused to plough over it.[38] Another formulation is the tale of a woman who was afraid to swallow the eucharist since she doubted Christ's presence in it, and who took it out of her mouth and fed it to her pigs. The pigs knelt in respect, so she tried to burn it but it was not consumed, rather it started bleeding and thus taught her of her error.[39] This woman's story could obviously instruct on the consequences of undeserving reception and of weakness of faith in the eucharist, and the blood flowed to strengthen her faith and that of the audience.

The prominence of women, of Jews, of heretics as protagonists in some very similar tales of eucharistic crime and its punishment reflects the symbolic equivalence which they possessed. These were figures who were, and who could be further constructed as, the Other.[40] A doubting man was perhaps too dangerous a phenomenon to be publicly acknowledged and discussed, except through the mouths of women, children and sometimes *rustici*, all of whom could be treated with cautious indulgence for their 'blindness', for their lack of reason and rigour, and be corrected through the miraculous and rhetorical transformation of the tale. As in the more extreme case of the Jews, their very error and transgression was a sign that only weakness and sinfulness could breed such abuses. But another identification around the eucharist was also possible, of an intimacy with Christ, in it.[41] The life-stories of female saints and mystics provided a large portion of exemplary tales of eucharistic miracles, which entered the same repertoire. So we can observe from the late twelfth century the creation of a systematic and necessary Other to that which was emerging increasingly clearly as the normative. And this is a process fundamental to the creation of any identity, in a confrontation of what is and what ought to be, through the construction of what is not and ought not to be. As the eucharist emerged in its central symbolic role, it was the inevitable locus for this construction.

All these cases strongly suggest that the widely disseminated hegemonic language of religion was deployed and applied, interpreted and given meaning and uses through the working of analogy, extrapolation and fantasy, to create and re-create its meanings. At the levels of uses it is impossible, both unfeasible and theoretically unappealing, to try and separate sections of language-uses, but rather to examine them in contestation and contact. The Church's *sacramentalia*, the offering of holy water, blessed crosses, chrism, and sometimes even the host for non-liturgical magical and ceremonial purposes, cannot be seen merely as a compromise. Analogies between the mode of power which worked the eucharistic miracles and the protection and fertility which people hoped to secure through the appropriation of the host were the product of meaning-bearing linguistic processes which underpin the vitality of any symbolic system.

The eucharist – elite and public; personal and private

In the public arena the eucharist's power was tapped within the discourse of political power and magistracy, in the feast of Corpus Christi.[42] This new liturgical feast possessed a processional element shared by other eucharistic practices such as the visitation of the sick with the sacrament in processional form, the procession having grown into the most suitable public manner of handling the eucharist. Throughout the fourteenth century this public, outdoor summer feast was turned into an important event in the civic ceremonial, especially in English towns. The eucharist, contained in a monstrance and carried by the clergy on a bier or under a canopy, was used as a symbolic measuring-rod of political power in its distribution between the processing corporations of the enfranchised sector of town-dwellers. Corpus Christi was soon chosen as the favoured theme for elite urban fraternities; the language of exclusivity captured by the eucharist was incorporated into the universal claims of patriciates to privilege and power.

The eucharist could thus restrain and exclude, but its polysemy also allowed for the exploration, even destabilisation, of normative roles and boundaries. In Margery Kempe's experience the eucharist allowed her an escape from expectations in family and neighbourhood, it provided the pretext for travel and self-exploration, and most importantly it allowed an identification of the female as *object* with Christ, the ultimate *object*, sacrificed, mutilated, all forbearance.[43] Thus everywhere, in towns and countryside, by peasant and gentry, men and women, priests and mystics, the symbolic system with the eucharist at its heart was being constituted and reconstituted, defining and being defined by experience and expediency, need and repressed desire. And this is inevitable in any cultural process. The arbitrary language becomes the site of infinite utterances, it mediates and expresses difference in the face of the ongoing demands for conformity made by language itself, and in response to the powers which aim at shaping hegemonic meanings. Yet determination cannot hold; powerful institutions can influence the frequency and shape of symbols, suggesting thereby normative readings of social relations, but users may go on to explore the gaps and create private, if not subversive, meanings.

The eucharist in the later Middle Ages – a symbol over-used?

So the central symbol of Christian culture, accessible and well taught and widely offered within the common language of religion, was destined to communicate some very disparate and changing personal and collective messages. Tracing the horizon of eucharistic reception (again, *Rezeption*), we have noted that some of the intangible and unspeakable associations will remain largely obscured and incommunicable to us, but other insistent objections, interpretations and uses have arisen and are enough to suggest the many uses of the eucharist.

By the mid-fifteenth century a tendency to withdraw, reclaim, shield and reappropriate the eucharist is everywhere in evidence, as the Church sensed that its perfect symbol of mediation became too charged and over-determined with conflicting meanings. The success of its enterprise of instruction was so great that most people possessed sufficient knowledge of the language of sacramental religion with the eucharist at its centre to attempt further departures from it. Exposition of the eucharist, its integration into civic ritual, its use for blessing of fields, its dispensation in sacramentals, its application in magic and healing, its status as a test of Christian adherence, all loaded the eucharist with conflicting and competing meanings in the uses of divergent and numerous discourses, some of which admitted little hegemonic privilege to the clergy within them. So an agitated attempt was mounted by theologians, friars and reformers to restore the eucharist to its pristine designed state.[44] The material manifestation of the divine had been exhausted through the development of edifices of images, meanings and uses which at once fragmented it as a central symbol and over-burdened it as a collective token. And these processes cannot merely be seen as 'popularisation' on the one hand, or 'dissent' on the other. What came to be branded as heresy was not only a question of context and contingency, it was often part and parcel of objections made within the 'orthodox' sphere. The process, at the end of which lay the two Reformations, was the inevitable transformation of a symbolic system, the inevitable working of the dialectics of form and meaning. The creative tension in signification is the life-blood of any culture. And when its gaps are furnished and filled with meanings, dense and conflicting, it is time for change of the system of symbols and realignment of the language which must service difference and experience.

We have concentrated our gaze on the possibilities of appropriation or 'making-own' of a symbol crafted on high with strong elements of power and persuasion invested into its design and presentation, all working to appeal and cajole. This has been a largely synchronic reading; only hints at the directions and dynamics of change have been given.[45] I have also attempted to suggest ways of *writing* about cultural forms which are shifting, and always re-created, without averting our gaze from the working of power and persuasion within the symbol itself. Furthermore, by looking at the English dialect of the language of religion, in its various idioms, some ways of considering cultural diffusion over the Christian world become clear through procedures of discipline, through the power of translation and the emphatic sense of legislation and authoritative compilation. Here too, resources and power further influence the suggestions and frequency of encounter with the symbolic world of the eucharist, introducing even further fragmentation to the world of change infinitely flexible, and strictly contextual in articulation.

Notes

1. G. Macy, *The Theologies of the Eucharist in the Early Scholastic Age*, Oxford: Oxford University Press, 1984, pp. 74–9.
2. See Augustine's images in the commentary on John: *In Iohannis evangelium tractatus CXXIV*, Corpus Christianorum, Series Latina, Turnholt: Brepols, 1954, tract 26, c. 1, p. 260; tract 27, c. 6, p. 272. N. Häring, 'Berengar's definitions of *sacramentum* and their influence on medieval theology', *Mediaeval*
    Studies, **10**, 1948, 109–46; esp. 109–10.
3. Macy, *Theologies of the Eucharist*, pp. 21–31.
4. On the oath, see M. Gibson, *Lanfranc of Bec*, Oxford: Oxford University Press, 1978, pp. 94–6; H. Chadwick, '*Ego Berengarius*', *Journal of Theological Studies*, new ser., **40**, 1989, 414–45, 421–3.
5. C. Walter, *Art and Ritual of the Byzantine Church*, London: Variorum Reprints, 1982, esp. pp. 184–9, 196–225.
6. J. A. Jungmann, *The Mass of the Roman Rite: Its origins and development*, trans. F. A. Brunner, 2 vols, New York NY: Christian Classics, 1951–5.
7. M. Rubin, *Corpus Christi: The eucharist in late medieval culture*, Cambridge: Cambridge University Press, 1991, p. 36.
8. On gesture during the mass, see J.-C. Schmitt, *La Raison des gestes dans l'Occident médiéval*, Paris: Gallimard, 1990, pp. 330–55.
9. At the Fourth Lateran Council of 1215, *Conciliorum oecumenicorum decreta*, ed. G. Alberigo, Bologna: Istituto per le Scienze Religiose, 3rd edn 1973, c. 1, p.230 and on communion see c. 21, p. 245. See the early diffusion of these canons through English councils in *Councils and Synods with Other Documents Relating to the English Church*, vol. II part 1, ed. M. Powicke and C. R. Chenev, Oxford: Oxford University Press, 1964: the statutes of Salisbury 1217–19, repromulgated for Durham 1228–36, pp. 57–96; the statutes of provincial council at Oxford 1222, pp. 100–25; the statutes for the diocese of Winchester 1224, pp. 125–37.
10. L. E. Boyle, 'The inter-conciliar period 1179–1215 and the beginnings of pastoral manuals', in *Miscellanea Rolando Bandinelli papa Alessandro III*, ed. F. Liotta, Siena: Accademia Senese degli Intornati, 1986, pp. 184–93; L. E. Boyle, 'Robert Grosseteste and pastoral care', *Medieval and Renaissance Studies*, **8**, 1979, 3–51.
11. 'De sacramentis', in *The 'Historia occidentalis' of Jacques de Vitry: A critical edition*, ed. J. F. Hinnebusch, Spicilegium Friburgense 17, Fribourg: Fribourg University Press, 1972, p. 219.

12. Rubin, *Corpus Christi*, pp. 39–45.

13. V. L. Kennedy, 'The moment of consecration and the elevation of the host', *Mediaeval Studies*, 6, 1944, 121–50.

14. E. Dumoutet, *Le Désir de voir l'Hostie et les origines de la dévotion au Saint Sacrement*, Paris: Gabriel Beauchesne, 1926, pp. 36–74; Macy, *Theologies of the Eucharist*, pp. 86–93; V. Reinburg, 'Popular prayers in late medieval and Reformation France', Princeton PhD, 1985, 185–201.

15. See the exposition and tales in the section 'The sacrament of the altar' in Robert Mannyng of Brunne, *Handlyng Synne*, ed. I. Sullens, Medieval and Renaissance texts and studies 14, Binghamton NY: Medieval and Renaissance, 1983, pp. 253–6, lines 10165–284.

16. See A. Bennett, 'A book designed for a noblewoman: An illustrated *Manuel des péchés* of the thirteenth century', in *Medieval Book Production: Assessing the evidence*, ed. L. L. Brownrigg, Los Altos Hills CA: Anderson-Lovelace, 1990, pp. 163–81; figures 11 and 12, p. 171.

17. R. H. Robbins, 'Levation prayers in Middle English verse', *Modern Philology*, 40, 1942–3, 131–46. See discussion in Reinburg, 'Popular prayers', Chapter 3, esp. 235–9.

18. *Selections from English Wycliffite Writings*, ed. A. Hudson, Cambridge: Cambridge University Press, 1978, tract 21a, p. 112.

19. See examples in Rubin, *Corpus Christi*, pp. 321–3.

20. On *exempla*, see C. Brémond, J. Le Goff and J.-C. Schmitt, *L'Exemplum': Typologie des sources du moyen-âge 40*, Turnholt: Brépols, 1982.

21. Caesarius of Heisterbach, *Dialogus miraculorum*, 2 vols, ed. J. Strange, Cologne: H. Lempertz, 1851; Caesarius of Heisterbach, *The Dialogue of Miracles*, trans. H. von E. Scott and C. C. S. Bland, 2 vols, London: G. Routledge & Sons, 1929.

22. J.-C. Schmitt, 'Recueils franciscains d'*exempla* et perfectionnement des techniques intellectuelles du xiiie au xve siècle', *Bibliothèque de l'Ecole des chartes*, 135, 1977, 5–22; D. L. d'Avray, *The Preaching of the Friars: Sermons diffused from Paris before 1300*, Oxford: Oxford University Press, 1985, pp. 64–70. On mendicant involvement in the collection of 'real-life' exemplary tales, see A. Murray, 'Confession as a historical source in the thirteenth century', in *The Writing of History in the Middle Ages: Essays presented to R. W. Southern*, ed. R. H. C. Davis and J. M. Wallace-Hadrill, Oxford: Oxford University Press, 1981, pp. 275–322.

23. On the work, see Robert Mannyng, *Handlyng Synne*, pp. xii–xviii. For a collection of *exempla* compiled in thirteenth-century Cambridge, see S. L. Forte, 'A Cambridge Dominican collector of exempla in the thirteenth century', *Archivum fratrum praedicatorum*, 28, 1958, 115–48.

24. See, for the history of the tale and its visual representation, M. A. Lavin, 'The altar of Corpus Domini in Urbino: Paolo Uccello, Joos Van Ghent, Piero della Francesca', *Art Bulletin*, 49, 1967, 1–24; esp. 2–10.

25. See W. C. Jordan, *The French Monarchy and the Jews: From Philip Augustus to the last Capetians*, Philadelphia PA: University of Pennsylvania Press, 1989, pp. 191–4.

26. An exception is the Croxton *Play of the Sacrament* discussed in this volume by Sarah Beckwith. This English rendition of the tale of host desecration, in a country which had no Jews, is humoristic and light-hearted, very different from the continental versions such as the French *Jeu de la sainte hostie*, L. Muir, 'The mass on the medieval stage', *Comparative Drama*, **23**, 1989, 316–30.

27. J. Cohen, *The Friars and the Jews: The evolution of medieval anti-Judaism*, Ithaca NY: Cornell University Press, 1982; esp. pp. 238–9.

28. R. Po-chia Hsia, *The Myth of Ritual Murder: Jews and magic in Reformation Germany*, New Haven CT: Yale University Press, 1988.

29. E. Wolter, *Der Judenknabe*, Bibliotheca Normannica 2, Halle, 1879. See visual representation of the tale in the miniature scenes of the Carew-Poyntz Hours of *c*.1350–60, Cambridge, Fitzwilliam Museum 48, fols 183r–185v.

30. See, for example, the version in William of Malmesbury, *Liber miraculorum dei genitricis semperque virginis*, Salisbury Cathedral MS. 97v, where the Jewish boy describes to his parents: 'In ecclesia se fuisse et azimum panem de cuiusdam infulati manu sumpsisse.' In the version told by Honorius Augustodinensis in the twelfth century, Christ the Child, seen painted in the altarpiece, was the image distributed by the priests to the communicants 'videbatur Judaeo puerulo quod puerum illi picto similem populo divideret. Qui cum aliis accedens crudam carnem a sacerdote accepit, quam patri domum detulit', *Patrologia latina* 172, col. 852. On William of Malmesbury's collection, see P. N. Carter, 'An edition of William of Malmesbury's treatise on the miracles of the Virgin Mary', 2 vols, Oxford, D Phil, 1959.

31. 'Pulcra femina, quam vidi in cathedra sedentem et cuius filius populo dividebatur, affuit michi in camino estuantis', Salisbury Cathedral MS. 97, fol. 97. See an image of the scene in the Queen Mary Psalter of *c*.1310, British Library Royal B VII 2, fol. 207v. On the tales, see R. Southern, 'The English origins of the "Miracles of the Virgin"', *Medieval and Renaissance Studies*, **4**, 1958, 176–216.

32. On ideas about the purity of children, see S. Shahar, *Childhood in the Middle Ages*, London: Methuen, 1990, pp. 17–19.

33. *La tabula exemplorum secundum ordinem alphabeti*, ed. J. T. Welter, Paris: E.-H. Guitard, 1926, no. 219. See the tale of another child's fear after viewing the celebrant in action, told by Thomas of Eccleston, 'De adventu fratrum minorum in Angliam', in *Monumenta franciscana* I, ed. J. S. Brewer, Rolls Series, London: Longman, 1858, pp. 67–8.

34. See again the image of sacrifice in the miracle tale depicted in Bennett, 'A book designed for a noblewoman', figures 11 and 12, p. 172.

35. Bennett, 'A book designed for a noblewoman', p. 172. See also Rubin, *Corpus Christi*, pp. 135–9.

36. See image in vision of St Hugh of Lincoln, *Magna vitae sancti Hugonis*, eds D. L. Douie and H. Farmer, Oxford: Thomas Nelson, 1962, p. 86; see also pp. 90–1.

37. *The Dialogue of Miracles*, book 9, c. 8, pp. 114–15.

38. *Ibid.*, book 9, c. 7, pp. 113–14.

39. See a Middle English tale, *The Alphabet of Tales* II, ed, M. M. Banks, Early English Text Society 127, London: Kegan Paul, Trench, Trübner, 1905, no. 695, p. 465.

40. On themes of labelling and marginalisation of groups in the eleventh and twelfth centuries, see R. I. Moore, *The Formation of a Persecuting Society*, Oxford: Basil Blackwell, 1987.

41. C. W. Bynum, *Holy Feast and Holy Fast: The religious significance of food to medieval women*, Berkeley CA: University of California Press, 1987.

42. M. James, 'Ritual, drama and social body in the late medieval town', *Past and Present*, **98**, 1983, 3–29; C. Phythian-Adams, 'Ceremony and the citizen: The communal year at Coventry 1450–1550', in *Crisis and Order in English Towns*, eds P. Clark and P. Slack, London: Routledge, 1972, pp. 57–85; M. Rubin, 'Symbolwert and Bedeutung der Fronleichnamsprozessionen in England', in *Laienfrömmigkeit im sozialen und politischen Zusammenhang des Spätmittelalters*, ed. K. Schreiner, Munich: Historisches Kolleg, 1992, pp. 271–80.

43. *The Book of Margery Kempe*, eds S. B. Meech and H. E. Allen, Early English Test Society 212, London, 1940. S. Beckwith, 'A very material mysticism: The medieval mysticism of Margery Kempe', in *Medieval Literature: Criticism, ideology and history*, ed. D. Aers, Brighton: Harvester Press, 1986, pp. 34–57.

44. See for example the review of Corpus Christi in York in the 1420s, A. F. Johnston, 'The procession and play of Corpus Christi in York after 1426', *Leeds Studies in English*, new ser., 7, 1973–4, 55–62.

45. See some consideration in late-medieval Germany: C. Zika, 'Hosts, processions and pilgrimages in fifteenth century Germany', *Past and Present*, **118**, 1988, 25–64.

Ritual, Church and Theatre: Medieval Dramas of the Sacramental Body

Sarah Beckwith

> I learned something from analysing drama which seemed to me
> effective not only as a way of seeing certain aspects of society
> but as a way of getting through to some of the fundamental
> conventions which we group as society itself. These, in their
> turn, make some of the problems of drama quite newly active.[1]

In a late-medieval East Anglian play, the *Croxton Play of the Sacrament* (*c*.1461), the host, central symbol of late-medieval 'community' and ecclesiastical power, is procured from the church, and sold by a merchant to a Jew.[2] Moving from ecclesiastical space to the *platea*, the very boundaries of Christ's body are delineated anew to take account of secular space and meanings.[3] The sacred, exclusively clerical words which consecrate the transubstantiation of bread to body, and wine to blood, are uttered by Jonathas the Jew as a parodic, testing gesture of profanation. The host is put to the test, made to articulate its miraculous powers. It is wounded, buffeted, scourged, beaten and immolated in an oven, from which, in an outrageously staged miracle, 'Christ' emerges in mock resurrection to chastise, but ultimately forgive the Jews. The Jews convert, the merchant confesses, and the entire cast, including the spectators, are invited to participate in a Corpus Christi procession, singing the eucharistic hymn, 'O Sacrum Convivium'.[4] The work of the play is to convert all its outsiders to insiders, to construct a world so totally incorporated and encompassed by the body of Christ that to be outside is no longer conceivable. And yet the very process of that incorporation cannot expel from its own dramatic rendering the riven ambiguities of the divided collectivity whose concerns it stages.

My contribution to this volume's investigation of medieval communities and subjectivities, and their subsequent representation in literary history, will be to effect a detailed analysis of one late-medieval staging of the symbol which laid hegemonic claim to embody and sacralise that community. As such it will investigate the relation between dramatic practice and religious practice. It will ask: what are the social and dramatic resources through which our belief is commanded? Do we believe what we see? Are we seeing what we believe? Is the body of Christ whole? Can its symbolism unify, can its ritual and liturgical modes cohere their spectators or practitioners? Can it incorporate everyone? How will its boundaries be drawn? Who will draw them? Who will threaten them? If, in this play, Christ's body is quite literally pulled apart in what Bakhtin called a 'comical operation of dismemberment', if the host is quite literally taken from its immolation in the church, if it is felt, pricked, cooked, trodden on, then we too are surely critically licensed to 'finger it familiarly on all sides, turn it upside down, inside out, peer at it from above and below, break open its external shell, look into its centre, doubt it, take it apart'.[5] For only by indulging the iconoclasm of the places to which our curiosity is likely to lead us might we begin to make 'quite newly active' the labile tensions, the contradictory tropes of such a drama.

Eucharist

Croxton is first and foremost a play of, and play with, the sacrament. In order to understand the dramatic mechanisms of its play, the limits and extension of eucharistic power need to be understood.[6] The host was simultaneously Christ's body, and in that daring clerical extrapolation, all of Christian society.[7] Transubstantiated by a guarded clerical power, it was only the priesthood who could consecrate bread to body, wine to blood. Christ's body was handled by them, held aloft by them; they were the keepers of its miraculous powers and the necessary medium of transformation.[8] It was in this way that the body of the Church and its universalistic claims could be coterminous with this meagre but mighty wafer. Its powers were unifying and cohesive, for they confirmed the unanimity of a social world and the sacrament of Christ's body was the very material of that unanimity. As *The Lay Folk's Catechism* says:

> . . . . halikirk our modir
> Is hali and allane thurgh-out the world,
> That is communyng and felawred of al cristen folk,
> That communes togedir in the sacrament3
> And in other hali thinges that falles til halikirk,

> In forgyfnes of synnes, and hele of thair saules
> For withouten halikirke nis 'na soule hele.[9]

Holy Church is both all-one and alone, and its unity is connected to its monopolistic claims on the sacred, as the means of salvation and the basis of community. As this passage also makes clear, it is the host that functions to create that community, to unite in the parish the local to the central, and centralising, ecclesiastical establishment. By the late Middle Ages, the claims of eucharistic piety were being contested by the explicit Lollard polemic, which attacked the relationship of eucharistic and priestly power.[10] For the Lollards the bread and wine in the mass did not actually or wholly become blood and body; rather they were signs for them. At issue was not simply an acute attack on clerical jurisdiction of the sacred, but an altogether different understanding of the nature of sign and symbol which disrupted a sacramental view of the world.[11] The price of such views was very high. In 1463 a man from Lincolnshire, and in 1467 William Balow from Essex, to pick two cases close in date and place to *Croxton*, were burnt for their anti-sacramentarianism.[12]

As well as being the object of an explicitly anti-clerical critique on the part of the Lollards, it is against the competing claims of other images, relics and icons that the Church is anxious to assert the centrality of the eucharist – the only relic, after all, which doctrinally endorses clerical power, and centralises it, rather than diffusing it to popular or other control. As Charles Zika reminded us, several theological reformers in the late Middle Ages saw the need to distinguish the cult of Christ from the cult of the other saints. Zika writes:

> Emphasis on the host as Christ's sacramental presence focuses on the act of producing the host and the role of those responsible for its production. In other words, the host is decisively located within the context of priestly power and the locally approved church and clergy.[13]

The eucharist, then, is the focus of competing claims which concern an intense debate about the very nature of sacramentality and social power. To stage a miracle play around the eucharist in the 1460s was to enter the very terms of that debate.

Miracle

At the centre of the *Croxton Play of the Sacrament* is a miracle. As the Jews test the host, as they pierce it in a mock crucifixion, as they immolate it in a tomb, inadvertently miming the burial, an image of Christ bursts out of the oven uttering words of lamentation and liturgical reproach. What the audience has witnessed is a demonstration of the miraculous efficacy of the host. The very act of profanation, the very act of torture, has merely produced the means of salvation in this Christian economy of redemption. The miracle in the miracle play will then induce belief. It will command consent through the evidence of the senses. It will speak incontrovertibly to the Thomases who doubt.[14]

But the very necessity to see what you believe is a testimony to the doubt which underlies the implicit logic of the miracle play. And the play can do nothing but intensify that doubt in the very act of alleviating it. For the miracle in a miracle play is a purely theatrical event. For this play in particular it is overtly, explicitly and outrageously theatrical, drawing attention histrionically to its sense of show. The host, the little biscuit, is a mere stage prop. Even the Christ who appears, as the stage directions state, is an image: 'Here the ovyn must rive asunder and blede owt at þe cranys, and an image appere owt with woundys bleeding.'[15] The second miracle, whereby Christ heals the dismembered hand of the very Jew who crucified him, is given such a palpable and visceral stage presence that it threatens to overwhelm by its remorseless physicality the sacred message it encodes.[16]

But even were the miracles not to be so blatantly theatricalised, even if they were to suspend our disbelief for the duration of their showing, what is apparent is that they occur here, outside of clerical jurisdiction.[17] Indeed the transformation that takes effect at the words of the bishop is not so much from bread to body, but from body back to bread. As the bishop prays for the balm of forgiveness, the stage directions read: 'Here shall the image change again into brede.'[18] It is this transformation of course that manoeuvres the host back into the 'solempne procession'.[19] Led by the bishop it becomes an act of enclosure that precedes his later enclosing injunction 'that your pyxys lockyd ye shuld se/And be ware of the key of Goddys temple'.[20] Momentarily, however, the effect is at least potentially parodic. The staging of miracle is hardly unequivocal. It tends to underwrite precisely that anxiety voiced by Lollard anti-clericalism in its widening of the separation between signifier and signified, between host and stage prop, Christ, image and actor.[21]

Merchant

In terms of the narrative of the play, the invasion of the sacred body of Christ works through the combined powers of doubt and money. The moneyed agent of the play is the merchant Aristorius. Aristorius is a 'mighty merchaunte' whose international activities extend as far as the geographical imagination, and as far as the alliterative range of the playwright can reach.[22] His display of wealth is cast in the vaunting terms of all late-medieval villains. He has the presbyter and the clericus in his pocket, for it is the presbyter who agrees to procure the host from the church at his behest. It is through his machinations that the body of Christ is turned into a commodity. It is the subject of haggling between merchant and Jew; the latter offers twenty pounds for it, but eventually has to part with a hundred.[23] The point here is not so much the final price of the host but the fact that in the process of being bargained for it is exposed to a different financial and symbolic economy. Its price has been relativised by the market economy from which it has been supposedly immune in the priceless realm of the sacred. It is not just the horrific possibility that the host can be bought that is at stake here, but that it becomes subject to a different economy of representation. As a commodity, the host assumes the nasty fluidity entailed by its susceptibility to barter and exchange. Its value, its worth, is no longer contained by, or activated in, the priests' handling. It becomes determined by an economy which is represented in the play as being outside ecclesiastical range and reach, with its value accruing as the result of a negotiated process of exchange.

Contemporary trial records show us that one of the mechanisms of Lollard attack was the attempt to debase the magical powers of the host by a bald reduction to its materiality. One means of doing this was *reductio ad absurdam* arguments which referred to its monetary worth. Bishop Chedworth's register at Lincoln, for example, provides us with the details of proceedings against the brothers William and Richard Sparke, of Somersham, Huntingdonshire. The date of 1457 places it very close to the putative date of *Croxton*. Among the articles submitted against William and Richard Sparke is the following:

> Item, quod triginta panes huiusmodi pre Vno Venduntur obolo, Vbi tamen christus venditus erat pro triginta denariis; Et quod huiusmodi fictione sacramentum propter auariciam sacerdotum erat primitus adinuentum.

> Thirty breads of this sort are sold for one halfpenny, but Christ was sold for thirty pence. The sacrament after this fashion is therefore a figment devised to enrich priests.[24]

If Christ's body were sold by Judas for thirty pennies (Matt. 36. 15), how could a wafer masquerade as Christ's body, for it was worth only one-sixtieth of a penny? The logic of the market in this context is, like the merchants's transaction in *Croxton*, to appropriate the body of Christ from the ecclesiastical establishment. But the logic of *Croxton* is not contained by the fixed price of the literal biblical interpretation. Its price is not fixed by Judas's price, but is as labile and subject to calculation as the transaction between merchant and Jew. What it means is no longer fixed, since its valuation is subject to repeated renegotiation. Thus its signification as the very materiality of social unanimity is no longer bounded by a sacred immunisation.

The merchant profanes the host because of his greed, and it is for his greed that he is enjoined to do penance at the end of the play. By making the merchant the sole vehicle of commercial transaction in the play, the Church can be expunged from its own thorough-going immersion in the world of the mercantile economy. For this of course is the thrust of the jeering comments of William and Richard Sparke and the basis of their accusation: the Church, they suggest, runs a veritable image industry.

If we look to the immediate vicinity of this play, which we can locate in the villages of the Norfolk/Suffolk border, and if we take John Wasson and Gail McMurray Gibson's suggestions seriously, it is evident that the play has definite connections with Bury St Edmunds, and was possibly written for performance there in the first instance.[25] Bury was a monastic borough administered by one of the richest of the English Benedictine abbeys. Housing the relics of the East Anglian king and martyr, it was a vast household corporation which 'through a combination of royal grants and favours and pious behests had managed to amass by the end of the fifteenth century most of the estates and Church tithes in southwest Suffolk'.[26] The majority of the abbey's profits stemmed from its vast landed endowment and the profits of land ownership.[27] Gottfried, Bury's most recent economic historian, informs us that the abbey held virtually all property within the borough and suburbs: 'Others might rent, trade, or sell land, bequeath, divide or alienate it, but in some way, at some point in time, the abbey reaped a profit on all property dealings in the banleuca.'[28] For our purposes it is important to note that the privileges granted to St Edmunds gave the monks control over all the marketplaces in the banleuca.[29] Though the regions of East Anglia were famous for their wool production before 1350, in the late fourteenth century it was cloth production that was the burgeoning and lucrative industry of that area. It was to the abbey-controlled markets of Bury that the merchants came and traded. In fact the greater urban region of Bury St Edmunds was one of the 'principal cloth-producing and marketing regions in England'.[30] As such it attracted not merely local trade, but also trade from London, Norfolk, Great Yarmouth, and aliens from the Low Countries, Germany and Northern Italy. As Gibson has noted:

Most of what we know of the late medieval history of the town of Bury comes from the records of litigation between the borough, growing increasingly rich in the Suffolk wool-cloth trade and zealous to grow richer, and the abbey, resolutely enforcing its economic monopolies and tithes.[31]

For the purposes of my argument here, I want to observe the currency of symbolic capital in this struggle, which has a bearing on *Croxton*'s unseemly fight over Christ's body.

The fifteenth century witnessed a movement for the formal incorporation of self-governing towns, a movement designed to ensure their ability to acquire common property that would be recognised by common law. When they were incorporated, towns were granted the right of perpetual succession, the power of suing and being sued as a whole and, by the name of the corporation, the legal power to hold land, to hold a common seal, and to have the legal authority to issue by-laws.[32] Bristol was the first town to be incorporated, but it was followed by a spate of others in the fifteenth century.[33] In Bury, the urban traders had long demanded the legal status of incorporation against the powers of abbatial control of the markets. In the town conflicts of 1327, as Lobel tells us, the term *communitas* was frequently used in the legal sense of a body of people incorporated by charter. Lobel describes the dispute in the following way:

> The burgesses' claim to be a corporate body was denied by the abbot on the grounds that they had no gilds merchant with power to hear pleas, no community, no common seal, no mayor. The justices, in the same case, criticised the technical point that the burgesses in defending the suit had not named any particular person as alderman – *aliquam certam personam* – who could represent them, nor had they claimed to plead as an incorporated body or produced any royal charters granting them an alderman. The judges gave it as their opinion that the burgesses could not be capable of acting as a corporation since they had no *unionem communitatis*, and that they were not '*libertatis aut hominii capaces tanquam una communitatis*', as they had no other head but the lord abbot.[34]

The notion of the body as a legal fiction raised the important question as to whom might be regarded as its head. The ecclesiastical control over Corpus Christi gave a sacred and organicist base to the pretensions of ecclesiastical unity. But rival bodies, rival corporations, threatened to puncture the seamless body of the Church. By the 1520s the abbey had declined financially. It was forced to sell its endowment outright to the merchants in order to make ends meet.[35]

It is the sacrament, brought back into episcopal jurisdiction, that is processed at the end of play, and unity is reiterated through the very mouths of the sinners who utter their repentance with 'on consent', with 'hertys stedfastly knitt in one'.[36] Their penance is not so much imposed on them as enjoined by them – a voluntaristic act which displays the depth of their contrition, and makes their confession valid.[37] Aristorius is enjoined to do good deeds and 'nevermore for to bye nore sell'.[38] And he is enjoined to chastise his body, perhaps to remind him who is its head.

J. A. Thomson, historian of late-medieval Lollardy, tells us that punishments for abjured heretics were often theatrical, and entailed a coercively therapeutic aptness: 'it is possible that an obligation to take part in a Corpus Christi procession may have been imposed on offenders who had denied transubstantiation'.[39] Moreover penances were often supposed to take place in the marketplace, because the 'public admission of offence' was crucial. Bishop Alnwick, for example, often made offenders appear bareheaded and bare-foot in the marketplace, or the offender would have to perambulate his parish church on Sunday, or often even more publicly in the cathedral city of the diocese.[40]

Such punishments demonstrate the coercive mechanisms of ritual incorporation, which were sometimes legally sanctioned. In the case of Aristorius, we are to understand that he is to depart, his sin has been absolved, and his threat assuaged by his own voluntaristic confession, induced by the power of miracle.

Jew

Like its sources, *Croxton* uses the figure of the Jew to explore the resources of doubt.[41] The Jew himself hardly needs to be persuaded of the benefits of Christian doctrine; it is evident that what we are exploring here is the doubt of the Christian community. But there is a particular relationship between Jew and eucharist which has to do with the way the drawing of the boundaries of that Christian society defined its own enemies. It was the Fourth Lateran Council that decisively articulated the doctrine of sacramentalism, and the relationship between Corpus Mysticum and Corpus Ecclesiae Mysticum. As Robert Moore reminds us, the Fourth Lateran Council 'promulgated a working definition (after baptism) of the Christian community, and stated the essential conditions of membership for the next three centuries'.[42] Defining the Christian community meant defining its enemies. The Fourth Lateran, as Moore documents, set up a decisive rationale and machinery for persecution:

> The last three canons required Jews to distinguish themselves from Christians in their dress, prohibited them from holding public office, and forbade those who converted to Christianity from continuing to observe any of their former rituals, to prevent them from avoiding the penalties of infidelity by means of false conversion.[43]

Anyone who is likely to become too confident about the wholesome organicism of late-medieval communities might do well to remember that Corpus Christi affirmed its own inviolable boundaries at the expense of those constructed as the enemies of Christ. The anti-Semitic stories which associate Jews with the profanation of the host intensified with the inauguration of the Feast of Corpus Christi in 1264.[44] Jews, in the fantasy of some Christians, boiled communion wafers in oil and water and stole and bought hosts to desecrate and profane the body of Christ. The bleeding host shrines of the late Middle Ages, which 'usually had their basis in miracles involving hosts which began to bleed', were often claimed to be the site of 'a claimed act of profanation or ritual murder by members of Jewish communities'.[45]

One of *Croxton*'s analogues, *La Sainte Hostie*, refers to a miracle of 1290 – although the play probably dates much later than that.[46] This version includes one of the commonest versions of the host profanation stories. A Christian woman is in debt to a Jewish moneylender and she promises her communion wafer to repay her debt. He gets the host and proceeds to stab it and to persecute and torture it. His family are disgusted at his activities. Subsequently he is reported and punished by being burnt alive. His wife and children are baptised. Versions of this story are treated dramatically in France, Italy, the Netherlands and Germany.[47] The French version is commemorated in enamels and stained glass in the Chapelle des Miracles. According to Lynette Muir, a mass was said in its honour on Low Sunday, and in 1328, Clemence of Hungary left £10 to the 'couvent ou Dieu fut bouilli [the monastery where God was boiled]'.[48]

In *Croxton* the figure of the Jew, the archetypal outsider, is brought inside, where he is not executed but not converted. He is the vehicle of a thorough-going and rationalistic doubt that is doctrinally sensitive. Many of the iconoclastic energies of the play derive from the thoroughness of his doubt. Thus, in this play, profanation is part of a quest for belief, rather than an unmotivated act of desecration. It is part of a search for insight:

> þe beleve of thes Cristen men ys false, as I wene;
> For þe beleue on a cake – me think yt is onkynd.
> And all they seye how þe prest dothe yt bind,
> And be þe might of his word make yt flessh and blode –
> And thus by a conceite þe wolde make us blind –
> And how þat yt shuld be he þat deyed on þe rode.[49]

To know the doctrine is not enough:

> Now, serys, ye have rehersyd the substance of ther lawe,
> But thys bred I wold myght be put in a prefe
> Whether þis be he that in Bosra of us had awe.[50]

So the Jew initiates the paradoxical formulation of the miracle play: the desire for proof which simultaneously negates belief as sufficient, and yet commands a belief sufficient for conversion. In the play the conflicted nature of such a production of the miraculous is underscored by the fact that it is Jonathas who produces the miracle, who elicits the appearance of the image of Christ. In the fashion typical of the didactic interpretation of these plays this could be read as an ironic proof of the triumph of the Christian scheme of salvation that rescues and redeems its torturers in their very act of torture.[51] But such a happy economy of salvation is subtly disrupted by the placing of the very words of consecration into the mouth of the Jew.

The use of York describes the priestly role in the act of consecration in the following stage directions:

Qui pridie quam pateretur, accepit panem in sanctas ac venerabiles manus suas, *Hic elevet oculos* et elevatis oculis in coelum, ad te Deum Patrem suum omnipotentem, tibi gratias agens, benedixit, ac *Hic tangat hostiam* fregit, deditque discipulis suis, dicens: Accipite, et manducate ex hoc omnes: HOC EST ENIM CORPUS MEUM.

Who on the day before he suffered took bread into his holy and most honoured hands. (*Here let him raise his eyes*) and with his eyes raised up towards heaven, unto Thee, O God, his Father almighty, giving thanks to Thee, he blessed and (*Here let him touch the host*) brake and gave to his disciples, saying, Take and eat ye all of this, for this is my Body.[52]

It is while saying the words 'Qui pridie quam pateretur' that the celebrant takes up the host from the altar table. Then as Young describes it, at the words 'Hic elevet oculos', he looks upward, and then lowers his eyes again.[53] The words of consecration, 'Hoc est enim Corpus meum', are said while he is bending over the altar. Then standing before the altar, he raises the host up before him so that everyone may see it. The bell is rung during elevation. In *Croxton*, it is Jonathas who utters those words, rehearsing the biblical precedent of the Last Supper by which the mass, the 'Sacrum Convivium', is re-enacted and commemorated:

On thes wordys ther law groundyd hath he
That he sayd on Shere Thursday at hys sopere:
He brake the brede and sayd, *Accipite*,
And gave hys disciplys them for to chere:
And more he said to them there
Whyle they were all togethere and sum,
Sytting at the table soo clere,
Comedite Corpus meum.[54]

Jonathas frames the words of consecration as the words of Christ at the Last Supper. But the theatrical effect of his presence works to blur the boundaries of identity, as it blurs the boundaries of direct and indirect speech. The words are uttered by Jonathas the Jew, and in that moment he becomes both Christ and priest.

Such a miraculous and subversive association is underscored by the events which succeed the mock communion. For the actions that follow are a parodic mimicking of the events of Passion week commemorated allegorically through the mass, and every week through the canonical hours. First Christ is put to a new Passion, then crucified again in a way which, unlike the economy and elegance of the subtle allusions of the mass, is a grotesque act of dismemberment which comically celebrates the miraculous plasticity and acceptance of the body of Christ. Then, Jonathas himself is crucified. For such is the zeal with which he wants to test the host, that he seizes it to sling it into the furnace the other Jews are stoking. It clings to his hand. It is as if the very boundaries of his own body are made coterminous with the boundaries of Christ's as it struggles to include him. In an effort to remove the sticky host from his hand, the other Jews nail him and the sacrament to a post. Thus both are crucified together: the Jew with Christ's body on his hands is irrevocably implicated in the act of crucifixion.[55]

The other Jews try to separate out Christ's body from Jonathas's body, but the cost of that separation is dismemberment; for the host comes away, and with it comes the hand of Jonathas. We might say that Jonathas's desecration, his attempt at puncturing the unity of Christ's body, and the concomitant unity of Christian society, results only in his own dismemberment. And yet to put it in those terms drastically reduces the grotesque materiality of enactment to which the play consistently returns us.

For what is this but a striking reduction to blood and body – both Christ's and Jonathas's? As the hand with the host still clinging to it is thrust into the cauldron, 'the hand ys soden, the fleshe from the bones'.[56] You don't believe the host is really blood and body? the play jokingly asks. Let's show you the meaning of Christ's substantial body. If you prick us, says the host, do we not bleed?[57]

Liturgy

Through an analysis of the complexities of impersonation in the play, I have been arguing for Jonathas as a grotesque form of Christ, a grotesque priest. Another way of looking at the voicing of the words of consecration is to examine the way they rebound on the histrionic qualities of the mass itself. They may well be contained by the stock anti-Judaism of this play, but the underlying point here is this: having the host on stage implies that the host can be staged. It opens up the possibility that the theatrical resources of the priesthood are not completely separable from the resources of theatre, thereby invoking that question asked by Blake in *Jerusalem*:

> . . . What is a Church? & What
> Is a Theatre? are they Two and not One? can they Exist Separate?
> Are not Religion and Politics the Same Thing?[58]

I have already alluded to practices such as the elevation of the host, and the ringing of the bell that marks the transformation of bread to body, wine to blood. As a 'visual theophany', the mass is a spectacular form of theatre.[59] All historians of the liturgy stress the extent to which, in the late Middle Ages, it is a clerical spectacle, rather than a participatory act.[60]

And yet in making this suggestion *Croxton* crosses a dangerous line. Historians of the drama and liturgical writers insist that the mass is not dramatic. As one of the early historians of the 'drama of the medieval church' has said:

> The central act is designed not to represent or portray or merely commemorate the Crucifixion, but actually to repeat it. What takes place at the altar is not an aesthetic picture of a happening in the past, but a genuine renewal of it.[61]

That is, the mass is not simply figurative, rather its cultic function is to induce a re-experiencing of the Nativity, Passion, Death and Resurrection of Christ in present time.[62] Thus a different economy of representation is supposedly at work in the liturgy than in the drama, one that rests on the actualising of event, rather than the re-creation of it, and one that therefore has no room for the concept of *impersonation*. For Young, for whom it is the key concept that differentiates liturgy and theatre, impersonation must be based on physical imitation. The performer must do more than simply represent the chosen personage, he must also resemble him.[63]

This relationship is subject to a great deal of critical attention in the early commentaries on the liturgy. The dividing line between church and theatre is sometimes insisted upon and sometimes happily dissolved. So Amalarius of Metz, one of the early commentators on the ninth-century mass, writes in his *De Ecclesiasticis Officis*:

> Sacramenta debent habere similitudinem aliquam earum rerum quarum sacramenta sunt. Quapropter, similis sit sacerdos Christo, sicut panis et liquor similia sunt corpori Christi. Sic est immolatio sacerdotis in altari quodammodo ut Christi immolatio in cruce.

> Sacraments are bound to some degree to have the resemblance of those things of which they are the sacraments. For this reason, let the priests resemble Christ, as the bread and liquid resemble the body of Christ. So the sacrifice of the priest on the altar may be likened to the sacrifice of Christ on the cross.[64]

Here the analogy rests and insists on resemblance, a legitimating resemblance of Christ to priest. The sacrifice of Christ on the cross is renewed in sacrifice of the officiating clergy. But in a later interpolation to this treatise by Honorius of Autun, the potential theatricality of this relationship is marked:

> Sciendum quod hi qui tragoedias in theatris recitabant, actus pugnantium gestibus populo repraesentabant. Sic tragicus noster pugnam Christi populo Christiano in theatro ecclesiae gestibus suis repraesentat, eique victoriam redemptionis suae inculcat.

> It is known that those who recited tragedies in the theaters represented to the people, by their gestures, the actions of conflicting forces. Even so, our tragedian (the celebrant) represents to the Christian people in the theater of the church, by his gestures the struggle of Christ, and impresses upon them the victory of his redemption.[65]

The analogy of the celebrant of the mass and the tragic actor is made with ease and little anxiety. Usually where that analogy is invoked, it brings a trail of anxiety in its wake.[66] For theatricality can seem dangerous because it threatens to foreground the gestures of representation over the thing itself, and so endanger the clerical control over the project by its capacity to defamiliarise, to highlight the mediators and the role of mediation.

It is precisely the negative sense of impersonation that is central to Lollard anti-theatricalism. That is, the Lollards attack the theatre, but the basis of their attack is not simply on theatre itself but on the false impersonation of the clergy. The clergy's representation of themselves as re-enacting the Nativity, Passion, Crucifixion, Resurrection is seen as a grotesque usurpation of the divinity and mystery of God. Miracle plays in the Lollard account are dangerous because they obscure the relationship between appearance and reality. When you've seen a play about the Last Judgement, you may believe that hell itself does not have the power to burn, hurt or punish you: 'And therefore many men wen that there is no helle of everlastynge peyne, but that God does but threaten us, not to do it in dede.'[67] Priests, in their immersion in sensible signs rather than ghostly things, reveal their own inauthenticity, their role as the false deceivers who elide that distinction between appearance and reality in a fearful manner. Anti-theatricalism and anti-clericalism in the Lollard account coincide, for both theatre and church inhere in each other; both play in a world of shimmering and bewitching surfaces.

The point I am making here is that the line between liturgy, church and theatre is a line that needs to be drawn and redrawn. It is anxiously policed to keep the labile potentialities of theatrical practice under control. In *Croxton*, as we have seen, that line is crossed and recrossed time and time again in acts of delightful and flagrant mockery.

The play closes with a procession, in which the spectators are allowed to join.

> Now folow me, all and summe,
> And all tho that bene here, both more and lesse,
> Thys holy song, O Sacrum Conviuium
> Lett us syng all with grett swetnesse.[68]

The 'Sacrum Convivium' is the hymn to the holy sacrament. It was originally the antiphon of the Magnificat for the Vespers of the Feast of Corpus Christi.[69] In the play, then, we may infer that at the behest of the bishop a Corpus Christi procession forms.

It was the Corpus Christi procession, in Mervyn James's influential account, which, using the body as an image of human society, was deployed as a mechanism of social order in late-medieval towns. Circumnavigating the town, the procession supposedly formed following the host in its pyx, with those first in precedence nearest in proximity to the host.[70] One way of seeing the end of this play is to see it as an exit from the stage, with a device which redefines audience as congregation, incorporated into the body of Christ. In this account the play triumphantly accomplishes the resurrection of the whole and wholesome community along with the body of Christ. This interpretation would put the play out of the reach of its own theatricalising modes and implications. It would affirm the Durkheimian function of rite: the 'symbolic means through which men worship their own society, their own mutual dependency'.[71] As such, to return to Williams's epigraph, it would provide the substance of the conventions which we group as society itself, subordinating drama to ritual's eternal recurrence.

But alternatively, it is possible to see this ending of the play not so much as the movement out of theatrical space, but rather the absorption of procession into theatre. The spectators, the 'congregation', become not so much processors, following the body of Christ (which is, after all, a stage prop), but actors, absorbed into the histrionic heart of the play.

We know that in late-medieval York, for example, there were complaints about the co-existence of the Corpus Christi plays and the Corpus Christi processions on the same day. In 1426, William Melton, a friar, complains about the unruliness which accompanied the production of the plays.[72] The town records of late-medieval York indicate that the procession and the plays are separated so that they can go on different days. This is partly, of course, a pragmatic gesture. The vast length and encyclopaedic range of the plays took the full day in and of themselves. But as the friar's complaint registers, it is also a question of the different forms necessitated by procession and theatre. In the Corpus Christi procession the host, in its little display cabinet, appeared firmly in ecclesiastical control.[73] On the day of the staging of the plays, Christ was ubiquitous in different form. Since he was played sometimes by carpenters, sometimes by butchers, sometimes by tilemakers, bakers or woolpackers, there were several of him playing in the town that day, presenced in the various bodies of the actors.[74] In a climate where such impersonation was being seen at least by some in mimetic rather than ritualistic terms, it was no wonder that there were those who preferred to have the procession on a different day, and to see Christ's body contained in the little wafer.

Croxton plays with these distinctions in subtle and sophisticated ways. In it, ritual and theatre hybridise each other, embarrassing the distinction between them.[75] In doing so the extraordinary elasticity of Christ's body, its grotesque lability, has been a central *theatrical* resource. Christ's body hardly unifies in Durkheimian harmony; it is rather made to fit a variety of different social meanings and readings. How hard it has worked to incorporate all its outsiders as insiders, how very much it has had to be manipulated, doubted, taken apart, before it could be put back together again.

Ritual

I stress this point because medieval drama criticism has generally been all too content to see an absolute dividing line between ritual and theatre. Either one discards the other to come into existence, or one must be subordinated to the other; theatre to ritual or ritual to theatre. Such critical categories are a hangover from the early criticism of the drama, which was severely evolutionary in its approach, showing how drama emerged out of the ritual form of liturgy.[76] More recent criticism has sought to use a much more pliable and nuanced version of ritual in its reading of the drama. The enormous advantage of the modern introduction of the category of ritual in the interpretation of the drama lies in its affirmation of the central relevance of drama and its symbolism to social life.[77] The dangers, however, especially given the vexed history of the category 'ritual' within the discourse of anthropology, are themselves not to be underestimated. For the very category of ritual has too often been reserved for societies deemed primitive.[78] Renewing the world as the same, abolishing time, ritual creates the word as eternally recurrent. It denies both histories and subjectivities to the agents supposed to enact its homogenising modes, and so it eviscerates them of the capacity to think and doubt, and act and play. Such a view is not a necessary concomitant of ritual studies of the drama, but it may be a consequence of certain importations of functionalist anthropology. As such, it joins that chorus of views that constructs the Middle Ages as pre-modern, making the medieval the tribal forebear of European historicity.[79] It succumbs to the piety of disenchantment in that it constructs a medieval world that is itself completely enchanted. Here is Durkheim again:

But if there is one truth that history teaches us beyond a doubt, it is that religion tends to embrace a smaller and smaller portion of social life. Originally it pervades everything: everything social is religious; the two worlds are synonymous. Then, little by little, political, economic, scientific functions free themselves from the religious function, constitute themselves apart, and take on more and more acknowledged temporal character. God, who was at first present in all human relations, progressively withdraws from them; he abandons the world to men and their disputes.[80]

Croxton has surely taught us to beware of such pieties. In its refusal to separate church, ritual and theatre, it creates a dramatic dialogue of the most extraordinary flexibility and power.

Dialogic drama

Rather than arguing over the relative valencies of a critical vocabulary of ritual and theatre, we might do better to consider the form of dramatic dialogue itself. Deploying a Bakhtinian terminology, Peter Womack has usefully described the theatrical word as the site of a fraught conversation between speakers – the writer, the dramatis persona and the actor. As Womack says:

> Although these three sources may converge on the moment when a line is actually spoken on stage, they remain separable because each has its own orientation: the writer is addressing himself to a reader, the dramatis persona to another dramatis persona, and the actor to an audience.[81]

Womack suggests that if we remove one of the lines of communication we change the theatrical mode; removing the writer–reader line would give us improvised theatre; the persona–persona line gives us recital or liturgy; finally, the actor–audience line produces, for example, closet theatre. Since it is characterised by a 'functional superfluity', there is no need for any one of the lines in the dramatic dialogue to hierarchise or determine the others.[82] It is this model which I believe is much more promising than importing ready-made and unexamined models of ritual into our consideration of late-medieval dramatic practice.

In *Croxton*, for example, liturgy is vital to the play's theatrical resources, but it never forecloses the play's readings, despite the endeavours of critics. Rather, in this play, the fact that liturgy is an extra-dramatic referent (not created by the author and having associations which function outside of the world of the play) means that the voice of the liturgy is played off against the voice of actor and persona. Such a play allows the maintenance of a division between actor and role that Brecht would have called *gestic*.[83] It allows that tension on which impersonation rests to play out the full range of its theatrical implication. Actor is never dissolved into persona, or vice versa; rather the tension felt through the impersonation allows us actively to see the use and abuse of the conventions, precisely, of social life.

'It was above all', writes Raymond Williams, 'in drama that the otherwise general processes of change in conceptions of the self and society are articulated and realized.'[84] At stake, then, in the description of the forms which this 'early' drama takes, are issues of wider concern than a merely literary history. At issue is the articulation of the possibilities of past imaginings which might free us from the pieties of our own disenchantment. The use of 'ritual' as a critical terminology for the drama has too often encouraged the projection of seamless unities on to the Middle Ages: the drama is then read like the clerical version of the host – whole in each of its little bits.[85] Such a projection is not simply inaccurate; it also encourages the perception of collective social forms as alien forms of life which belong to other cultures. Worse still, it encourages us to read clerical fantasy as late-medieval reality, and so to disavow the effects of its hegemonic reach. It is just such strategies of closure that *Croxton* has sought to disable. For *Croxton* demands that we see the body of Christ as a dramatic process of relation and not a static object of perception. Like Augustine, in one of his Easter sermons, it offers its ambiguous message: 'If you receive well, you are what you have received.'[86]

Acknowledgements

I would like especially to thank Peter Travis for sharing with me some of his fascinating and illuminating insights in relation to the medieval body of Christ, and in particular for pointing me in the direction of *Croxton* in the first place. Anthony Gash shared my first reading of the play, and it will be apparent to anyone who has read his work on late-medieval drama how much his perspectives have informed my own. Both in print and in conversation, Miri Rubin has helped to shape my understanding of the social-historical dimensions of eucharistic practice. Many thanks to Lee Patterson, Gail Gibson and Michael O'Connell. Thanks too to David Aers for his sharpening editorial comments and to the participants of the English Colloquium at Duke University for their enlivening responses, and to my 'Politics and Piety' class of autumn 1990. Finally, thanks to John Twyning for his meticulous and numerous readings of various drafts of this essay.

Notes

1. Raymond Williams, *Writing in Society*, London: Verso, 1983, p. 20.
2. *The Croxton Play of the Sacrament* is found in a manuscript containing various sixteenth- and seventeenth-century texts: Trinity College, Dublin F. 4.20, Catalogue no. 652, ff. 338^r–56^r. My citations are from Norman Davis's edition: *Non-Cycle Plays and Fragments*, Early English Text Society, ss. 1, Oxford: Oxford University Press, 1970, pp. 58–89. For the dating of the play, see Ian Lancashire, *Dramatic Texts and Records of Britain: A chronological topography to 1558*, Toronto: University of Toronto Press, 1984, p. 122.
3. For a gloss on my usage of *platea*, see Robert Weimann's chapter '*Platea* and *locus*: Flexible dramaturgy' in *Shakespeare and the Popular Tradition in the Theater: Studies in the social dimension of dramatic form and function*, Baltimore MD: Johns Hopkins University Press, 1978, pp. 73–85.
4. Davis, *Non-Cycle Plays*, p. 84. The hymn was originally the antiphon of the Magnificat for the Vespers of the Feast of Corpus Christi. For further details, see Davis, *Non-Cycle Plays*, p. lxxiii and Sister Nicholas Maltmann, 'Meaning and art in the Croxton play of the sacrament' in *English Literary History*, **41**, 1974, 2, 151.
5. Mikhail Bakhtin, 'Epic and novel' in *The Dialogic Imagination*, ed. Michael Holquist, trans. Caryl Emerson and Michael Holquist, Austin TX: University of Texas, 1981, p. 23. The context of this quotation is Bakhtin's discussion of laughter's demolition of the pieties of 'epic distance': 'Laughter demolishes fear and piety before an object, before a world, making of it an object of familiar contact and thus clearing a ground for an absolutely free investigation of it.' It is this 'uncrowning', this destruction of the distanced plane in the 'zone of maximal proximity' that Bakhtin calls the 'comic operation of dismemberment'. See pp. 23–4. For a fine treatment of Christ's social body in relation to the mystery cycles, see Peter Travis, 'The social body of the dramatic Christ in medieval England', *Early Drama to 1600, Acta*, XIII, 1985, pp. 17–36.
6. My understanding of eucharistic practice is indebted to Miri Rubin's incisive analysis. See her *Corpus Christi: The eucharist in late medieval culture*, Cambridge: Cambridge University Press, 1991. See also Chapter 2 of my forthcoming book, *Christ's Body: Symbol and social vision in late medieval English culture*, London: Routledge, which gives a much fuller treatment of the socio-political ramifications and potentialities of the imagery surrounding Christ's body in relation to late-medieval affective piety than I am able to provide here.
7. For the importance of the Fourth Lateran Council of 1215 in this articulation, see Robert Moore, *The Formation of a Persecuting Society*, Oxford: Basil Blackwell, 1987, Chapter 1, and Ernst Kantorowicz, *The King's Two Bodies*, Princeton NJ: Princeton University Press, 1957. See also Charles Zika, 'Hosts, processions and pilgrimages: Controlling the sacred in fifteenth century Germany', *Past and Present*, **118**, 1988, 25–64.
8. For the increasing spectacularisation of eucharistic power in the late Middle Ages, see Zika, 'Hosts, processions and pilgrimages' and Edouard Dumoutet,

Le Désir de voir l'Hostie et les origines de la dévotion au Saint-Sacrament, Paris: Gabriel Beauchesne, 1926. See also the historians of the liturgy, Dom Gregory Dix, *The Shape of the Liturgy*, London: Dacre Press, 1949; and Theodor Klauser, *A Short History of the Western Liturgy*, London: Oxford University Press, 1969. For the relation between the elevation of the host and the Easter rites of resurrection, see Pamela Sheingorn, *The Easter Sepulchre in England*, Kalamazoo MI: Medieval Institute Publications, 1987, p. 58.

9. *The Lay Folk's Catechism*, ed. T. F. Simmons and H. E. Nolloth, Early English Text Society, Original Series 118, Oxford: Oxford University Press, 1901, p. 24.

10. For Lollard views on the sacrament, see *English Wycliffite Writings*, ed. Anne Hudson, Cambridge: Cambridge University Press, 1978, pp. 110–15. Also see Margaret Aston, 'Wyclif and the vernacular', *Studies in Church History*, Subsidia 5, Oxford: Basil Blackwell, 1987, pp. 281–330, and J. I. Catto, 'John Wyclif and the cult of the eucharist', *Studies in Church History*, Subsidia 4, Oxford: Basil Blackwell, 1985, pp. 269–86. Catto relates the scholastic dimensions of eucharistic controversy – could appearances subsist without reality? – to their social and political dimensions. For a typical 'Lollard view' recorded in early-fifteenth-century trials of Lollards, see Johannes Reve of Beccles, glover: 'Also that Y have holde, beleved and affermed that no prest hath poar to make Goddis body in the sacrament of the auter, and that aftir the sacramentall wordis said of a prest at messe ther remaneth nothying but only a cake of material bread', Norman Tanner, ed., *Heresy Trials in the Diocese of Norwich 1428–31*, London: Royal Historical Society, 1977, p. 111.

11. At the centre of Wyclif's views on the eucharist, for example, was his powerful sense that the eucharist was an idol *par excellence*, where sign was mistaken for reality. See Catto, 'John Wyclif', pp. 274–5. For a lengthy discussion of the relationship between image and signified, see *Dives and Pauper*, ed. Priscilla Heath Barnum, Early English Text Society no. 275, Oxford: Oxford University Press, 1976, esp. pp. 81–7.

12. J. A. Thomson, *The Later Lollards 1414–1520*, Oxford: Oxford University Press, 1965, p. 133. Ann E. Nichols, 'The Croxton play of the sacrament: A re-reading', *Comparative Drama*, 22, 1988/9, 119, mentions both these cases, citing them against Cecilia Cutts, 'The Croxton play: An anti-Lollard piece', *Modern Language Quarterly*, 5, 1944, 45–60 as merely sporadic instances of local Lollardy. Both men were burnt in London; see *The Historical Collections of a Citizen of London*, ed. James Gairdner, London: Camden Society, 1876, rpt 1965, p. 233, cited by Nichols, 'The Croxton play', 132. My point in mentioning the stark fact of these executions is to remind my readers that arguments about the relations of what a modern terminology might like to call signifiers and signifieds were literally life-and-death issues.

13. Zika, 'Hosts, processions and pilgrimages', 58.

14. Gail McMurray Gibson points out that late-medieval devotion makes the apostle Thomas, that 'insistent believer in the sensory concrete', the archetypal doubter, a 'positive emblem' because it is through his doubts that the doubts of others may be resolved. See her *Theater of Devotion: East Anglian drama and society in the late Middle Ages*, Chicago IL: University of Chicago Press, 1989,

p. 16, For an exemplification of this view, see Theodor Erbe, ed., *Mirk's Festial*, London: Kegan Paul, Trench, Trübner, 1905, p. 18. For *Croxton's* mention of Thomas in the mouth of Jasdon, see Davis, *Non-Cycle Plays*, p. 71. In an early-fifteenth-century translation of Aquinas's *Lauda, Syon*, written for the feast of Corpus Christi, 'Of the Sacrament of the Altere', the necessity of belief (and therefore the inevitability of doubt) is expressed in the following way: 'In syȝt and in felyng, þou semest bred,/In byleue, flesch, blod, and bon;/In syȝt and felyng, þou semest ded,/In byleue, lyf, to speke and gon;/In syȝt and felyng, noþer hond ne hed,/In byleue, boþe god and man;/In syȝt and felyng, in litil sted,/In byleue, grettere þyng nes nan.' See *Twenty Six Political and Other Poems*, London: Kegan Paul, Trench, Trübner, for Early English Text Society, 1904, pp. 103–7, 11, 113–120.

15. Davis, *Non-Cycle Plays*, p. 80. For a photographic representation of a modern staging, see Meg Twycross, 'Beyond the picture theory: Image and activity in medieval drama', *Word and Image*, 4, July–December 1988, p. 11.

16. Davis, *Non-Cycle Plays*, p. 82 and see below.

17. Cecilia Cutts notices that it is after 1380, when Wyclif's views on the eucharist were condemned as heretical at Oxford, that host miracles are given prominence in the chronicles. See Cutts, *The English Background to the Play of the Sacrament*, PhD dissertation, University of Washington, 1938, 57. Cutts discusses the elaboration of host miracles as a concerted and conscious attempt to refute Lollard heresy on transubstantiation, (121–45). Such a chronology makes obvious the relation of eucharistic miracles to clerical maintenance of sacred power. According to her, the first 'bleeding host' miracle in England is attributed to Archbishop Courtenay in 1381. Courtenay becomes Archbishop during the revolt of 1381. Knighton recounts a host miracle revealed to one knight, Cornelius Cloune, who insisted on his belief that there remained true material bread even after transubstantiation. During the elevation of the eucharist in the mass he sees 'true flesh, raw and bleeding, divided into three parts'. (Henry Knighton, 'Chronicle', ed. J. R. Lumby, Rolls Series, vol. 92, 1895, II, 163–4, cited Cutts, in translation, 132. I have omitted the Latin original for the sake of brevity.) The doctrinal implications are stressed by Knighton: 'Amazed and overcome, he called his squire so that he also could observe, but he saw nothing except what he was in the habit of seeing. But the knight, on the third piece which was to be dipped in the chalice, saw the same white colour as it first had had, but in the midst of that piece he saw the name *Jesus* written with letters of flesh, raw and bloody.' In the chronicle account, the miracle is carefully framed by a procession, and a sermon at St Paul's Cross where the knight promises that 'he would fight and would die in that cause, that in the sacrament of the altar is the true body of Christ, and not material bread only, as he himself had previously believed'. For other late-medieval host miracles, see W. O. Ross, ed., *Middle English Sermons from MS. Roy. 18 B. xxiii*, Early English Text Society no. 209, Oxford: Oxford University Press, rpt, 1960, p. 130, and Erbe, ed. *Mirk's Festial*, pp. 170–5.

18. Davis, *Non-Cycle Plays*, p. 83.

19. Davis, *Non-Cycle Plays*, p. 84 and see below.

20. Davis, *Non-Cycle Plays*, p. 86.
21. Of course we know that there were concerted 'Lollard' attacks on miracle playing: however, the point here is that anti-theatricalism works to condemn the entire basis of clerical sacramentalism. See *A Middle English Treatise on the Playing of Miracles*, ed. Clifford Davidson, Washington DC: University Press of America, 1981, for medieval versions of this criticism, and for a discussion of dramaturgy and belief in Lollardy, see Ritchie Kendall, *The Drama of Dissent*, Chapel Hill NC: University of North Carolina Press, 1986.
22. Davis, *Non-Cycle Plays*, pp. 60–1.
23. Davis, *Non-Cycle Plays*, pp. 67–8.
24. The articles submitted against William and Richard Sparke are reproduced in *Lincoln Diocese Documents 1450–1544*, ed. Andrew Clark, Early English Text Society no. 149, Oxford: Oxford University Press, 1914, pp. 91, 93. In the Sparkes's analogy, of course, the church becomes Judas.
25. Gibson, *Theater of Devotion*, pp. 35 and 186 n. 72. Gibson's suggestion is that the play may possibly have been produced by one of the religious guilds of the town, perhaps one whose members included the clergy (p. 38). Arguments about the authorship and production of the play are inevitably speculative; the Bury St Edmunds connection seems, however, irrefutable. See Cutts, *English Background*, 155.
26. Gibson, *Theater of Devotion*, p. 118.
27. See Robert S. Gottfried, *Bury St. Edmunds and the Urban Crisis 1290–1539*, Princeton NJ: Princeton University Press, 1982, p. 74. Also see the older M. D. Lobel, *Bury St. Edmunds: A study in the government and development of a monastic town*, Oxford: Clarendon, 1935.
28. Gottfried, *Bury St. Edmunds*, p. 74.
29. *Ibid.*, p. 78, and see, in addition, p. 169.
30. *Ibid.*, p. 23.
31. Gibson, *Theater of Devotion*, p. 119.
32. A. R. Myers, *English Historical Documents 1327–1485*, Andover: Eyre & Spottiswoode, 1969, p. 391.
33. Martin Weinbaum, *The Incorporation of Boroughs*, Manchester: Manchester University Press, 1937, especially Chapter 4, 'The classic age of incorporation', pp. 63–96. See also James Tait, *The Medieval English Borough: Studies on its origins and constitutional history*, Manchester: Manchester University Press, 1936, esp. pp. 234–47.
34. Lobel, *Bury St. Edmunds: A study*, p. 82, and see Tait, *Medieval English Borough*, p.238.
35. Gottfried, *Bury St. Edmunds*, p. 43.
36. Davis, *Non-Cycle Plays*, pp. 87 and 88.
37. For the relation of the sacrament of penance to contrition, confession and the eucharist, see Cutts, *English Background*, p. 146. It was axiomatic to the views of the clerical establishment on confession that contrition and forgiveness could not be won on one's own, but only through the sacrifice of Christ; confession *to priests* was the sacramental medium through which the grace and forgiveness of Christ was mediated. See Thomas Tentler, *Sin and Confession on the Eve of the*

Reformation, Princeton NJ, Princeton University Press, 1977, p. 25;

> In scholastic language, the sacraments produced grace not from the work of the person receiving them, as would be the case if contrition were the efficient cause of forgiveness, but from the actual performance of the sacrament itself. The first way (*ex opere operantis*, from the work of the worker or recipient) emphasizes the disposition and effort of the penitent, even when theologians, anxious to avoid Pelagianism, declare love or sorrow to be infused by God. The second way (*ex opere operato*, from the work worked or performed) also requires the proper disposition of the penitent – he could not be drunk, asleep, joking, or, in this case, dissimulating sorrow or the intention to stop sinning – but it emphasizes the automatic power of the sacramental sign. By explaining the sacrament of penance in terms of its efficacy 'from the work worked', St. Thomas had made clearer than any theologian before him why it was necessary to receive the absolution of the priest.

Perhaps as a result of the Lollard belief that contrition in itself legitimises penance, the clerically administered sacrament of penance is given its due weight in the play.

38. Davis, *Non-Cycle Plays*, p. 86.
39. Thomson, *Later Lollards*, p. 234 and see Gibson, *Theater of Devotion*, p. 34.
40. Thomson, *Later Lollards*, p. 231.
41. For *Croxton*'s sources, see Davis, *Non-Cycle Plays*, Introduction, p. lxxiii, and for a more extensive consideration of the European analogues, see Cutts, *English Background*, pp. 207–316. It is perhaps important to state that the expulsion of the Jews from England in 1290 reinforces the purely fantastic quality of anti-Judaism. See Lester Little, *Religious Poverty and the Profit Economy in Medieval Europe*, Ithaca NY: Cornell University Press, 1978, pp. 42–59, for a discussion of Christian–Jewish relations within the context of economic change.
42. Moore, *Formation of a Persecuting Society*, p. 6.
43. *Ibid.*, p. 7.
44. *Ibid.*, p. 38, and see Zika, 'Hosts, processions and pilgrimages'.
45. Zika, 'Hosts, processions and pilgrimages', 48.
46. See Davis, *Non-Cycle Plays*, p. lxxiii, and L. Petit de Julleville, *Les Mystères*, 2 vols, Paris: Hachette, 1880, pp. 574–6.
47. Davis, *Non-Cycle Plays*, p. lxxiii.
48. Lynette Muir, 'The mass on the medieval stage', *Comparative Drama*, **23**, 1989/90, 317.
49. Davis, *Non-Cycle Plays*, p. 64.
50. Davis, *Non-Cycle Plays*, p. 71. 'Substance' may be punning on the scholastic technicalities and terms by which eucharistic transubstantiation was discussed.
51. Cutts, *English Background*, insists that the play's impact is doctrinal; so do Nichols, 'The Croxton play' and Homan, although they differ as to the doctrine being communicated. See Richard Homan, 'Devotional themes in the violence and humour of the *Play of the Sacrament*', *Comparative Drama*, **20**, 1986/7, 327–41.
52. The York Order of Mass in *The Lay Folk's Mass Book*, ed. T. F. Simmons, Early

English Text Society no. 71, London: Trübner, 1879, pp. 106–7. See also Adrian Fortescue, *The Mass: A study of the Roman liturgy*, London: Longman, 1912, p. 335.

53. Karl Young, *The Drama of the Medieval Church*, 2 vols, I, Oxford: Clarendon Press, 1933, p. 36.

54. Davis, *Non-Cycle Plays*, p. 70. Jonathas's elision of the definite article in the words of consecration emphasises the visceral, feastlike qualities of the mass, rather than its figurative and communicative qualities.

55. Davis, *Non-Cycle Plays*, pp. 70–3.

56. Davis, *Non-Cycle Plays*, p. 80.

57. William Shakespeare, *Merchant of Venice*, III, 1.1. 58.

58. *The Complete Poetry and Prose of William Blake*, ed. David Erdman, New York NY: Anchor Press, 1982, p. 207.

59. Zika, 'Hosts, processions and pilgrimages', 31.

60. See Dix, *Shape of the Liturgy*, and Klauser, *A Short History of the Western Liturgy*.

61. Young, *Drama of the Medieval Church*, pp. 84–5.

62. See Clifford Flanigan, 'The Roman rite and the origins of the liturgical drama', *University of Toronto Quarterly*, **43**, 1974, 265.

63. Young, *Drama of the Medieval Church*, pp. 80–1.

64. J.P. Migne, *Patrologiae cursus completus, Series Latina*, 221 vols, Paris 1841–64; here vol. cv, col. 989, quoted Young, *Drama of the Medieval Church*, p. 81, my translation. In subsequent quotations from Migne, only volume and column number will be cited.

65. Reprinted in Young, *Drama of the Medieval Church*, p. 83, and Bevington, *Medieval Drama*, Boston MA: Houghton Mifflin, 1975, p. 9, with translation.

66. See, for example, Aelred of Rievaulx's famous explosion against priestly histrionics in his *Speculum charitatis*, Migne, cxcv, 571 cited by Young, *Drama of the Medieval Church*, p. 548.

67. Hudson, *Selections*, pp. 103 and 98.

68. Davis, *Non-Cycle Plays*, p. 84.

69. Davis, *Non-Cycle Plays*, p. lxxiii.

70. Mervyn James, 'Ritual, drama and social body in the late medieval English town', *Past and Present*, **98**, 1983, 3–29.

71. This interpretation of Durkheim's definition of rite is taken from David Kertzer, *Ritual, Politics and Power*, New Haven CT: Yale University Press, 1988, p. 9.

72. From the A/Y Memorandum Book, reprinted in *Records of Early English Drama: York*, ed. Alexandra F, Johnstone and Margaret Rogerson, Toronto: University of Toronto Press, 1979, p. 43, and translation, vol. 2, p. 728. It is the very same friar, William Melton, who has such strong objections to the weepings and cryings of Margery Kempe when he visits Lynn; see *The Book of Margery Kempe*, ed. H. E. Allen and S. Meech, Oxford: Oxford University Press, 1940, p. 155.

73. See Pamela Graves, 'Social space in the English medieval parish church', *Economy and Society*, **18**, 3, 1989, 297–322, for the way in which mercantile patronage and redesign of the architectural space of church buildings could literally change the shape of the processional route, and in this way modify the

shape of 'ecclesiastical control'. It is important to note here that the York civic records, for example, show that it was the city fathers who determined the route of the Corpus Christi procession, going so far as to fine the craft guilds who refused to participate; however, as Douglas Cowling points out, although the corporation maintained jurisdiction over the procession, 'they could not carry the Host'. See Douglas Cowling, 'The liturgical celebration of Corpus Christi in medieval York', *Reed Newsletter*, 1, 2, 1976, 7. Cowling also makes the (for our purposes) important observation that the 'parochial clergy and laity cele-brated Corpus Christi with the city fathers independent of the monastic and cathedral foundations' (7). This meant that there were occasionally competing processions on the same day (see 6–7). The local details of the complex relations between the Corpus Christi processions and the plays are still emerging; what it does seem possible to say at this stage is that there is enough information to indicate some pronounced tensions over jurisdictional control.

74. In York, for example, there were regularly between ten and sixteen stations, and each play in each cycle was supposedly performed at each station. See Richard Beadle, *The York Plays*, London: Edward Arnold, 1982, p. 32.
75. David Mills notes the 'dissolution of the boundaries of mimesis and sacramental rite, of illusion and reality', but sees this as working in the service of 'fideistic affirmation' in the audience, in A. C. Cawley, David Mills, P. F. McDonald and Marion Jones, *The Revels History of Drama in English*, vol. I: *Medieval Drama*, London: Methuen, 1983, p. 148.
76. For a critical account of the evolutionism of early medieval drama history, see O. B. Hardison, *Christian Rite and Christian Drama: Essays in the origin and early history of modern drama*, Baltimore MD: Johns Hopkins University Press, 1965, especially Essay I, pp. 1–35.
77. For a consideration of the Chester Cycle as ritual, see Peter Travis, *Dramatic Design in the Chester Cycle*, Chicago and London; University of Chicago Press, 1982, pp. 22, 108, 117, 121 ff. For a useful distinction in the use of the category of 'ritual' in medieval drama studies which I unfortunately read after this essay was completed, see Kathleen Ashley, 'An anthropological approach to the cycle drama: The shepherds as sacred clowns', *Fifteenth Century Studies*, 13, 1988, 128:

> Much drama criticism has been focused on the issue of what divides ritual from drama, but contemporary anthropological and performance theory suggests that the lines cannot be easily or sharply drawn. I prefer to use 'ritual' in its broad rather than narrowly religious sense.

Finally, for a recent consideration of 'ritual' (as derived from the anthropologist Victor Turner) and medieval drama, see C. Clifford Flanigan, 'Liminality, carnival and social structure: the case of late medieval biblical drama', in *Victor Turner and the Construction of Cultural Criticism: Between literature and anthro-pology*, ed. Kathleen Ashley, Bloomington and Indianapolis IN: Indiana University Press, 1990, pp. 42–64.
78. See, for example, Jack Goody, *The Domestication of the Savage Mind*, Cambridge: Cambridge University Press, 1977.

79. This is partly because the familiar usage of 'ritual', especially as mediated through the contemporary anthropological writings available to the early critics of medieval drama (Durkheim, Radclyffe Brown) was used precisely for tribal as opposed to historical religions. For a recent analysis of such 'primitivism', see Julian Stallabrass, 'The idea of the primitive: British art and anthropology 1918–1930', *New Left Review*, **183**, 1990, 95–116. For a discussion of the intertwining of fantasies of cultural coherence and integration and views of traditional societies, see Margaret Archer, *Culture and Agency: The place of culture in social theory*, Cambridge: Cambridge University Press, 1988, p. 8. The influence of anthropological primitivism on medieval studies, in its role as – in Patterson's lucid phrasing – the 'custodian of the formative history of the cultures of the European nation states' has been underestimated to date. See Lee Patterson, 'On the margin: Postmodernism, ironic history, and medieval studies, *Speculum*, **65**, 1990, 87.

80. Emile Durkheim, *The Elementary Forms of Religious Life*, London: Allen & Unwin, 1964, p. 169.

81. Peter Womack, *Ben Jonson*, Oxford: Basil Blackwell, 1986, p. 31.

82. *Ibid.*, p. 32.

83. For a consideration of the possibilities of Brechtian readings for medieval drama, see Martin Stevens, 'Illusion and reality in the medieval drama', *College English*, **32**, 1970–1, 448–64.

84. Raymond Williams, *Culture*, Glasgow: Fontana, 1981, pp. 146–7.

85. Aquinas maintained that the entire body of Christ was present in each particle. For a late-medieval doctrinal representation of such a view see, for example, William of Shoreham's *De sacramento altaris* in *William of Shoreham's Poems*, Early English Text Society, Extra Series 86, 1902, edited by Dr Konrath, where Shoreham discusses the doctrine of *concomitance*, which expresses the union of his Blood, Soul, and divinity with his Body. Should the sacramental species break in the mouth of its recipient, it is not Christ that is broken any more than an image is broken in a glass that has been smashed. Rather, Christ is present whole and entire on each and every altar. See also *The Holy Eucharist in Middle English Homilectic and Devotional Verse* (PhD dissertation, Catholic University of America, 1936), pp. 77–8. For a discussion of such doctrine, see Caroline Walker Bynum, *Holy Feast and Holy Fast: The religious significance of food to medieval women*, Berkeley CA: University of California Press, 1987, pp. 51 and 325, n. 84.

86. Sermon 227, Migne, xxxviii, 1099. Quoted Nichols 'The Croxton play', p. 128.

Imagining Communities: Theatres and the English Nation in the Sixteenth Century

Peter Womack

Imaginary puissance

> But pardon, gentles all,
> The flat unraised spirits that hath dar'd
> On this unworthy scaffold to bring forth
> So great an object: can this cockpit hold
> The vasty fields of France? or may we cram
> Within this wooden O the very casques
> That did affright the air at Agincourt?[1]

The Chorus's embarrassment seems odd, even disingenuous. This is, after all, Shakespeare's ninth history play. Most of the earlier ones have been notably successful, and *Henry V* itself has several confident allusions to them. The banal problems which seem to be troubling the company's spokesman (the discrepancy of size, the inauthenticity of costume) have been overcome many times over the previous decade; the spectators, experts in the genre and treated as such, can surely be expected to manage the business of 'minding true things by what their mock'ries be' (IV, 53) without this officious apology.

This is not, in other words, a real discussion of the quandaries of representation. Rather, it is a rhetorician's aporia – an assumed, figured doubtfulness which is actually a hyperbolic mechanism. This is confirmed by the charming gap between the humility and incapacity of the choric speaker's self-description and the passionate, buttonholing confidence of his verse:

> O, do but think
> You stand upon the rivage and behold
> A city on th'inconstant billows dancing;
> For so appears this fleet majestical
> Holding due course to Harfleur. Follow, follow!
> Grapple your minds to sternage of this navy,
> And leave your England. . . .
>
> (III, 13–19)

The deictic immediacy, the mouth-music of fricatives and sibilants, the doubled image (think a city so that you can see the fleet), the daring conceit in which the spectators' minds concretely board the ships – the rhetoric has a sort of strained opulence which is winning because of the generous intensity of the speaker's desire to take the audience with him. He confesses the theatre company's impotence only in order to make the gesture of empowering the spectators; they are royally and subtly flattered ('For 'tis your thoughts that now must deck our kings', I, 28) with being needed in what he is already making sound like a radiant adventure.

So one could invert the Chorus's own description of the project: it is not that the audience's imagination is being enlisted in order to repair the deficiencies of the theatre, but that the deficiencies of the theatre are being advertised in order to motivate the enlisting of the audience's imagination. This inversion has the advantage of rendering the formulation open-ended: now we can ask – enlisting it for what? What has this audience got that this play wants?

It is illuminating to contrast the Chorus with the Prologue from Shakespeare's previous history play: Rumour. He describes himself as

> a pipe
> Blown by surmises, jealousies, conjectures,
> And of so easy and so plain a stop
> That the blunt monster with uncounted heads,
> The still-discordant wav'ring multitude,
> Can play upon it. But what I need I thus
> My well-known body to anatomise
> Among my household?[2]

As in *Henry V*, the audience is invited to 'entertain conjecture'; but here the invitation is ironic, offered in the consciousness that such imaginative prodigality produces truths and lies, message and noise, anarchically mixed up together. The theatre, teasingly, is Rumour's household, the disreputable space where blown surmises and false reports are indulged in. *You* all know who *I* am, he implies: otherwise you wouldn't be here.

The social body which corresponds to that cognitive faithlessness is the populace, the monster whose uncounted heads contain the uncounted tongues of Rumour's monstrous costume.[3] The incorrigible plurality of the people, bubbling up through the fissures in the unity of government, expresses itself in the treacherous and many-voiced utterance of the Vice. Here too the theatre provides a provocative actualisation of the image: nothing enacts the emblem of many-headedness so literally as the crowded yard and galleries of the wooden O:

> Storeys of men and women, mixed together,
> Fair ones with foul, like sunshine in wet weather;
> Within one square a thousand heads are laid,
> So close that all of heads the room seems made. . . .
>   then, sir, below,
> The very floor, as't were, waves to and fro,
> And, like a floating island, seems to move
> Upon a sea bound in with shores above.[4]

For this prologue, in the populist theatre of Dekker and Middleton, the instability of the actor's stance on the platform stage, floating on a sea of heads, is a source of excitement and pleasure; nevertheless, the components of the image – numerousness, fluidity, heterogeneity, illusion – are identical with those of the contemptuous patrician topos of the *mobile vulgus*.[5] The ambivalence is a radical one: that ocean, the solvent of all discursive order and truth, is also the element of the theatre's productivity. Like the sea for Shakespeare, and like the public for all box offices, the crowd is a chaos containing fabulous riches.

In this light, *Henry V*'s self-conscious cultivation of 'imaginary puissance' looks like an attempt to harness the fictive energies of Rumour's household to a myth, grappling the floating unreliable thoughts of the multitude to the sterns of the royal fleet. The audience's corrupting, boundary-rotting facility for imagining things which are not so is asked to conceive of a positive imaginary entity. This entity can, I think, be named very simply: it is England. Imaginary in the sense, expounded by Benedict Anderson, that a nation 'is *imagined* because the members even of the smallest nation will never know most of their fellow-members, meet them, or even hear of them, yet in the minds of each lives the image of their communion'. Other kinds of loyalty can be directly located – a ruler can be seen, hearth and home directly experienced, a sacred text read – but the nation needs to be imagined. It cannot particularise itself because it is not a thing but a mode of connectedness:

'It is imagined as a *community*, because, regardless of the actual inequality and exploitation which may prevail in each, the nation is always conceived as a deep, horizontal comradeship.'[6]

Anderson is mainly talking about the more or less democratic post-Enlightenment nationalisms which correspond to the modern global system of sovereign states. His observations cannot automatically be applied to the patriotic culture of late-Elizabethan England. But certainly *Henry V* sometimes sounds like a dramatic commentary on his text – for example in the famous moment of Henry's rhetoric where the heroism of Agincourt dissolves the distinctions of rank:

> We few, we happy few, we band of brothers;
> For he today that sheds his blood with me
> Shall be my brother; be he ne'er so vile
> This day shall gentle his condition:
> And gentlemen in England now a-bed
> Shall think themselves accurs'd they were not here. . . .
>
> (IV, iii, 60–5)

The conceit draws attention to the social stratification whose suspension it declares: this is the very transient egalitarian moment of a deeply hierarchical order. It is not an accident that these lines passed, through Churchill's allusions and Olivier's film, into the British iconography of World War II, at once the 'people's war' and the last throw of a class-ridden Empire.[7] Then, analogously, the gentlemen of England had to reach for the most vital sources of the state's cohesion, which turned out to include the concept of 'a deep, horizontal comradeship'; and the ideology of nationhood struggled to resolve the contradiction. As Anderson argues, nationalism must contain a strand which is ineradicably, often inconveniently, democratic.

Graham Holderness, in one of his recent essays on these plays, notes that Henry's army at Agincourt glowingly represents the nation, and that this trope is facilitated by the explicit way the army is, in turn, represented by 'four or five most vile and ragged foils': 'The theatre is the ideal medium for the representation of such an image of union: since a small group of characters can symbolize a nation as well as they can symbolize an army.'[8] I think this is not exactly true. A small group of characters can fairly easily represent an army because armies are hierarchical and uniform: they can be formally represented in real life by their leaders, and if you see a small part of one, you can take it that the rest is, roughly speaking, more of the same. Representing a nation is problematic in a different way because of the concept's irreducibly 'horizontal' orientation. Its totality must transcend formal hierarchy, which means that its presence cannot be fully signified by that of its leaders. And its unity must be compatible with heterogeneity, which means that it cannot be simply extrapolated from a random sample. The movement from part to whole, which is a logical procedure in the case of an army, is in the case of a nation an imaginative leap.

It is precisely this leap that the audience is invited to make. The dangerous 'imaginary forces' of the crowd are to invent the grandeur of a national essence underlying the smallness of contingency:

> O England! model to thy inward greatness,
> Like little body with a mighty heart,
> What might'st thou do, that honour would thee do,
> Were all thy children kind and natural!
>
> (II, 16–19)

This inward England which is greater than its outward appearance is graspable not in spite of the disjunctions between stage and kingdom, beleaguered army and nation, but through them. In piecing out the imperfections of the performance with their thoughts, the spectators are at the same time piecing out the imperfections of the historical events.

For example, the Chorus says at the outset that if the company really had the impossible national stage he imagines –

> Then should the warlike Harry, like himself,
> Assume the port of Mars; and at his heels,
> Leash'd in like hounds, should famine, sword and fire
> Crouch for employment.
>
> (I, 5–8)

At first, that looks as if it is saying that with a kingdom for a stage there would be no need for impersonation: Henry V would appear 'as himself', as they say in the cinema. But then the visualisation of that actuality is strikingly emblematic: Mars with a trio of allegorical dogs. The *real* Agincourt would be purged, not only of the stage's material inadequacies, but also of its own. At Harfleur, Henry's own vision of his troops is similarly transfiguring:

> For there is none of you so mean and base
> That hath not noble lustre in your eyes.
> I see you stand like greyhounds in the slips,
> Straining upon the start. The game's afoot. . . .
>
> (III, i, 29–32)

This climactic image is at once followed by a farcical scene in which Bardolph, Nym and Pistol are driven into reluctant action by Fluellen ('Up to the breach, you dogs'!). The united and indomitable army of Henry's rhetoric is not exactly there – not on the stage, and not in the story either. The heroic idiom of the Chorus and the King is repeatedly disconfirmed by clownish codes of individuality: self-preservation, logic-chopping, humours. But on the other hand, the miraculous victory is there, and the Chorus's uniquely direct access to the audience ensures that the disconfirmations are not working in any simple way to discredit it. Rather, the rhetoric of national endeavour rides over the imperfections of the (theatrical *and* historical) actors to seek out its 'kind and natural' community in the audience, eliciting its patriotic identification by being incoherent without it.

It is an audacious tactic, basing its appeal not on the show's capacity to display the truth, but on the fictive productivity of its relationship with its audience. Its paradoxes pose, in exemplary and provocative fashion, the questions I am concerned with in this essay. On what terms is the 'imagined community' of the nation staged by the Elizabethan theatre? What are the conditions of possibility of its national drama, as these can be traced in its formal resources, its relations with its audience, and its political situation? These are questions about the interpretation of nationalism as well as of drama. And given Shakespeare's continuing presence in the construction of English identity – given, too, the undiminished strength of nationalism as a political motive across Europe and the world – they refer, not only to the audiences of the 1590s, but also to ourselves, studying, performing and watching the plays now.

1576

Histories of Elizabethan theatre regularly begin at 1576 because it was in April of that year that James Burbage signed the lease on the plot of land in Shoreditch where he proceeded to build the first specialised playhouse.[9] It is also a good year to choose because of a second, somewhat less celebrated document. In May, the Diocesan Court of High Commission in York wrote to the mayor and corporation of Wakefield, effectively banning the Corpus Christi play which would otherwise have been performed there during the following month.[10] To put these two documents side by side is to raise interesting questions about the relationship between theatre and the Elizabethan state. The Wakefield letter is part of the government offensive which brought the religious drama of the provincial towns to an end. The pageants were played for the last time at Norwich in 1564, at York in 1569, at Chester in 1575, and at Coventry in 1579, and in most of these cases there was official pressure to close, whether from the ecclesiastical authorities, the Council of the North, or the Privy Council.[11] All the major organs of state power were working against the plays, sometimes despite the apparent wishes of the urban authorities themselves. Burbage, on the other hand, seems to have made his risky investment *despite* the hostility of the City authorities, and because he was reasonably confident that he had the *support* of the Privy Council.[12] Government policy on theatre, then – whether or not there was anybody actually thinking it through in such terms – was to promote a particular kind of drama in the capital while suppressing another kind in the provinces.

Why did the provincial drama go under at this point? The obvious answer is that it was banned by a Protestant establishment because it bore too many traces of its pre-Reformation origin. Certainly this was important; what has to be added, though, is that the establishment, whose general commitment to Reformation principles was by no means unambiguous, had particular reasons for insisting on its Protestantism in the north, and particularly at that time. The rising of the northern earls in 1569–70 had revealed that a regional culture of Roman Catholic belief and dynastic loyalty, although much weakened since the 1530s, was still capable of threatening royal authority. In the aftermath of the insurrection, Edmund Grindal was made Archbishop of York, and the Earl of Huntingdon Lord President of the Council of the North. Both were firm Calvinists, and under their influence, diocese and Council co-operated in an effective *Kulturkampf* which involved not only persecuting Catholics directly, but also depriving suspect clergymen, planting a preaching ministry, and inspecting local traditions by the light of the Gospel.[13] Grindal's case is precisely illustrative of the tensions involved. After his translation to the see of Canterbury in 1575, his Protestant principles rapidly led him into a direct confrontation with Elizabeth, but so long as he was at York, his reforming militancy met the political needs of the moment: ironically, the 'struggle for a reformed church', which in London found itself in conflict with the Crown's concern for uniformity, was official policy in the north precisely for the sake of uniformity. Thus the attack on the cycle plays was part of a somewhat ambiguous programme. It was carried out by agents for whom its key theme was Protestant doctrine, but for the state which they served, the key theme was national unity. In other words, the suppression of the urban drama is not a purely doctrinal question, but a doctrinal question in a determining political context.

The doctrinal issues, after all, were not new. The distinctively Catholic features of the texts had naturally been under intermittent attack since the 1530s. Up until now, however, it had apparently been permissible to meet such objections by cutting or rewriting the offensive passages.[14] And the possibility in principle of more radical amendment is shown by plays such as John Bale's *John the Baptist* (1536) and Lewis Wager's *Marie Magdalene* (1566), which used the motifs and conventions of medieval devotional theatre for irreproachably, even militantly, Protestant purposes.[15] The Wakefield letter decisively closes that door. It requires that

> no pageant be used or set furthe wherein the Ma'ye of God the Father, God the Sonne, or God the Holie Ghoste or the administration of either the Sacramentes of Baptisme or of the Lordes Supper be counterfeyted or represented, or anything plaied which tende to the maintenance of superstition and idolatrie.

There are two striking things about this edict. One is that it is not mainly directed against Catholicism. The Protestant plays I mentioned would themselves have violated these requirements, and the sacraments which are banned from the stage are not the seven Catholic ones but precisely the two which the reformed Church had itself adopted. The objection is not that the actors would, from a Protestant point of view, be propagating religious falsehoods, but on the contrary, that they would be profaning religious truths by performing them in a play. The concern is not with the content of the show, but with its form. Second, the Diocesan Court's objections are clearly insuperable. There are thirty-two plays in the extant Wakefield cycle, and God appears in twenty-three of them. That the majesty of God the Son, in particular, be 'counterfeited or represented', is the organising principle of the event. The censors are striking not, as they seem more or less disingenuously to imagine, at alterable details, but at an entire cultural practice.

Two classic studies have contributed immensely to an understanding of what this practice was.[16] The Corpus Christi plays were the drama *of* the late-medieval urban community, taking shape only in towns whose craft guild structure was powerful and diverse enough, and making sense as part of an elaborate municipal-cum-ecclesiastical ceremonial year. Considered as components of a single observance, the procession and pageants that marked the festival were an exposition of the doctrine of the fall and redemption of man, and also, in the same breath, an affirmation of the communal identity of the town which mounted the spectacle. As the corporation of Chester put it in response to attack from the Privy Council, the plays were staged

> acordinge to an order concluded and agreed upon for dyvers good and great consideracons redoundinge to the comon wealthe, benefit and profitte of the saide citie in assemblie there holden, according to the auncyente and laudable usages and customes there hadde and used fur above remembraunce.[17]

Mervyn James draws on anthropological theory to suggest the structure of these good and great considerations: by affording a moment of particular self-assertion to each occupational group, but at the same time incorporating them all in the iconographic totality of Christ's body and the dramatic totality of the Creation-to-Doomsday narrative, the festival effected a ritual reconciliation of social wholeness and social differentiation. The universal scope of the extant texts – astonishing to a modern reader habituated to the post-1576 assumption that really ambitious drama is always metropolitan – is grounded in the *universitas*[18] of the corporate town, and in the symbolic acts which reproduced its integrity and renegotiated its contradictions.

One striking concomitant of this function is the ritual and theatrical importance of the community's being *literally present*. For example: scholars have balked at the evidence about processional presentation in York, which appears to show that nearly fifty plays, with a total minimum cast of 300, each played up to twelve times in different locations in the course of the day.[19] Since Christ appears in over half the plays, which were all cast separately, this account of the staging asks us to imagine several hundred performances of the sacred role, scattered about the city at different times and places. The whole thing seems 'intolerably wasteful and fragmented'[20] until we abandon modern assumptions about what is theatrically practical and think a quite different dramatic intention. There were between 8,000 and 11,000 people living in late-medieval York:[21] something like one-tenth of the total male population must have been directly involved in the show, and even making generous allowance for visitors, an overwhelming majority of the rest of the people must have watched it, especially since it is hard to imagine much chance of doing anything else in the town while it was happening. It is thus not fanciful to suggest that this type of theatre involved the urban community *as a whole*. In that case, the spectacular proliferation of Christs, so far from being redundant, seems extraordinarily eloquent. The figure of the Redeemer permeates the town, endlessly subdivided, yet one and entire in each embodiment, just as, when the host is broken into pieces, the *verum corpus* is wholly present in each fragment. To perform that consecration of the ordinary environment is much more important than to achieve an economical rendering of the written text. The whole real town – its people, its material resources, its social structure and its topography – is organised into a single spectacle, in which it recognises itself as the mystical body of Christ.

This can be seen in practice in the numerous points at which the show makes direct use of the presence of the crowd. In the York 'Entry into Jerusalem', for example, it seems likely that Christ rides a real donkey in the street, and is formally welcomed by eight 'burgenses' positioned on the pageant-wagon. As recent editors have suggested, this arrangement makes the play resemble a ceremonial civic welcome in which the speakers *represent* the watching people: there is an easily accessible level at which Christ is riding into York.[22] There is a slightly more complex effect in the vaunting which always characterises the secular rulers in the story – Pharaoh, Caesar, Herod, Pilate. These potentates commonly begin by claiming to rule the world, and commanding the crowd to be silent on pain of terrible punishments. In one sense, they are speaking directly as actors, who need to get an unconfined holiday audience to quieten down before anything significant happens. But the device is of course also a comic one: it is understood that the speaker does not really rule the world – because he is only an actor who cannot carry out his threats, but also because the Christian spectators know that he is not, as he seems to think, the central character in the story, but an ancillary and ignoble one. So the watching group is drawn together by its shared transcendence to the gaudy individual who is pretending to dominate it. Such moments depend a lot on the familiarity of the story: details presumably change from one year to the next, but the overall shape remains massively stable over lifetimes. It is the play of *what everyone knows*, and so works to focus the self-presence of the 'everyone'.

What might be called the community politics of this process can be seen exceptionally clearly in the N-town Passion Plays, partly because they have an unusually integrated structure (together the two plays form a single continuous sequence almost as long as an Elizabethan playhouse text), and partly because the script is unusually generous with stage directions.[23]

The events leading up to Christ's arrest occupy most of the first play, and are ordered like this:

1. Annas and Caiaphas confer with their Doctors about how to proceed against Christ.
2. The Palm Sunday entry into Jerusalem.
3. Another council scene like (1).
4. The first part of the Last Supper, incorporating the anointing of Christ's feet by a woman who in this play is identified as Mary Magdalen.
5. Judas goes to the high priests, they strike their bargain, and their followers position themselves around the acting area ready to make the arrest.
6. The rest of the Last Supper, going straight into the events in Gethsemane.
7. The arrest.

This intercutting produces an effect of simultaneity which is intensified because both the priests in council and the disciples at supper are in settings which can be curtained off. Thus from (2) through (7) nobody leaves the acting area, the alternations being marked by a temporary screening off of each group during the other's scenes. Powerfully, this enables Judas to walk out of the supper at the end of (4) and, after a short soliloquy in the open *platea*, cross to the council house to make his offer. The show holds the two groups separate and vibrantly connected until they come together in the long-prepared moment of violence in the garden.

The opposition is strongly marked by costume. All the actors on the priestly side are gorgeously dressed, the priests in the formal robes of 'buschopys, prestys, and jewgys sitting in here astat' (397–8), and the knights who make the arrest 'in white arneys and breganderys . . . wih swerdys, glevys, and other straunge wepon' (670). Jesus and the disciples are not described in the text, but the citizens who welcome them to Jerusalem in (2) are 'barfot and barelegged and in here shirtys', and Simon Leprows, the owner of the house with the upper room, is described as 'a pore man in simpyl aray' (670). The sartorial contrast is already value-laden because the play opened with an exceptionally dandyish Satan, who boasted about his clothes in enough detail to identity him as a fifteenth-century courtier (65 ff.). The opposition of elaborate and simple is repeated in the action: the priestly group's scenes are all about plans, reports, jurisdictions and deals, while the actions in Christ's group are all free gifts – the man who simply hands over his ass, the washing of the disciples' feet, and so on. It is one such unconditional gift – Magdalen's ointment – which prompts Judas to switch from one group to the other. In the earlier part of the sequence, the same contrast is stated yet again by the blocking. Annas and Caiaphas sit established in 'a litil oratory with stolys and cusshonys, clenly beseyn lych as it were a cownsel hous' (123), while the events of Palm Sunday and the impending Passover swirl fluidly around them in the *platea*.

Simple dress and rich robes, freedom and institutional fixity, the people and the establishment, gift and law, openness and conspiracy: an eloquent theatrical rhythm ironically amplifies the priests' exposition of the danger as they see it:

> The pepyl so fast to him doth falle
> (By prevy menys as we aspye),
> Yif he procede, son sen ye shalle
> That oure lawes he wil distrye.
>
> (133–6)

The populist and utopian import of the dramatic structure is unmistakable, even without the provocative decision to dress the murderers of Christ as members of the ecclesiastical hierarchy (were the costumes *real* church vestments?). This Christ's ministry is not to the authorities, but to the poor and meek.

This is a vigorously anti-establishment theatre, then, consistently displaying diabolical princes and princely devils to the sort of socially comprehensive public a modern populist director can only dream about. But then how are we to place this apparent social and ecclesiastical subversion? After all, the doctrinal content of the drama, its festive occasion, and almost certainly its scripts, all emanated from the Church: it can be convincingly argued that ecclesiastical control was not so complete as scholars used to think,[24] but the predominance of the laity in the organisation of the event hardly amounts to an open door – or even a desire – for secular or heretical meanings. In any case, the urban community whose structure was being reproduced was not in the least 'communal' in an egalitarian or collectivist sense, but was minutely graded, horizontally and vertically, by occupation, seniority, gender, wealth and civic position. We can say that the plays functioned as a realisation of urban community, but they were not actuated by the democratic impulse which typically informs the community plays of our own time: it was a community under authority, projected ultimately on to the host, which remained in the possession of the priests. So the inclusiveness represented by the cosmic universalisation of the crowd beats against the rigid exclusions of the social order to which the show belonged. In all the circumstances, it is clear that if the scripts seem to us to be undermining social and ecclesiastical authority, we must be reading them wrong. Even when the plays were suppressed, it does not appear to have been on the grounds that they were destructive of hierarchy.

To back out of this interpretive wrong turning, we can look more closely at the anthropological reading proposed by James. Its source is Victor Turner, who says:

> It is as though there are two major 'models' for human interrelatedness, juxtaposed and alternating. The first is of society as a structured, differentiated and often hierarchical system of politico-legal-economic positions with many types of evaluation, separating men in terms of 'more' and 'less'. The second . . . is of society as an unstructured or rudimentarily structured and relatively undifferentiated *comitatus*, community, or even communion of equal individuals who submit together to the general authority of the ritual elders.[25]

It is the relationship between the two which is the uncertain point of this powerful formulation. It would be easy, for example, to think of the models as different 'ways of looking at society', with the implication that some kinds of people are going to prefer one, some the other, and the sensible citizen a judicious blend of the two. That would be a misunderstanding, I think. 'Structure and anti-structure' are not competing opinions but systemic opposites; they are models of society which are at once jointly comprehensive and mutually exclusive; you cannot compromise between them, as you cannot compromise between heads and tails, because each is *constitutive* of the other. That is why they are not in a fixed relationship, but 'juxtaposed and alternating' – that is, their totalisation requires, not a discursive closure, but something like a dramatic form. To put it in older terms, the spectacle of Corpus Christi embodies the community as both One and Many, the body in its singleness and the members in their diversity.[26] The imagery of the One dissolves intra-communal distinctions and tends towards a utopian and egalitarian vision; to that extent, it can be read, can even function, in an oppositional way. But the hierarchy has to accept that degree of challenge because the underlying unity which is so expressed is the deep source of the hierarchy's own validity. This is the reason, so to speak, why the bishop agrees to lend his cope to the actor playing Caiaphas. Precisely in order to maintain the coherence of its differentiating structures, the town passes periodically through a ritual in which it *both* parades those structures *and at the same time* recognises itself as a 'community, or even communion of equal individuals'.

This 'both-and' – juxtaposing and alternating – consequently pervades the spectacle. Bringing up the rear of the procession, there is the host, the ultimate repository of *communitas*, but also, next to it, there is the Mayor. At Wakefield, famously, the nativity of Christ is doubled by the discovery of a stolen sheep in Mak's unsanctified manger.[27] The absurd bragging monarchs are only (exactly) half of the drama's image of kingship; the other half is the majesty of the Risen Christ.[28] The York Crucifixion is at once a dramatic making of the universal image of Christ and a comic exhibition of the skills of the Pinners, the craft guild responsible for the performance.[29] Examples could be multiplied indefinitely; and what underlies all of them is the plays' wonderful, aggressive and *structurally motivated* anachronism. In scene after scene, two dramatic modes confront each other: one which locks characters into time and into the immediate practicalities of their own play, and the other which presents them as medieval Christians, revering the saints and quoting the Latin liturgy, always already in contact with the timeless truth of the cycle as a whole. The actor moves easily between the world of the story and that of the audience, not because the authors are historically naïve, but because it is only when the figures of the Christian story become the common property of the crowd that the crowd realises its common membership of the body of Christ.

It is precisely this communion which is unacceptable to the censors of the 1570s. For them, the collective appropriation of divine majesty is a kind of blasphemy, and the converse consecration of the common body a kind of idolatry.[30] The syntax of the ritual had become unintelligible; and to enquire why that was may give us a more concrete understanding of its collapse.

It has to be seen, first of all, as only one part of the broader dismantling of the urban communal year. Many other ceremonial observances, connected with Christmas, Shrove Tuesday, Midsummer and so on, were also discontinued at some point in the second half of the century. Each ceremony has its own history and its own terminal point, but if, as Phythian-Adams argues, they formed between them 'a coherent ceremonial pattern',[31] then their abandonment amounts to a general change in the way towns represented themselves.

One context for this change, which Phythian-Adams himself highlights, is the fact of sheer material decline in the mid-sixteenth century: 'at no other

period since the coming of the Danes have English towns been so weak . . .
for the most part smaller in size, industrially debilitated, commercially
vulnerable, and increasingly prone to structural strains'.[32] These strains, at
least in the case of Coventry, had the effect of unravelling the network of
urban institutions – craft guilds, socio-religious guilds, parish organisa-
tions, civic authorities – which the ceremonial calendar depended on and
reflected. Increasing imports undermined domestic self-sufficiency and
skewed the relationships between craft guilds; customary controls on
economic life became burdensome or unworkable; a decline in urban
population, both relative and absolute, meant that the elaborate corporate
superstructures could no longer reproduce themselves. Economic historians continue to debate the general applicability of this description, but it
seems clear that some corporate towns were under severe strain, and
(equally to the point here) were felt to be.[33] In so far as 'urban decline' was
a contemporary reality, it meant that the town came to lack both the
resources and the structures for the expensive cultural self-assertiveness of
which Corpus Christi had been a central component.

The other side of this diminution was the unprecedented expansion of
London, which was already under way by the 1570s, and which took the
form, not only of raw demographic increase, but also of a growing domination, as a port and as a manufacturing and financial centre, over the
economic life of other towns.[34] The greater this domination, the more the
other towns became components in a set of relations which overrode their
autonomy – that is, in a national economy.[35] As Christopher Hill has
argued, this was not simply an unplanned economic tendency; it was also a
sequence of political and ideological events,[36] driven partly by specific
government policies designed to centralise the administration of justice and
the ministry of the Church. The greater the tendency for legal, mercantile
and financial business to migrate to London, and the greater the Privy
Council's success in transferring power from the great regional families to
its own agents,[37] the harder it was to understand the life of a particular
provincial town without constant reference to the over-arching order of the
state. Without that internal wholeness, that capacity to represent itself
concretely as a type of *universitas*, the town's annual rehearsal of a universal
history lost some of its point.[38]

The forces of national integration were mediated not only through
politics but also through language. The Corpus Christi plays were part of a
ministry whose relation with its authoritative texts was indirect, because
they were transmitted in Latin, while the vernacular forms, such as preaching
and the plays themselves, were oral. By contrast, Protestantism, as it was
consolidated in the first half of Elizabeth's reign, was fundamentally dependent on the distribution of a limited number of crucial books in English: the
Bible, the Paraphrases of Erasmus, the Book of Common Prayer, the

Homilies and, in the 1570s, Foxe's *Actes and Monuments*.[39] The Act of
Uniformity was assisted by the literal uniformity afforded by printing: the
state could plausibly require a single form of worship because it was tech-
nically possible to place the same book in every church. Instead of the
institutionally transmitted manuscripts of the religious drama, with their
irregular combinations of inter-urban borrowing and local uniqueness, and
their habit of mixing scriptural paraphrase together with traditionary or
authorial invention, there was now the single authorised text, emanating
from the capital and affording equal access to the truth to anyone who could
read.

Apart from anything else, this distribution of books and university-
trained preachers was a major piece of linguistic standardisation. To be a
good Protestant in Yorkshire it was necessary to master an unfamiliar
dialect, and in parts of Wales and Cornwall, a second language.[40] English,
an emotive issue because of the past struggles for biblical translation, and
the related history of exile, became the language of the godly nation in a
newly unified sense as a direct result of its diffusion through the Church. Its
form was that of the metropolitan centre (London, Canterbury, Oxford and
Cambridge), whose cultural predominance it thus expressed and reproduced. The language of the provincial plays suffered a corresponding loss of
authority.

Besides, the propagation of the word was the immediate effect of government policy. The books were printed, the liturgy fixed, the episcopal powers
exercised, under statutes passed by Parliament in London. The churches,
bare of crucifixes, were adorned with the royal coat of arms.[41] Moreover,
the implicit identification of doctrinal uniformity and national unity was
also explicitly, not to say aggressively, insisted on by the government. When
Catholics were persecuted, they were tried for treason, not heresy: this was
not only a tactic to avoid accusations of religious intolerance, but also a real
assertion that loyalty to the Protestant faith and loyalty to the queen were
the same thing.[42] As the Elizabethan settlement came to look permanent,
and was confirmed by political events, it became inescapably clear that the
social unit to which the Church corresponded was not Christendom in
general, and not the urban community in particular, but the nation.

This is not to suggest that the dismantling of the ceremonial year simply
led to a decline in religious-civic *consciousness*. On the contrary, Reformation
principles produced, in the minds and programmes of local oligarchs, the
image of their town as a potential 'godly commonwealth'. But as Collinson
argues, that Genevan ideal is not to be realised through ceremony:

> The new order, presided over by a tight alliance of 'ministry and magistracy', was
> as much concerned as the old to . . . conserve the harmony and wholeness of the
> town: indeed this was an objective now made more explicit. But the objective was

now connected with obedience, disorder with disobedience, that is to say with disobedience to God, sin. Therefore order was to be spelt out in the spoken word and enforced by coercive discipline, not achieved in the charmingly roundabout fashion of 'pastime' and instinctive ritual and carnival.[43]

It is not necessary to share the odd assumption that rituals are 'instinctive' to see the importance of this distinction. The 'both-and' structure of the festival and its plays – York and Jerusalem, sacred and profane, hierarchy and *communitas*, civic order and holiday licence – is incompatible with a didactic monologism where holiness and unholiness meet on the same plane of reality and are therefore in a relation of 'either-or'. The town's sanctification, now, is to be encompassed less through symbols than through executive actions: preaching, punishing immorality, providing for the poor. Grindal's dual policy at York is typically Protestant in this sense: at once suppressing ritual observances (including plays) and labouring to establish a learned ministry in the parishes, he was expressing, and enforcing, a shift in the centre of doctrinal gravity from ceremony to discourse, from image to word. What this does is to *delocalise* the language of religious truth. Whereas symbolism ties the universality of Christian doctrine to particular times (festival days) and places (church building, shrines, the routes of processions and pilgrimages), the word is immaterial and ubiquitous, its validity quite unaffected by where and when it happens to be uttered.[44] From this point of view, the *connection* between the immediate locality and the cosmos, which the medieval drama was designed to make, becomes one which *does not matter*.

The primacy of the word has another implication as well. If the gospel is in a book, then its implied recipient is a reader: that is, he is an individual, he is the subject of knowledge, and he is a member of the literate elite. All these assumptions mark a withdrawal from the public mode of the urban pageants, which sought to dissolve personal difference in the revelation of *communitas*, and confer membership through ritual participation rather than personal knowledge. This implication forms part of what Phythian-Adams calls a general movement of privatisation:[45] belonging in Christ ceases to be a *common* thing, and becomes rather something which is threatened by the miscellaneous material presence of a crowd. The difference which counts is no longer that between the members and non-members of a given urban community, but that between the godly and the godless. To put Christ in a public show, then, seems a scandalous degradation, a wanton confounding of the most with the least precious objects. The popular character of the drama ceases to make sense, and becomes a matter of reproach.

Thus the great drama of the medieval urban community was by no means simply shut down by Puritan bureaucrats. Its material base was under strain, its characteristic imagery was becoming incomprehensible, the social space in which it worked was closing up. A document from Chester is painful evidence of many of these elements of cultural defeat. The last performance there was in 1575, but it seems that the resistance to closure was unusually vigorous. At some point in the struggle, someone wrote a new version of the 'banns', the rhyming announcement which was delivered in the streets a week or two before the plays were to be performed.[46] Traditionally, the banns were an exuberant kind of publicity: large promises about the splendours in prospect were made by a rider dressed as St George. This late text, though, is strikingly apologetic. Apparently in order to forestall Protestant objections to the inclusion of 'some thinges not warranted by anye wrytte', the speaker explains that the plays were written long ago by a monk; he also appeals to the antiquity of the script to excuse some 'groosse wordes . . . which importe at this daye smale sence'. In conclusion he warns:

> By craftsmen and meane men these pageauntes are playede,
> and to commons and contry men accustomablye before.
> If better men and finer heades now come, what canne be sayde?
> But of common and contrye players take yow the storye,
> and if anye disdayne, then open is the doore
> that lett him in to heare. Pack awaye at his pleasure!
> Oure playeinge is not to gett fame or treasure.[47]

The awareness of historical change is at once acute and pitiful: the speaker is unhappily conscious of his disadvantages in terms not only of scriptural orthodoxy but also of fashion, correctness, class, and what he calls 'the fine witte, at this day aboundinge'. Even his closing declaration of independence has a sort of churlish humility. The loss of confidence could hardly be more graphically expressed than in the description of the citizen-actors as 'common and contrye players': a tradition of both communal drama and urban status is relinquished in the phrase.

Chester in the late sixteenth century retained and even enhanced its medieval prosperity,[48] so the abjectness is not simply a symptom of declining resources; rather, the town has been commercially, politically, linguistically and culturally *provincialised*. That is to say, the gaze under which St George blushes and loses his words is that of the metropolis. The urban drama has been swamped by the idea of a centralised national culture. It remains to be seen on what terms that larger and less immediate 'community' could find theatrical expression.

The royal bastard

The provincial diffidence of the Chester banns finds its counterpart a decade or so later in the conscious metropolitan disdain of Marlowe's famous prologue (1587):

> From jigging veins of rhyming mother-wits,
> And such conceits as clownage keeps in pay,
> We'll lead you to the stately tent of war,
> Where you shall hear the Scythian Tamburlaine
> Threatening the world with high astounding terms
> And scourging kingdoms with his conquering sword.
> View but his picture in this tragic glass,
> And then applaud his fortunes as you please.[49]

'Mother-wits' – the sneer at infancy, naturalness, domesticity – announces the arrival of a different kind of universality, one which is intimately linked to the structure of the new theatre which Burbage's venture of 1576 had inaugurated.

First, it is fully professional. The Theatre, the Curtain (1576–7) and their successors each represented a major outlay of borrowed capital which made sense only on the expectation of significant profits at the box office.[50] To say that the old kind of writing (presumably meaning the semi-improvisatory theatre of Tarlton) was 'such as clownage keeps in pay' is to imply that it is not capable of pulling an audience unaided: suddenly we are in a recognisable commercial theatre, with its nervy contempt for the unfashionable and the flop. The promoters of *Tamburlaine* are not only in possession of the cultural high ground, but also are confident – rightly, as it turned out – that they have got a hit. Since the actors are now mainly dependent on a paying audience (unlike the performers of either cycle plays or court entertainments), they necessarily advertise not, like the 'contrye players' of Chester or the cast of 'Pyramus and Thisbe', merely their good will, but their talent. Their playing *is* to get fame and treasure.

This is not simply an access of arrogance on the part of the actors. The audience is being constituted in a new way, because it is now enclosed in a building which belongs to the company. Whereas earlier actors, whether amateur or professional, had played either as guests in somebody else's house, or in common spaces that were the property of everybody, the new shows define the spectators as visitors to the actors' house. The effect is to weaken the communally appropriative anachronism which had rooted the events of the religious drama in the social reality of their enactment. This scene is not part of any community, but takes you *out of it* – 'We'll lead you to the stately tent of war', as if the price of admission bought a ticket to Asia Minor. The all but oxymoronic phrase, 'stately tent', glances superbly at the new mixture of ambition and illusionism, the majestic and the makeshift. Besides being thus 'away from home', the audience is also randomly collected: one or two thousand people out of a population of over a hundred thousand, having nothing in common with each other except that they all happened to choose the same diversion on the same afternoon. Thus, whereas the medieval urban audience was *the same* crowd as the one which assembled for other civic and religious purposes, the audience of Burbage and Marlowe is a casual grouping of individuals, whose coherence must come, if at all, from the show itself. 'View but his picture in this tragic glass, / And then applaud his fortunes as you please': the spectacle refuses to be held accountable, either for the events (to which it claims merely to be a neutrally reflecting mirror) or for the spectators (who are invited to react as they please). Sealed off from the order of everyday reality by the walls of the playhouse, the actors lay claim to the autonomy of fiction. This is the theatre irresponsible; or, to put it less romantically, the entertainment is now a commodity.[51]

However, that is not the whole story. Theatre does not really spring up, as if in some Friedmannite fairy tale, from the virgin soil of individual preference. Burbage's, certainly, was built in a definite social and political situation. The political context was a continual if intermittent struggle for control between the Elizabethan Privy Council and successive Lord Mayors of London.[52] The Lord Mayors mostly disapproved of plays, which they thought conducive to idleness, immorality and bubonic plague; the Privy Council mostly approved of them, if only because experienced actors were periodically needed to adorn the court. Both these opinions had broad ideological implications, but the immediate point was that half a dozen extremely important Privy Councillors were individual patrons of acting companies, empowered under the terms of the 1572 Poor Law to authorise them to play without fear of prosecution as vagabonds; while the city authorities were apparently enjoined by a royal proclamation of 1559 to license, or refuse to license, all theatrical performances within the territory of their jurisdiction. So the conflict was not only a debate about whether plays were a good thing but also a contest, in the shadow of a legislative ambiguity, for the right to permit them.

What seems to have prompted Burbage's initiative in Shoreditch is a notable coup brought off in 1574 by the court party in this long-running dispute. Burbage's company, as servants of the Earl of Leicester, were granted a unique royal patent which licensed them to play anywhere.[53] The only exception was that they could not play in London in time of common plague or of common prayer; and even this concession was really part of Leicester's victory, since by specifying conditions for London at all, the patent implicitly overrides the city's authority. Burbage must have felt that in the game of competing permissions he now held the ace. However, the document says nothing about venues: the expectable next move was that the Common Council of London would negate the patent's effects by refusing to license any London householder to let his premises be used for playing. Burbage therefore needed a place of his own; while at the same time, the security which the patent afforded meant that investing in such a place was a reasonable gamble. Under the circumstances, a site in the city would have been problematic (as well as expensive); so he did the obvious thing and found one just outside its boundaries, within the more amenable jurisdiction of a Middlesex JP.

The gamble came off, as everyone knows, and Burbage's arrangement became in time the general model for theatrical enterprise in London. All the same, it is worth recalling how many practical obstacles the actors still faced.[54] Playing was regularly prohibited in Lent, irregularly but frequently suspended because of plague, and more occasionally stopped as a result of outbreaks of disorder more or less vaguely connected with theatre attendance, or because of exception taken to a particular play. Almost every acting season was interrupted for one reason or another; and in some years, such as 1593 and 1603, there were virtually no London performances at all.[55] The pressure on the Privy Council to close the playhouses for good, from pamphlets, sermons, and city council resolutions, was intense for at least the first decade after 1576,[56] and Privy Councillors – who were of course senior residents of London as well as courtiers – shared enough of the aldermen's anxieties to afford some chance that they might one day be persuaded.[57] In the constant struggle to stay in business, the managers of companies naturally fell back on their strongest positions – their individual status as the servants of this or that influential courtier,[58] and the argument that they must be permitted to play so as to be in a state of readiness to perform for the queen.[59] Both these tactics had their attendant drawbacks: as aristocrats' protégés, the actors were inconveniently exposed to the fluctuations of court politics; and as royal servants, they came under the authority of the Master of the Revels, whose power to censor scripts grew steadily, his commission of 1581 gaining new teeth in 1589, 1598 and 1606.[60] In order to be allowed to make money by entertaining the people, the theatre had to prove that it was serving the Crown.

In other words, Elizabethan theatre was a political paradox – an intermittent, dubiously legitimate commercial enterprise which, precisely because of its low status, was compelled to appeal for legitimation to the highest authority. The historical context of the paradox was the phenomenon whose negative face we have already seen: political, legal and economic centralisation, and the consequent growth of London. The theatre was organically linked to the capital by virtue of both its 'high' and its 'low' identity. Its legitimacy depended on its claiming to be, and to some extent actually being, a department of the court, which was almost immovably located at Westminster from the late fifteenth century on.[61] And as a commercial enterprise, it was locked in to the metropolis by its need for a regular paying audience: only London had enough people, and enough spare cash, to sustain a permanent playhouse.[62] However, London was not *only* the seat of national government. It was also a city on its own account, governed by a traditional civic oligarchy whose power was if anything being enhanced during these years.[63] With this corporate London the theatre had no such organic links: on the contrary, each experienced the other as an abiding source of inconvenience. The theatre's eventual position in the suburbs was thus a highly determined one: what it signified was that the theatre was *nationally* central but *locally* marginal. The social entity to which the actors were affiliated was the nation – an invisible collective, too numerous and diffused ever to be literally present – while on the other hand they had disaffiliated from the immediate urban body in whose neighbourhood they happened to work.

As a result, there is something inescapably factitious about the institution's prestige: it had a special freedom, but also a special fraudulence, like an imposing edifice which is not quite touching the ground. This was enacted with parodic literalness in December 1598, when the Theatre was dismantled and clandestinely carried from Shoreditch, through the city and across the river to another dubious suburb, there to be re-erected and renamed (with a rhetorical universalism proportionate to its municipal marginality) the Globe.[64]

Consciously or not, Shakespeare provides a reverberant image of this contradictory situation in the figure of Philip Faulconbridge, the hero of *King John*. Faulconbridge is the first major non-historical character to appear in a Shakespeare history play, and his story has the suggestiveness of a legend.

It is about a country gentleman who discovers he is the bastard son of the heroic king, Richard I. He is legally entitled to deny his bastardy and so secure his modest paternal inheritance. On the other hand, if he renounces both his legitimacy and his estate, he will be precipitated into the world of the court, where he might do much better, or much worse. He must choose –

> Whether hadst thou rather be a Faulconbridge,
> And like thy brother, to enjoy thy land,
> Or the reputed son of Coeur-de-lion,
> Lord of thy presence and no land beside?[65]

Shakespeare probably took this story from a slightly earlier chronicle play, *The Troublesome Raigne of King John*. For the author of that version, the most conspicuous point about the choice is that it elicits a biological mystique of royalty. Wrapped in a Marlovian trance, the Lionheart's bastard finds that he is physically unable to deny his true nature: as the play's dedication hints,[66] this is Tamburlaine *anglicé*, casting aside his shepherd's weeds and assuming the imperial appearance that goes with his essence. As Shakespeare tells it, the story is rather more complicated.

For one thing, Faulconbridge is choosing, not simply what to go for, but *who to be*. Whichever option he takes, the act of choice itself is a strikingly individuating one: if a man can decide which paternally given identity he wants, then clearly neither identity really determines the being of the chooser. Faulconbridge picks this up, commenting, rather like a later Shakespearean bastard, 'I am I, howe'er I was begot' (i, i, 175). It follows naturally from this moment of unconditional individuality that he opts for the individualist alternative, rejecting the safe continuities of legitimate inheritance to become a landless 'lord of his presence'. The situation which enables him to do this has a bizarre particularity, depending on his father's documented absence from home at the time of his conception. But it also makes him powerfully typical, a representative of the monetarisation of social relationships associated with the growth of both the metropolis and the court.[67] Upwardly mobile to a spectacular degree, Faulconbridge is a concentrated version of the assorted careerists and unauthorised courtiers of 1590s satire, sacrificing his respectability (and, scandalously, that of his mother) to become a gambler – 'Brother, take you my land, I'll take my chance' (151) – and a social climber: as soon as the choice scene is over, he launches into an exuberantly cynical soliloquy (180–26) about the tricks and affectations he will learn now that he is on his way up.

It is in this character that he follows the king to France, where for the following scenes he operates as a comic interpreter, at once satirical and complicit, of the stately hypocrisy and diplomatic haggling on view. He can fulfil this role because while his meteoric rise places him among the nobility, his 'baseness' (a false but influential etymology for 'bastard') detaches him from them. Pushy, fashion-conscious and shrewd, he stands in between the action and the audience, disrupting the iambics of the officially located speakers:

> KING JOHN: Doth not the crown of England prove the King?
> And if not that, I bring you witnesses:
> Twice fifteen thousand hearts of England's breed –
> BASTARD: Bastards and else.
> KING JOHN: To verify our title with their lives.
> KING PHILIP: As many and as well-born bloods as those –
> BASTARD: Some bastards too.
> KING PHILIP: Stand in his face to contradict his claim.
>
> (ii, i, 273–80)

If we place these interjections in their theatrical context, they are not very different from the playhouse behaviour which Dekker sardonically recommends in *The Gull's Hornbook*:

> Let our Gallant . . . presently advance himself up to the Throne of the Stage. I meane . . . the very Rushes where the Commedy is to daunce, yea, and under the state of *Cambises* himselfe must our fethered *Estridge*, like a piece of Ordnance be planted, valiantly (because impudently) beating downe the mewes and hisses of the opposed rascality. . . . It shall crowne you with rich commendation to laugh alowd in the middest of the most serious and saddest scene of the terriblest Tragedy: and to let that clapper (your tongue) be tost so high that all the house may ring of it.[68]

The Bastard is identifying himself with the most individualistic elements in the play's audience: the young men – gallants, apprentices, students at the Inns of Court, discharged soldiers, masterless men – who are the least tightly attached to the framework of inheritance, patriarchy and service which ensures social cohesion.

For the aldermen of the city, this was also the meaning of the theatre itself. The actors are people who have forsaken their lawful calling, and are trying to make a living out of what ought only to be a pastime. And those who go to see them are

> of the base & refuse sort of people or such yoong gentlemen as have small regard of credit or conscience . . . vagrant persons & maisterles men that hang about the Citie . . . (which by experience wee fynd to bee the very sinck & contagion not only of this Citie but of the whole Realm). . . .[69]

These phrases are from a mayoral letter to Burghley, and are of course painting the blackest possible picture in the hope of getting his support for the suppression of the theatre. The hard evidence about theatre attendance, fragmentary as it is, makes it clear that the audience was not simply the semi-legal *demi-monde* it appears to be in the aldermanic imagination.[70] What the alarmed rhetoric registers, though, is the sense of London as a licentious space, a gathering point for rootless and illegitimate individuals from all over the country, and, then, of the theatre as the very focus of this disorderly urban assembly.[71]

This interpretation of the theatre is quite understandable if we recall that the civic oligarchy was an 'essentially gerontocratic'[73] authority unsure of its capacity to control an asymmetrically youthful population. The court, the Inns of Court, the apprenticeship system and the mushrooming suburbs were all in their different ways magnets for the ambitious or supernumerary young from elsewhere in the kingdom, and each of them seems to have brought young men together in sufficient numbers to generate its own volatile subculture,[73] which included, in most cases, conspicuous attendance at the playhouses. One such subgroup, particularly relevant to the figure of Faulconbridge, was that of 'gentleman apprentices' – that is, the younger sons of gentry, impelled by the strict conventions of primogeniture to seek alternative sources of status and profit.[74] Peter Burke suggests that this group, which was quite significant even in flat numerical terms, may have been strategic in mediating between elite and popular cultures; and Faulconbridge looks very like an exploitation of that nexus, with his success as a landless adventurer, his colourfully expressed contempt for his stay-at-home brother, and his roughly demotic interventions in the councils of the great. It is not just that such figures were vocally present in the audience, but also, clearly, that the theatre itself was in an analogous cultural position, as a commercial venture whose style and connections elevated its performers above their station without ever quite dissolving their degrading links with the 'base & refuse sort of people' who dropped a penny at the door.

But Faulconbridge's legend has another meaning too. His choice means that he loses his land in the sense that he ceases to be a landowner. But his other 'father's land' is the realm: in choosing that inheritance he sacrifices a specific and enforceable relationship with a little piece of land in order to enter into an unsecured, dynamic relationship with England as a whole. He turns his back on local rootedness and joins the order of a general sovereignty, acquiring an authority which derives from the whole nation because it is not attributable to any lordship in particular. His placing in the royal dynasty confirms this paradoxical centrality. Like Prince Arthur, he is the son of one of John's elder brothers, and so is closer to the true succession than the king himself. He does not have a claim to the throne because of his illegitimacy, but he resembles his father physically, and after he has proved himself in battle against his father's old enemies, he inherits his national role in an alternative, imaginative sense. Looked at in this frame, his choice is not the disreputable option but precisely the noble one: the opposite of 'land' is not so much 'chance' as 'honour', the Bastard's decision a rejection of private comfort for the sake of public patriotism. Here, potentially, is a much more grandiose claim for the drama: that as the model to England's inward greatness it does not so much violate the City's order as soar above its reach.

So Faulconbridge, as he emerges from the first act, is a deeply hybrid figure, rootless swaggerer and national champion, cynical and noble, illegitimate and royal. The tension is generalised early on when the French king is informed of the arrival of an English army which includes

> . . . a bastard of the king's deceas'd,
> And all th'unsettled humours of the land;
> Rash, inconsiderate, fiery voluntaries,
> With ladies' faces and fierce dragons' spleens,
> Have sold their fortunes at their native homes,

> Bearing their birthrights proudly on their backs,
> To make a hazard of new fortunes here:
> In brief, a braver choice of dauntless spirits . . .
> Did never float upon the swelling tide
> To do offence and scathe in Christendom.
>
> (II, i, 65–75)

The motivation of this speech in its context is itself double: the speaker is a warning messenger, stressing the gravity of the threat to France, and also a French spokesman expressing contempt for the bastard magnificence of the enemy. The English volunteers, whose rejection of their native homes in favour of personal presence and new fortunes makes Faulconbridge their type, are both admired and derided, sometimes in the same line. The rash and dandyish gallants are familiar satiric targets: compare, for example, Donne's courtiers, their clothes 'as fresh and sweet . . . as bee/The fields they sold to buy them. . . . Naturall/Some of the stocks are, their fruits, bastard all'.[75] The dragons' spleens and dauntless spirits, on the other hand, are part of a different discourse, not satiric but jingoistic. But the flaunting gamblers and the patriotic warriors are the same people. In their combination of high fashion, archaic chivalry, and reckless speculation, they seem particularly to echo the style of Essex and his following in the 1590s.[76] But the historical sensitivity goes beyond topicality: the speech juxtaposes two ways of seeing the whole field of forces which draw people in from domesticity and locality to the ambitions and illusions of a national centre.

The pleasure and energy which characterise the writing no doubt reflect the fact that the royal bastard's story, thus generalised, is also that of many actors, arguably including the author. But more inwardly, the character, in his provocative mixture of centrality and alienation, his embracing of a precarious national totality instead of an institutionally ratified grounding, wittily mirrors the situation of the theatre itself. Like Faulconbridge, this theatre has not been *given* a birthright to the community to which it truly belongs. It has to reach it through 'the hazard of new fortunes'.

It is interesting, then, that the role's ambivalence does not at all take the form of a 'complex character' in whose consciousness self-interest and patriotism conflict. What happens instead is that he is quite consistently the comic *parvenu* until III, iii, when he exits for his only extended period off-stage; and when he reappears at the end of IV, ii it is as the principled defender of the nation's integrity which he remains for the rest of the play. Shakespeare runs first one meaning of the story and then the other, staging the change of emphasis from bastardy to royalty, not as an integration of the two, but as a narrative break. The royal–national recuperation of that venturing, individualistic energy is prompted, not by any new impulse within the character, but by the broader events of the play. So what is it that happens to redeem the Bastard?

Enter England

The story of King John was already firmly imprinted with Elizabethan meanings.[77] Like Henry VIII, John expropriated the Church in the name of English honour; and like Elizabeth, he was excommunicated by the Pope and had to beat off an invasion by a Catholic enemy. Both in Foxe's *Actes and Monuments* and in the Elizabethan *Homily against Disobedience*, he appears as an unsuccessful precursor – someone who was defeated where the Tudors later won.[78] Shakespeare's immediate source, *The Troublesome Raigne* of 1591, includes, in the middle of a blank-verse play, a ribald scene in fourteeners in which the Crown's search for ecclesiastical gold turns up monks and nuns compromisingly concealed in cupboards[79]: here, very clearly, the history of King John carries a rough tradition of Reformation libelling into the theatre of the 1590s. A more interesting dramatic parallel, from our point of view, is John Bale's ambitious and innovative *King Johan*,[80] written in the 1530s, and revived (perhaps for Elizabeth herself) in 1561, but apparently not known to Shakespeare.

King Johan is an agitational morality play, first performed under the patronage of Thomas Cromwell in the middle of the Henrician Reformation. The legislative revolution of 1532–4, which brought about the English government's break with Rome, had been, among many other things, an effective declaration of national independence. In order to reform the Church, in order to contain the power of the episcopate, and even in order to achieve so limited an aim as the king's divorce from Catherine of Aragon, it had proved necessary to designate England 'a sovereign state, with a King who owed no submission to any other ruler and who was invested with plenary power to give his people justice in all causes'.[81] Despite the internationalist attitudes of many reformers, the political circumstances of the Reformation inevitably gave it a national form, mobilising, against the supra-national claims of the Church, the idea of England. This project called for new departures in both historiography and drama – partly because the traumatic break in institutional and ideological continuity produced the need to reread the Catholic centuries and discover a 'usable past',[82] and partly because the inter-state conflicts surrounding the Reformation entailed a desecularisation of national history.[83] England could no longer be simply an instance of temporal statehood; it was, perforce, a realm with a difference.

The play registers this newly distinct object of consciousness in the most literal way. At the outset of the play the king identifies himself and what he sees as his function, that is:

> To reforme the lawes and sett men in good order,
> That trew justyce may be had in every border.
>
> (20–1)

Immediately England enters, having heard this declaration. She rejoins:

> Then I trust yowr Grace wyll waye a poore wedowes cause,
> Ungodly used, as ye shall know in short clause.
>
> (22–3)

The allusion is to Isaiah, 1.17: 'Learn to do well; seek judgment, relieve the oppressed, judge the fatherless, plead for the widow.' So that at the very outset, the play makes 'Ynglond Vidua' the acid test of the just king.

Like all the play's personages, this one works on several typological levels. Her widowhood is partly a type of oppression: she is the victim of hypocritical clerics, the 'scribes, which desire to walk in long robes . . . which devour widows' houses, and for a shew make long prayers' (Luke, 20.46–7). But it is also an allegory of the spiritual condition of England under Catholicism: England is a widow because her husband, God, has been exiled by 'popych swyne' (106), for 'Ye know he abydyth not where his word ys refusyd' (116).

It is an ideologically potent combination of meanings. At the social level, the widow represents 'Christ's poor' – that is, not just the generalised object of Christian charity, but the vehicle of a specifically Reformation contrast between ritual and welfare as wrong and right ways of serving God. Just as in the cycle plays, the priestly order denounced by Christ is identified with the Catholic clergy. But now the contradiction between *communitas* and ecclesiastical hierarchy, so far from being ritually resolved, is deliberately inflamed: the gospels are being used, not to reaffirm the Church's legitimacy, but to demolish it. At the same time, the doctrinal level of the allegory makes that politicisation a distinctively national one, according to which the widow is the whole of England, and her bereft state a symptom of Rome's usurpation of God's authority over her. Considered as propaganda, the move gives each issue access to the rhetorical advantages of the other: on the one hand, the pursuit of social justice is a charge laid specifically on the nation state; and on the other, the assertion of England's rights against the papacy is made into a fully Christian duty, enjoined by scriptural authority. In short, the attack on the Catholic Church is being mounted in the name of the national community.

This crucial conception allows Bale to adopt a strikingly critical attitude to his material. His king is a hero – one of his purposes is to defend John's reputation against what he takes to be the biased accounts of clerical chroniclers (583–9) – but that does not prevent the play from pressing the question of whether he adequately upheld the interests of England the Widow. Its answer is at once forthright and political: the king is shown as *willing* but *unable* to right her wrongs. The analysis is made clearest in a later exchange between Johan and England.

Johan's estates, Cyvyle Order, Clergye and Nobylyte, have all deserted him. Left to face the papal onslaught alone, Johan seeks to know the mind of his Commynalte. England then introduces Commynalte, who is her son. He would like to take Johan's side against Usurpid Power (the Vice who is also the historical Pope Innocent III), but is prevented by two impediments:

> The first is blyndnes, wherby I myght take with the Pope
> Soner than with yow, for, alas, I can but grope,
> And ye know what full well there are many nowghty gydes.
> The nexte is poverte, which cleve so hard to my sydes
> And ponych me so sore that my powr is lytyll or non.
>
> (1560–4)

The blindness signifies lack of Christian knowledge, and the poverty is a symptom of ecclesiastical exploitation. England promises that if only she can have her husband and her lands returned to her, she will cure her son of both his disabilities and make him fit to serve the king. Johan replies:

> I wold I ware able to do to the that offyce,
> But, alas, I am not, for why my nobelyte,
> My lawers and clargy hath cowardly forsake me.
> And now last of all, to my most anguysh of mynd,
> My Commynnalte here I fynd both poore and blynd.
>
> (1575–9)

The king and the blind beggar confront one another, each one willing but powerless to help the other. The stalemate is savagely broken by the entrance of the Cardinal, who reproves Commynalte for talking to Johan when he has, apparently, promised not to. Commynalte, terrified, says '*Peccavi, mea culpa!* I submit me to your holynes' (1600), and, through his reverence for 'Holy Chirch', allows himself to be ordered off the stage. The vices' ruthless dismantling of Johan's ability to govern continues.

The scene's use of morality conventions is astonishingly political. The genre's capacity for strong, simple generalisation enables it to stage quite a complex idea about the relationship between the king, his realm, and different sections within it. At the same time, the presentation is quite *un*moralistic. Johan and Commynalte are both shown to fail, but both failures are determined by the situation: Johan needs Commynalte's service *in order* to win back the widow's rights, and Commynalte needs the rights to be restored before he can offer his service. The political point seems very clear: it is that the Reformation will be defeated if it is nothing more than a switch of royal policy. The king needs to build support for his own position by allowing it to be, also, a social and ideological revolution – an expropriation of the Church and an 'unblinding' of the commonalty. Since this is exactly the reality which Henry VIII would attempt to resist,[84] the play's 'line' is impressive both for its relevance and for its correctness. Under the pressure of urgent requirements, Bale has rapidly evolved a form capable, not merely of generalised anti-Catholic satire, but of political analysis.

In what is arguably the first English history play of all, Bale has thus solved, with one inventive stroke, the problem of how to put the 'imagined community' on the stage. But the solution necessarily remains at a fairly high level of abstraction. One could put it like this: Bale's innovative national reference comes out of a temporary exploitation of theatre by producers who are not really interested in the medium, but are using it for immediate propaganda purposes. As far as we can tell, it was written for occasional performances in the houses, or at any rate under the auspices, of sympathetic notables such as Cranmer. Its performing context, that is, was quite unstable – its playing spaces ad hoc ones, its theatrical language neither nourished nor shackled by tradition, its patrons insecurely placed on the dangerous heights of Henrician politics. Its image of England has the sharpness, but also the limitations, of its situation of cultural homelessness. Utterly unlike ritual and communal drama (it quotes liturgical elements only in strident, argumentative parody),[85] it offers its national figures for understanding rather than for identification. The audience was perhaps an elite one: whether or not that was so, it is treated as such; the space it occupies is extra-social; it is not invited to recognise itself as a community, but to study an externally seen community with the intention of directing it differently. This outsideness reflects not only Bale's own embattled and precarious relations with the polity, but also the divisiveness and openness of a general revolutionary moment: one could say that Commynalte comes on to a national stage precisely as an object of controversy. Shakespeare's version of Bale's pregnant stage direction, 'Enter England', is at once more dynamic, more integral, and less clear.

For most of the second and third acts of *King John* the representation of national identity is elementary, not to say two-dimensional. The words 'England' and 'France' are used to denote the kings of those countries, or at most the kings backed by their respective armies. The action, which largely consists of highly public inter-state diplomacy, is informed by the assumption that the monarch is the effective embodiment of his realm – that the individual who represents the nation for a rather narrow set of legal and political purposes really is its equivalent for all purposes whatever. However, this assumption is not substantiated by the play. The comically arbitrary events, the magniloquent postures and grubby deals, have the effect of hollowing out the royal claims to representative status. Each king announces that he is the ruler of Angiers; the symmetry of their positions discredits both; the claim that sovereignty is a self-evident character looks silly when it can so easily be switched by means of a battle or a marriage. Precisely because it is divorced from any sense of a national polity, monarchy is made to seem unreal: 'Mad world! mad kings! mad composition!' (II, i, 561). It is amid this empty political formalism that the Bastard flourishes as a satirical rogue-hero, debunking, as we saw earlier, both sides' spurious rhetoric of legitimacy.

The Bastard leaves the stage for his extended break early in III, iii, and immediately the brackish comedy of state begins to shift into a new register. Shortly afterwards, the meaning of the change is explored in a scene between the Dauphin Lewis and Cardinal Pandulph. Lewis is in despair because the French have lost a battle. He is 'green . . . and fresh in this old world' (III, iii, 145), and imagines that the ceremonial display of power we have been watching is power itself. Pandulph explains that John's apparent victory is actually a disaster for him, because, having captured Arthur, he will have to murder him:

> and then the hearts
> Of all his people shall revolt from him,
> And kiss the lips of unacquainted change,
> And pick strong matter of revolt and wrath
> Out of the bloody fingers' ends of John.
> Methinks I see this hurly all on foot:
> And O, what better matter breeds for you
> Than I have nam'd! The bastard Faulconbridge
> Is now in England ransacking the church,
> Offending charity: if but a dozen French
> Were there in arms, they would be as a call
> To train ten thousand English to their side,
> Or as a little snow, tumbled about,
> Anon becomes a mountain.
>
> (III, iii, 164–77)

So long as the two kings were confronting each other, they could sustain a spectacle of pure sovereignty: the very rigidity of each one's position confirmed the stance of the other. Pandulph's insinuations unlock that formal stasis by introducing two previously overlooked elements in the political situation. The first is time. In the pageant theatre of state, the various treaties, victories and vows all declare themselves as final and certain to last for ever; but the slippery, sexual imagery of this speech is all about process, cumulation, 'unacquainted change'. Pandulph is initiating the prince into a world in which no word is ever final. The second unfixing element is the people. They are the ones who 'revolt', 'kiss', 'pick strong matter'; they can be called, trained, tumbled about to make a mountain. John's kingship suddenly ceases to be a simple fact of his identity, and is restated as an insecure and multiple relationship.

Time and the people are analogous. Both are formless, polysemous, interminable, subversive of sovereignty. They both make the world more confusing and less heroic than it was when they were excluded. They reveal the king's authority to be less than absolute; and in a sense they are absolutely powerful themselves – you cannot either negotiate with them or stop them existing. But as Pandulph concludes, of the people, ''Tis wonderful/What may be wrought out of their discontent' (178–9): if their unsettling capacity for transformations is in principle unlimited, then so, by the same token, is their malleability – at least from this profoundly cynical point of view.

It is the point of view, intriguingly, of the Vatican: Pandulph is the accredited representative of the Pope. (As such, he actually featured as one of Bale's Vices.) Shakespeare makes him a diplomatic manipulator, orchestrating inter-state conflicts, in which he is really on no side, always in order to promote the transnational authority of the Church. He is thus opposed, not just to English interests, but to national sovereignty as such: his insight into the nature of kingly authority is that of someone who himself acknowledges none. The pressure he puts on John's power is consequently more critical than any threat from a rival national ruler could be. Confronted with the Pope's pretensions to universal suzerainty, the sovereign is thrown back on his base in the people: as in Bale's play, John turns out in the crisis not to *be* England, but to *need* England. That royal necessity opens up the dramatic space in which the nation can appear, not as a personal patrimony, but as an autonomous presence.

In the immediately following scenes, Pandulph's words are borne out in detail. As he predicted, the logic of events leads to the death of Arthur; and as he advised, Lewis embarks on an invasion of England. These events are accompanied by more intimations of the strange labile quality Pandulph has attributed to the people. John receives reports:

> I find the people strangely fantasied;
> Possess'd with rumours, full of idle dreams. . . .
> I saw a smith stand with his hammer, thus,
> The while his iron did on the anvil cool,
> With open mouth swallowing a tailor's news;
> Who, with his shears and measure in his hand,
> Standing on slippers, which his nimble haste
> Had falsely thrust upon contrary feet,

> Told of a many thousand warlike French,
> That were embattailed and rank'd in Kent.
> Another lean unwash'd artificer
> Cuts off his tale, and talks of Arthur's death.
>   (IV, ii, 144–5, 193–202)

Although nothing very alarming in itself is being described, these images carry an odd menace because of the intimate inadvertence of the gestures (the listening mouth, the slippers on the wrong way round) which are so pointedly itemised. The people appear, not as a distinct political constituency, but rather as the unconscious of the state, whose disturbed condition is revealed through little slips and anomalies. The 'strangeness'[86] of foreign invasion is echoed by the domestic strangeness of the people's dreams. The naturalistic fragments are therefore of a piece with the supernatural interventions in the same scene: Peter of Pomfret's true-and-false prophecy (147–59) and the appearance of five moons in the sky (182–6). The play's turn to the people is numinous, an encounter, in a highly rhetorical play, with an anti-discursive entity expressed in magic, and in an untypically concrete and suggestive verse.

So that this central section of the play (III, ii–IV, ii) combines at least three changes in the dramatic situation:

1. John himself is redefined as a tyrant by his attempt to murder a child.
2. A foreign army lands on English soil, where it will remain for the rest of the play.
3. The image of formal sovereignty is undermined by the numinous idea of the people.

Together with the absence of Faulconbridge, these amount to a radical change of gear, a sense confirmed by a simultaneous shift in the dramatic technique. Until now, uncharacteristically for Shakespeare, the action has been organised almost entirely in three long, formal single-focus scenes of public and legalistic negotiation (I, II, i and III, i). Now this is replaced by a much more recognisable pattern of shorter scenes, centring on action, switching between public and private modes of communication, and intercutting disparate but related plot elements. Even at a formal level, the play has responded to Pandulph's invocation of time and change.

The most obvious effect of all these shifts is that they comprehensively demolish the authority of the king himself. Just as Pandulph deconstructs his sovereignty rhetorically, so the ensuing action undermines it conceptually (as his subjects form an independent dramatic presence), morally (through the attempted murder), politically (as he loses control of part of his territory) and dramaturgically (as his ability to control the events of the play is overwhelmed by their increased pace and density). This uncompromising handling of the title role is carried through in detail: shallow and opportunistic from the start, John displays as the crisis deepens an interesting but hardly admirable alternation of bravado and timidity. There are even signs that Shakespeare has gone out of his way to tarnish the character: the play makes his title to the throne look weaker than it does in the chronicles, and reduces Arthur's age so that the pathos of his suffering is enhanced.[87] The effect of the murder is complicated, first by the murderer's decision not to carry out the order, and then by Arthur's accidental death. The episode turns into a fiasco: John is denied the prestige of successful villainy because the murder does not happen, but then when Arthur dies anyway his lords believe that he was somehow responsible for it, so he is denied the advantages of clemency as well. This sets the tone for the second half of the play: John's second coronation, by which he intends to cement his authority, only unsettles it; his submission to the papal legate, which is provoked by the French invasion, demeans him without producing a French withdrawal; when the invaders are eventually confronted in battle he falls ill and has to leave the field. In the end he seems not so much a tyrant as a *failure*, neither unscrupulous enough for his stratagems to work nor principled enough for his defeats to be honourable. His last scene falls into the convention of a *sinner's* death, the raging fire of the poison inside him being likened to (though not identified as) hell (v, vii, 46). But what is revealed is not so much apocalyptic judgement as common mortality: the physical sensations of sickness are harshly insisted on, and John's last words speak of the imminent moment when 'all this thou seest is but a clod/And module of confounded royalty' (57–8). The king dies in sin and pain, just like anybody else.

Against this image of physically, morally and politically 'confounded royalty', there is the King John who appears in the rhetoric of his adherents. The contrast is activated by the rapid reversals of Act v. In v, i John submits to the Cardinal; he has clearly lost all his confidence, and when the Bastard upbraids him, he replies feebly, 'Have thou the ordering of this present time' (77). In v, ii, however, the Bastard addresses the French leaders as John's representative – 'Now hear our English king,/For thus his royalty doth speak in me' (128–9) – and delivers a tirade of regal contempt for the invaders. In v, iii the king, sick at heart, is carried from the battlefield, but then in iv the English barons who had defected to the other side return to their national loyalty, resolving to

> Stoop low within those bounds we have o'erlook'd,
> And calmly run on in obedience
> Even to our ocean, to our great King John.

(55–7)

A relentless irony exacerbates the gap between the king who speaks and the king who is spoken about; yet the point of the irony is not to expose John's followers as either deluded or dishonest. Rather, the effect is to detach 'our English King' from the questionable individual who happens to be occupying the throne at the moment. Whatever John may say, his *royalty* speaks differently; he is great, oceanic, not because of what he is like, but because of what he is. In other words, the play is staging the distinction between the king's two bodies: the natural body which is subject to minority, error, sickness and death, and the politic body which is invisible, incorruptible and sempiternal.

As we know from the classic study by E. H. Kantorowicz, the duplex royal body was a political and metaphysical conundrum of practical importance to Elizabethan jurists. The conundrum can be schematically expressed like this: since monarchical sovereignty refuses to function either on the basis that the king is mortal, or on the basis that he is not, he must necessarily be both. But it is a logical absurdity to suppose that the same body can be both mortal and immortal. Therefore the king must be supposed to have two bodies, which are distinct because they are of opposite characters, but identical in the sense that they partake in the single identity of the king.

Kantorowicz's genealogy of the theory shows its indirect descent from earlier ecclesiastical doctrines about the duplex body of Christ. But he also highlights a particular difficulty which arises when the formula is translated from church to kingdom. The immortality of the body of Christ could be taken for granted: as God the Son he was eternal by his nature. In the case of the politic body of the king, there was no equivalent divinity in play, so the value of immortality 'had to accrue to the king from some other source'. The source of this supplement was the realm itself:

> the value of immortality or continuity upon which the new polity-centred rulership would thrive, was vested in the *universitas* 'which never dies', in the perpetuity of an immortal people, polity, or *patria*, from which the individual king might easily be separated, but not the Dynasty, the Crown, and the Royal Dignity.[88]

Thus the king-who-is-spoken-about, 'that strange being who, like the angels, was immortal, invisible, never under age, never sick, and never senile', owes his sempiternal nature to the perpetuity of the realm. It is the national *universitas* which saves his royalty from his mortality.

This is a legal fiction devised for legal purposes, and it cannot be automatically applied outside its specialist context. But drama is also in the business of producing fictional representations of kings, subject to similar dilemmas. Its monarchs too are required to be immortal and mortal, majestic and frail. And the logic of doubleness gives rise to a particular paradox in the theatre because it is only the natural body, the fallible creature, which is visible on the stage. The paradox is that the more the king is characterised as kingly, self-complete, royal *in himself*, the more he covers up the ulterior source of his royalty in the body of the realm. Conversely, it is precisely through the monarch's natural frailties, as if through the holes in a tattered robe, that one sees his politic body, the true object of patriotic loyalty, the *corpus mysticum* of the nation. The second half of *King John* pursues this audacious dialectic in exceptionally schematic fashion, eventually arriving at its royal-nationalist conclusion, not despite the imperfections of the king whose troublesome reign it displays, but through them.

This, then, is the enabling context of the Bastard's apparently arbitrary transformation from rogue-hero to national champion. He could not figure as a patriot in the first half of the play because there was, effectively, no *patria* to which such a role could refer, only the patently empty formalism of a monarchical rhetoric. Only with the delegitimation of the monarch through his personal failures does that blank surface start to break up and disclose a national principle of rule. The Bastard's language acquires the authority of that principle, decisively, as he watches Hubert picking up the body of the dead Prince Arthur:

> How easy dost thou take all England up
> From forth this morsel of dead royalty!
> The life, the right and truth of all this realm
> Is fled to heaven; and England now is left
> To tug and scamble, and to part by th'teeth
> The unow'd interest of proud swelling state.
> (IV, iii, 142–7)

As the son of John's elder brother, Arthur arguably had a stronger claim to the throne than John himself. The Bastard would of course never have acknowledged this while Arthur was alive; now he almost (but not quite) does so. The density of the speech then comes from the way it does two things simultaneously: it identifies the body of the prince with the realm, and it mourns the loss of that identification through the parting of body and soul. The combined effect is to situate 'the life, the right and truth of all this realm' in a space beyond the actual persons on the stage: it is not in Arthur who has gone, and not in John who is left, but it is intensely present in that double absence. It is because the interest of the state is now 'unow'd' – not identifiable with any individual – that it can suddenly be seen as a general interest, belonging not to a person but to a community in danger. Hence the importance of the dreamlike fragments and portents which intimate the 'strangeness' of the people: the invisible collective which is the ultimate source of visible power is brought on to the stage by these obscure but strategic traces of its agitation.

The Bastard is empowered to represent that collective in the action because, as we saw, his illegitimate royalty gives him rights over the 'land' as a whole while at the same time ensuring that these rights are not real: he speaks in the name of England because he himself has no name, upholds the 'unow'd interest' because he himself owns nothing. At the very end of the play, standing over another morsel of dead royalty, he asserts the immortality of an England true to itself, appealing from the ruin of John's body to 'the *universitas* "which never dies"'. Marginal, like the theatre itself, to the institutional continuities of law, church, property, legitimacy, he becomes the chorus for a sort of secular theophany, in which the attrition of those orders manifests what can then be conceived of as prior to all of them – the life of all the realm which is at once an origin and a fiction; the imagined community.

Infinite numbers

As we have seen, one condition of this realisation in *King John* is the *bringing home* of the action halfway through the play. So long as the locus of significant conflict is France, the representation of England remains formal – that is, both abstract and unproblematic. For John, as for Henry V later, France is a sort of pageant theatre where English sovereignty can present itself in ideal form; it is when deprived of its French alibi – or released from it – that it is compelled to make its turn to the people. In this, *King John* is repeating within a single play the logic of *Henry VI*: there too, almost exactly halfway through, the abandonment of a programme of conquest in France leads to a re-emergence of the question of England. Within the relatively schematic confines of *King John*, this shift gives rise to obscure alarm; in the ampler design of the first tetralogy, to terror.

The reason for the pattern lies in the nature of the claim which is being asserted by the French expeditions of *King John*, *Henry V* and *1 Henry VI*. It is not a claim that France is somehow part of England; nor is it that, in the manner of modern imperialisms, the English have a duty to rule over the French because of their alleged racial or cultural superiority. It is only that the individual who happens to be the King of England says he also has a hereditary right to the lands held by the King of France. Regardless of whether this claim is advanced sincerely or cynically, it implies a concept of royal sovereignty which is not national but dynastic. The king who can define his possessions in such terms is behaving like a great landowner who has inherited several different estates. The inhabitants of the various estates all acknowledge the superiority of the same man, but this does not confer any unity on them or generate any horizontal connections between them; in short, it does not form a community. Moreover, there is no thing particularly inalienable about the bond between the king and the bits of his patrimony: provinces can change hands almost routinely in the course of peace settlements or marriage treaties. The realm, in short, is not necessarily *one*; it is the monarch who is that.[89]

In other words, so long as the plays show the Crown of England as mixed up with the matter of France, the depicted polity remains, in crucial ways, a feudal and pre-nationalist one, defined in terms of personal lordship and allegiance, and effectively devoid of the idea of *national* sovereignty. It is only when royal power is thrown back within its 'natural' boundaries of language and geography[90] that a national identity starts to define itself in the drama, an England which can meaningfully be urged to be true, not just to a dynastic ruler, but to itself.

The *Henry VI* plays execute this transformation, not only at the level of the kind of politics which are represented, but still more in the *mode* of their representation. We can see this by recalling the narrowly theatrical problem which I raised at the outset of this essay: how can historical drama, with a company of a couple of dozen actors at the very most,[91] show, as it must, the actions of thousands, the conflicts and the fate of whole communities? The Chorus of *Henry V* has his answer in a sort of mental arithmetic which converts one into many:

> Into a thousand parts divide one man,
> And make imaginary puissance.
>
> (I, 24–5)

But the logic of this process is not so innocent as he suggests. *How* one man can 'stand for' thousands is, as we have seen, precisely the (political) point.

1 Henry VI, despite its superficial air of theatrical naïveté, is sophisticated about this question. In II, iii, a French countess patriotically ensnares the English hero Talbot in her castle. Apparently caught, Talbot laughs and says that she has not caught Talbot's substance, only his shadow. The countess asks him to explain the riddle – that he is there and not there – and he replies, 'That will I show you presently' (59): [*Winds his horn. Drums strike up; a peal of ordinance. Enter Soldiers.*] The countess sees the point, and apologises for underestimating him:

> I find thou art no less than fame has bruited,
> And more than may be gathered by thy shape.
>
> (67–8)

The comedy is subtle and brutal. Talbot is greater than he looks: he looks like an ordinary individual, whereas what he is is a legendary English champion and scourge of the French. In that sense the person is like the actor who plays him – the shadow of a hero whose real substance is elsewhere. But then the substance, which the riddle projects as a mystery, turns out to be blankly literal: Talbot's 'greatness' consists in a squad of soldiers who do what he tells them. The countess's obeisance to this savagely inverted Platonism is rather ambiguous: she may be accepting, or satirising, her introduction to the metaphysics of armed force.

The scene is playing with one possible principle whereby a single actor can stand for 'a thousand' – that the representation can base itself on the character's actual authority. The play has already made use of this principle in the brawling between the serving men attached to Gloucester and Winchester in I, iii. Amplifications of their respective masters, the peer's men identified by blue coats and the ecclesiastic's by tawny ones, these extras at once dramatise the conflict between the two men and clarify its importance: it is not simply a personal question because of the contestants' 'greatness' – that is, the extent of the disorder which is implied by their enmity. Conversely, what speaks in the proud and formal rhetoric of Gloucester and Winchester themselves is not just individual feeling, but also the passions and commitments of a following.

This is consistently the means by which *1 Henry VI* tells its story. In the second half of the play, the struggle between Gloucester and Winchester is displaced by that between York and Somerset: we see it flare up between two otherwise insignificant characters who are adherents of each (III, iv), move up the hierarchy so that it involves the principals (IV, i), and spread outwards so that it obstructs the movement of men and resources needed for the war in France (IV, iii–iv). Just as in the earlier disorders, and in the presentation of Talbot, what enables the individual transactions of the play to denote the collective transactions of the realm is the personal power of the barons over their respective followings.

So that when Talbot's scene with the countess is immediately followed by the famous roses scene in Temple Garden, Warwick's prophecy – that in time this brawl 'Shall send between the Red Rose and the White/A thousand souls to death and deadly night' (II, iv, 126–7) – is in harmony with the dramatic syntax. The slightness of the action – half a dozen men on the stage, each picking a red or a white rose – draws ironic attention to the substance of which it is the shadow. But then the irony is extremely far-reaching; for just this mechanism of multiplication, on which the play depends, is also shown as destructive, because it means that the individuals on view have the power to draw everybody else into their quarrels. Warwick is right: the flare-up between a handful of barons in a garden inescapably contains within it a bloody and interminable war.

Because of the dominance of this personal-dynastic syntax in *1 Henry VI*, the play is distinguished from the rest of the cycle by two striking absences. First, there is nothing about the question of the throne itself. There is much baronial jockeying for power within the political vacuum produced by Henry VI's minority, but no one, not even Richard Plantagenet, is plotting to become king at this stage. The historical controversy about Henry's title is reopened by the dying Mortimer only to be explicitly deferred (II, v, 118–19). And second, there are no significant dramatis personae from outside the ranks of the nobility: it is *only* as the adherents of this or that aristocrat that the commons appear at all. The combined effect of these two restrictions on the scope of the action is that, as the play tortuously traces the various factional interests and their conflicts, there is no stage image of a general interest, nothing which all the factions share in common, or which they all want. If this is national historical drama, it is of a paradoxical kind, because the totality of the nation remains out of sight: England as a whole is not what is being fought for, but it is not, either, a principle powerful enough to bring the factional struggles to an end. The idea of England is not inconceivable – it is quite crudely present, for example, in the rhetoric of the war in France. But it is an idea which remains a 'shadow' because there is no formula comparable to that whereby Talbot makes his 'substance' appear on the stage. What makes that manifestation possible is that the lord's authority confers a unity on those who acknowledge it: these men are, so to speak, present in the singular as their leader's 'power'; and that is how they can be represented collectively on the stage. England has no such representable unity – if anything, the imagery is of its absence, of what the play begins by taking leave of in the form of Henry V's coffin, and leaves further and further behind as it elaborates the terms of its own action. In the course of that action, what is happening in principle is that the cohesion of the nation is being ruptured, as the uniform but temporary black of the state funeral splits into the clashing colours of subnational allegiances. But all that is directly shown suffering from the dissension is the conduct of the war, which therefore becomes the surrogate form of the national community, substituting for, and so postponing, the nation's appearance in its own right.

2 Henry VI breaks decisively with this entire structure. In the first scene, Henry's new queen, Margaret, is presented to the English court, and the disastrous articles of peace accompanying the marriage are read out. Gloucester declares that France is effectively lost and leaves; the Cardinal immediately denounces him:

> 'Tis known to you he is mine enemy;
> Nay more, an enemy unto you all,
> And no great friend, I fear me, to the King.
> Consider, lords, he is the next of blood. . . .

What though the common people favour him,
Calling him 'Humphrey, the good Duke of Gloucester'. . . .
(I, i, 148–59)

Here are all the suspended themes entering together: the idea of England without France; the language of a contest, not just for power, but for the throne; and the evocation of the attitudes of the common people, giving the baronial struggles the external dimension which they lacked in *1 Henry VI*. Taken together, they define the new agenda for Part Two. The baronial power games are to continue, with many of the same players, but the environment in which they are played has changed. France disappears from it, leaving the field of political action coterminous with England. And as a result, two complementary totalities supervene on the competing partialities of the nobles: the Crown and the people.

The figure of Jack Cade unites these elements, being at once the leader of a popular rising and a claimant to the throne. And his entrance strikingly marks the changed *theatrical* terms of the new configuration: [*Enter Cade, Dick butcher, Smith the weaver, and a Sawyer, with infinite numbers* (IV, ii, 30).] This must be almost the only Shakespearean stage direction which is not practical, but reaches out beyond playhouse notes to an intended impression. The little break in the adequacy of the dramaturgic repertoire reflects the illicit nature of Cade's leadership: just as the royal representatives who meet the rebels refuse to treat with Cade, but address everyone within hearing as a leaderless mob, so the play itself cannot use the normal arithmetic of representation to show a group of 'followers' which is not recognisably constituted and authorised. They are 'infinite' in the sense that they have no definition; their numerousness is not accidental but constitutive; there is no code for representing them because it is by virtue of being outside or prior to the codes that they are what they are. This is the many-headed monster, and the company can show it only by flooding the stage with extras.

This is not only an artistic disturbance, but much more insistently a political and moral one. The infinite numbers are the solvent of all truth and permanence. Sidney puts it neatly in the rebellion sequence of the *Arcadia*, a stylish anthology of anti-populist commonplaces: 'Oh weak trust of the many-headed multitude, whom inconstancy only doth guide to well-doing! Who can set confidence there where company takes away shame, and each may lay the fault on his fellow?'[92] Having no shame, and therefore no morality, the multitude is absolutely unpredictable – it can change unconditionally what it does or believes or feels from one moment to the next, because, paradoxically (that is, 'monstrously'), it is an entity with no identity. For Sidney, the spectacle is horrific and comical, but more comical than horrific because it follows that the multitude is self-defeating: unable to draw its endlessly heterogeneous interests into any kind of coherence, it is effortlessly defeated by the harmonious virtue of his courtly protagonists. How could this grotesquely self-cancelling creature ever arrive at any kind of community? How could it be represented, whether artistically or politically? But then the courtly narrator of the *Arcadia* sees it from the outside: a leisured and self-conscious individual – the author, or the reader – is imagining a crowd. The theatre's images are different because they are designed to be seen *by* a crowd as well.

The difference does *not* take the form of a softening of the anti-populist images. In the play, as in the topos generally, the many-headed monster is a kind of devil – not because of the cruelty and stupidity with which it behaves (there are cruel and stupid aristocrats too), but because it is opposed by its very nature to good order in general. Cade is first characterised in a soliloquy of York's, which recalls him as a soldier in Ireland, fighting on when stuck all over with arrows:

> I have seen
> Him caper upright like a wild Morisco,
> Shaking the bloody darts as he his bells
> (III, i, 364–6)

and working as a spy, disguised as a 'shag-hair'd crafty kern'. Of this carnivalesque and double-faced figure York says, 'This devil here shall be my substitute' (371). Cade is a grotesque embodiment of the ambitious passions and intrigues of York himself; his wildness is non-human in its schematic and total negativity. As he says of himself and his troops, 'then we are in order when we are most out of order' (IV, ii, 189–90) – they are actuated, in the play, by a principle which is the *systematic* opposite of government.

But in the popular theatre, this diabolism gives them access to what might be called the privileges of *stage* devils. The stage has a space for their thorough-going inversion of truth and reason – that of comedy. They are clowns, unleashing upon the society of the drama the torrent of violent horseplay, nonsense, parodic doubletalk and metatheatrical jokes which characterises the devils and vices of medieval theatre. For example, Cade's fairy tale about his royal birth (he is the son of Edmund Mortimer, 'by a beggar-woman stol'n away') is explicitly untrue:

STAFFORD:	And will you credit this base drudge's words,
	That speaks he knows not what?
ALL:	Ay, marry, will we; therefore get ye gone.
BROTHER:	Jack Cade, the Duke of York hath taught you this.
CADE [*aside*]:	He lies, for I invented it myself.

> (IV, ii, 151–5)

The plebeian answers here are parodies, pointed up by their mocking conformity to the iambic pentameters of the government spokesmen. The reasonable answer to Stafford's rhetorical question would be to argue that Cade does know what he is saying, and the appropriate counter to the brother's accusation would be to maintain that the story is true. The rebels' refusal to observe these discursive rules is at once anarchic and funny. The metalinguistic exchange is roughly this: Cade and his followers are accused of being liars and fools, and reply, unanswerably, that they *choose* to be liars and fools. Neither Cade nor his followers believe a word he says: the rebellion has the absolute (but circumscribed) subversiveness of a *joke*. What makes this possible is the theatrical context: in their colloquial energy, their easy commerce with the audience, and the festive utopianism of their aims, the rebels come on stage as entertainers. They strike heroic attitudes and instantly collapse them in a flurry of realistic allusions; their coup d'état is more theatrical than real, a fantastical playing with the signs of power (as when Cade prepares himself to meet with a knight by quickly knighting himself). It is never quite possible to say whether they are clear-sighted ironists or deluded bumpkins: the reason for this doubleness is that they are what Robert Weimann calls *platea* figures,[93] inhabiting the real time of the performance as well as the fictional time of the story, disrupting and travestying the speech world of the serious characters. Seen from within that official speech world, of course, they have the unambiguous negativity of Sidney's rioters: an instance of 'gross and miserable ignorance' (IV, ii, 161). But that is not the only available viewpoint: they establish their own relationship with the audience – a more intimate one in some ways – on terms wholly different from those of the nobles.

The only figure in Part One who came close to forming such a relationship was La Pucelle, who has the same transgressive comic energy, the same direct line to the audience, the same diabolic associations. She does not work in the same way, however, because besides being plebeian she is heavily marked with two extra signs of otherness: she is female and foreign. The comparison is interesting because it further defines the nature of what 'comes home' in Part Two. It is as if France was the space for an external projection; as soon as this is closed off, its elements surface at home. A Frenchwoman becomes Queen of England, the Lord Protector's wife is caught making use of witchcraft, a Kentishman emerges with pretensions as absurd and dangerous as Joan's own. The nobles – that whole group of rigid honourable men with the names of English counties – rediscover the fluid and tricky antithesis of their order, not, this time, in a form which can be conveniently anathematised and burnt, but swirling round the very foundations of their own power.

It is vital to this effect that the comic-diabolic dimension of the play's society is not confined to Act IV. Cade is the monarch of this anti-order, but his accession is heralded by an odd series of episodically presented plebeian forerunners: Margery Jourdain the witch of Eie, Simpcox the religious fraud, Horner the armourer and his man. It seems that every time the play ventures outside the restricted code of aristocratic politics, it gets entangled in the same twilight world which we glimpsed in *King John*: rumour, fantasy, absurdity, change, reversal, superstition, deception, monstrosity. The Duchess of Gloucester resorts to the witch in an attempt to circumvent the official hierarchy and advance her husband's claim to the throne; however, her contact is an agent of Suffolk and the Cardinal, and she is arrested by York; all three of them are using the episode to try and discredit Gloucester. Horner is accused of treason by his man, but then the case comes by accident to the attention of Suffolk, who pushes it to its farcical climax because it offers a chance of discrediting York. York, in turn, has fed Cade the Mortimer story with the double purpose of testing popular attitudes to the Yorkist claim and destabilising royal government while he himself is away in Ireland so that he has a pretext for bringing his army with him when he returns. What repeatedly *takes* the action into the twilight world is that individual noblemen move covertly out into it in attempts to outflank their immediate opponents in the internal power struggles of the ruling class. The popular voice is a double one, full of dreams and lies – but many of the dreams and lies are the barons' own.

The doubleness is, as we have also seen, a matter of parody. This works in small, sharp ways: in the clownish linguistic reversals of the rebels, or in the way the unctuous pieties of the con-man Simpcox guy those of Henry VI himself. But beyond that, the whole Cade rebellion, with its grandiose gestures of regal authority and its brutal and arbitrary violence, holds up a mocking mirror to the civil war whose curtain-raiser it is. In the reckless mendacity of his claims, and the barbaric frivolity with which he has people killed, Cade is a highly fashionable figure: he is doing to the best people what they will very soon be doing to each other at St Albans, Wakefield, Towton, Tewkesbury. The point is economically made through the figure of Iden, the modest country squire who kills Cade. The model of a loyal subject, Iden lays the traitor's head before his king, is knighted, and then stands silent for 150 lines, watching the greatest families of the realm argue about who really is the king, and who the traitor.

The hereditary nobility, in other words, has lost its capacity to represent the principle to which the loyal subject is loyal. This is the simplest and most fundamental reason why the confident condemnation, *de haut en bas*, of the many-headed multitude is deprived of its monologic authority. The elite is now many-headed as well. What connects the barons with the comic-diabolic sphere of the populace is not only that they attempt to make use of it, and not only that they are parodied by it, but also that they *produce* it through their own collective failure to form a single polity. As the idealised (and presumably dismayed) spectator of this disintegration, Iden embodies a point of view which is clearly distinct both from what he is watching and from its popular mirror-image. He says nothing, but he does not need to, because the place where he is standing is also the place where the play as a whole locates its audience. In the comic objectivity of its representation of the relations between nobles and populace, the drama offers a subject-position which is aligned with neither.

It is tempting to conclude, with Stephen Greenblatt, that Shakespeare has here discovered his national principle in a freeholder's private garden:[94] that the imagined community of England, in the play as in Marxist historiography,[95] takes shape only when a property-owning middle class emerges to do the imagining. This overlooks the significance of the one aristocrat who is shown as able to think beyond the interest of himself and his house: Gloucester. As Lord Protector of the realm, he has been first and foremost the guardian and adviser of the young king. But once Henry has ignored his advice – as he does at the very beginning of Part Two over the marriage to Margaret – Gloucester is increasingly forced to found his *locus standi* not simply on his loyalty to the king, but on his loyalty to England. Paradoxically, the decline of his power is an enhancement of his autonomy. The more his less principled fellow peers spiral into mutually destructive antagonisms, the more his moral uprightness comes to look like a political position, a commitment to the commonwealth. This sense of a national alignment is confirmed by his popularity with the commons. It is logical, then, that York and the Queen, the mighty opposites of the first phase of the ensuing civil war, are involved together in plotting his death. He is the last thing that can make them co-operate; after he has been killed, there are no more aristocratic voices which articulate the general interest even of the aristocracy.

This gives the murder a pivotal importance. It comes directly after the soliloquy in which York sets out his plan to use Cade (III, i/ii): Gloucester's death is thus juxtaposed with the play's two most total images of the realm's crisis: the Crown and the people. And it provokes an intervention by the commons which is surprisingly lacking in comic-diabolic character. The Commons – the source suggests that this means the Commons in Parliament, but Shakespeare makes them simply an off-stage 'rude multitude' (III, ii, 134) – have got hold of a rumour that Suffolk is responsible for the murder, and tumultuously insist on his banishment: although it is part of the *mobile vulgus* convention that crowds are agitated by rumours, our attitude as spectators to this one is affected by the fact that we know it is true. It is as if the commons are relieved from their demonic and anarchic typology by virtue of their temporary status as partisans of the good Duke. By its very atrocity, the crime creates a space for civic action, because the interest which has been violated has a generality that goes beyond that of the nobility. It remains, it is true, a cramped and compromised space: the commons do not get on to the stage, and their outrage is transmitted by Salisbury (III, ii, 241–68), who may, as Suffolk reasonably points out, be rephrasing their sentiments to suit his own factional purposes. But the message is not reducible to the messenger; the new presence in the political arena is undeniable.

And it soon acquires a voice of its own, after a fashion, in the extra-ordinary scene of Suffolk's death. He is murdered by pirates, not randomly, but precisely because of who he is and what he has done. The Lieutenant who commands the ship denounces him in a speech which is remarkable both for its rhetorical vigour and because it is the most coherent account of the state of the realm to be found in the play (IV, i, 70–102). Playing on Suffolk's family name, Poole, it begins by calling him the puddle 'whose filth / Troubles the silver spring where England drinks', and proceeds to place him in relation to the king, the queen, Gloucester, Warwick, York and the Kentish rising in a single analysis which is neither Yorkist nor Lancastrian, but national.

Suffolk, meanwhile, is more obsessed by his killers' lowly rank than by either the content of their accusations or his impending death: he claims that the Lieutenant used to hold his stirrup and wait in his antechamber (this seems like a generic imputation rather than a literal one), and exclaims, in a paroxysm of class-consciousness –

> O that I were a god, to shoot forth thunder
> Upon these paltry, servile, abject drudges! . . .
> It is impossible that I should die
> By such a lowly vassal as thyself.
>
> (IV, i, 103–10)

So that for Suffolk himself, his death is precisely the same kind of image as the deaths of Lord Say and Sir James Cromer in the immediately following Cade sequence: an atrocity made the more barbaric by its being perpetrated on the high-born by the low-born, as if the order of nature itself is being upset by the 'mad-bred flaw' threatened by York (III, i, 354). But it is not quite like that. The Lieutenant is not identified with Cade's rising: on the contrary, he mentions it in his catalogue of the disasters for which he holds Suffolk responsible. He speaks, and acts, as a man loyal to the king. It could be that the appropriate analogy is not so much Cade's execution of Say as Iden's execution of Cade. In so far as the scene is comic, the joke is not any presumption on the part of the pirates, but Suffolk's scrabbling attempts to hold on to a status difference which circumstances have rendered finally irrelevant:

> – Jove sometime went disguis'd, and why not I?
> – But Jove was never slain, as thou shalt be.
>
> (48–9)

Here the play's interrogation of lordship is at its harshest. Suffolk's 'great-ness', unlike Talbot's, has no substance; it is his nameless accuser who speaks for thousands, for the misused and deranged kingdom. But if this is another of the play's fugitive 'national' voices, its tones are not the same as those of Iden. The speaker is a semi-legal figure, and the scene is dark and violent, set on the sand between England and the sea, beginning with a lurid *chronographia* of the night and ending with the visual image of the headless corpse. Iden's normativeness seems by comparison to be a matter of naïveté: he admirably believes in an order which is destroying itself as he speaks. The Lieutenant is a more mysterious figure, partaking, in his black humour and the shadowy nature of his occupation, in the twilight world of the populace. He is thus capable of speaking as the interpreter of the Cade scenes which immediately follow: through him, and through the violent clowns of the rebellion, the many-headed monster takes revenge on the aristocratic order which has failed to govern it.

National theatre

To read *Henry VI* through the lens offered by *King John*, then, suggests an answer to what might otherwise be a puzzling question: why did the company, in mounting this immensely ambitious national cycle a year or two after the Armada, choose the most inglorious and unsuccessful period of English history it could find? The answer is that so long as the dynastic legitimation of the monarch and the nobility is more or less working, the stage does not afford any space for anyone else. The community of the nation is not needed, so to speak, and so there is no call to imagine it. It is only when that hierarchical order fails that the undifferentiated totality of the realm appears, as *that which is harmed by its failure*. The theatre's obsession with the contentions of noble houses is not a reflection of con-temporary political reality: Elizabeth by the 1590s seems not to have been particularly threatened either by lawless magnates or by rival claimants to her throne. Rather, the *enactment* of such conflicts operates like a ritual, in which the degradation of the institutional forms of the realm generates a manifestation of the *comitatus*, the prior, underlying body to which all – characters and spectators – can feel they belong.

In this sense, Shakespearean historical drama, comparable in scale and scope to the provincial cycle plays of a few decades earlier, does bear out Mervyn James's epigrammatic suggestion that 'under Protestantism, the Corpus Christi becomes the Body of the Realm'.[96] Just at the point where the Catholic ceremonial calendar was giving way to a growing list of national celebrations and commemorations,[97] the metropolitan theatre was seeking to draw its miscellaneous audience into a new kind of unity by rehearsing the fall and redemption of England.

But just as the late-medieval drama could not be the unproblematic reflection of a pre-existent 'community', but on the contrary took its formal character from the need to negotiate the tensions between communion and stratification, heterogeneity and belonging, so the new drama of the putative national community was handling several models of that community's cohesion.

One such model was what I have been calling the 'dynastic' one. The coherence of the polity, according to this model, is fundamentally a system of personal loyalties, an aggregation of lord and servant relationships corresponding to a hierarchical image of both the state and the cosmos. The unity of the realm is here not immanent, but is a reflection of the person of the monarch. The land is what Gaunt famously called it in *Richard II*: a royal throne of kings, its history an aspect of the history of the ruling family. One influential version of Elizabethan political culture regards this 'frame of order' as defining its limits: the Tudor monarchy, in this view, was in most respects a late-medieval one. Even if the cult of the monarch had a 'national aureole', this was 'in reality contingent and borrowed';[98] 'the day of national consciousness and national interest had not yet appeared'.[99]

What is questionable in that account is not only the dating, but the linear notion of emerging nationhood within which the dating works. 'From divine cosmos to sovereign state':[100] the confident mapping of a route leaves us with nothing to decide except which milestone Shakespeare had got to. The experimental theatre of John Bale shows that this neat teleology will not quite do. We cannot see the hierarchical kingdom as 'residual' and the nation state as 'emergent' when the theatrical language of a long generation before had accommodated both concepts with such clarity. Rather, the *air* of antiquity which hangs about Elizabethan representations of monarchy and nobility is the effect of a *constructed* archaism – that 'imaginative re-feudalization of culture'[101] of which Shakespeare's medieval history plays were themselves a part. That is to say, the relationship between the different versions of the realm – hierarchical and populist, 'kingdom' and 'commonwealth', the Queen's subjects and Christ's people – is not one of chronological sequence but of conflicting emphases within the frame of late-medieval *and* Elizabethan thought.

These conflicts ran, as I have suggested, right through the middle of the Elizabethan theatre. As the protégés of noblemen, and festive entertainers of the court, the actors were firmly defined within the quasi-feudal structure of lordship and service. But as common players, 'servants of the people',[102] they were no less committed to addressing an unstructured and freely assembled crowd – a *public*. What decisively distinguishes these two modes of address is not simply the social rank of the respective patrons. The point is rather that in the first the show belongs to a community whose membership is a matter of degree, so that an individual is more or less a part of it according to his (or her) distance from the centre; while in the second, it belongs to a community which is defined as including everyone equally. The plays reproduce that opposition as a dramatic process, in which the two Englands – the one which descends from its hereditary rulers, and the one which ascends from the people as a whole – collide, transform one another, negotiate.

In a way, the outcome of these negotiations is very clear. The principle which alone turns out to be capable of embodying both Englands at once is that of divine monarchy. As the tetralogy is wound up in *Richard III*, the terms of the national narrative get ever more insistently eschatological, until finally the whole diffused identity of the nation is concentrated in the dreams of the two leaders on the eve of the last battle. It is a literally violent centripetal move, breaking the polity to pieces so that it can be reconstituted in the single person of the king. This is absolutist theatre – not in the relatively trivial sense that it blackens the characters of the Tudors' historical opponents, but in that the monstrous many-headedness of the multitude is evoked, in the last analysis, in order to be resolved in, and so to substantiate, the all-embracing oneness of the monarch.

But the last analysis is not the only possible one. What that absolutist closure overlooks above all is the place which the theatre is claiming for itself when it offers the monarchy this spectacular public legitimation. 'Nation', as John Pocock points out,

> is a symbolic entity under which are grouped a diversity of social institutions and activities, many of which possess pasts of their own, and yet, at the same time, 'nation' attracts to itself myths and symbolic stories suggestive of a common past which may or may not be related to the institutional pasts.[103]

By moving out from the circumscribed past of institutional traditions (great families, the Crown) into the 'common past' of the nation as a whole, the theatre was inviting its audience not merely to contemplate the 'imagined community' but to *be* it. Nashe wrote, defending the theatre by invoking *Henry VI*, that 'our forefathers' valiant acts . . . are revived, and they themselves raised from the grave of oblivion and brought to plead their aged honours in open presence'.[104] The 'open presence' is that of a notional 'everybody'; in recognising 'our' forefathers we recognise our shared identity. Even if the royal orientation of that identity prevented the full expression of an autonomous 'national consciousness' within the text, the experience in the theatre will have made it possible to imagine that too.

Acknowledgements

Drafts of this essay have been read by my colleagues Tony Gash and David Aers, and greatly improved by their detailed and supportive criticisms.

Notes

1. William Shakespeare, *King Henry V*, ed. J. H. Walter, London: Methuen, 1954, ɪ, Chorus, 8–14. Subsequent references in the text.
2. William Shakespeare, *King Henry IV, Part Two*, ed. A. R. Humphreys, London: Methuen, 1966, Induction, 15–22.
3. The image is proverbial; for its Elizabethan and Jacobean currency, see Christopher Hill, 'The many-headed monster', in *Change and Continuity in Seventeenth-Century England*, London: Weidenfeld & Nicolson, 1974, pp. 181–204.
4. From Thomas Dekker and Thomas Middleton, *The Roaring Girl*, I, i, cit. Michael Hattaway, *Elizabethan Popular Theatre*, London: Routledge & Kegan Paul, 1982, p. 45.
5. See *Oxford English Dictionary*, 'mobile' *sb*^{2}. The commonplaces of vulgar fluidity are extravagantly displayed, in a courtly context, in Philip Sidney, *The Countess of Pembroke's Arcadia (The New Arcadia)*, ed. V. Skretkowicz, Oxford: Clarendon Press, 1987, pp. 280–94.
6. Benedict Anderson, *Imagined Communities: Reflections on the origin and spread of nationalism*, London: Verso, 1983, p. 15.
7. The paradoxical legacy of World War II is noted by Tom Nairn, *The Break-Up of Britain*, London: New Left Books, 1977, pp. 60, 273. The politics of the Olivier film are discussed by Graham Holderness in *Shakespeare's History*, Dublin: Gill & Macmillan, 1985, Chapter 2.
8. Graham Holderness, Nick Potter and John Turner, *Shakespeare: The play of history*, London: Macmillan, 1988, p. 80.
9. See E. K. Chambers, *The Elizabethan Stage*, 4 vols, London: Oxford University Press, 1923, II, pp. 383–8.
10. The document is printed in A. C. Cawley, ed., *The Wakefield Pageants in the Towneley Cycle*, Manchester: Manchester University Press, 1958, p. 125.
11. H. C. Gardiner, *Mysteries' End: An investigation of the last days of the medieval religious stage*, New Haven CT: Yale University Press, 1946, pp. 65–93.
12. See Glynne Wickham, *Early English Stages*, 3 vols, London: Routledge & Kegan Paul, 1959–81, vol. II, part 1: *1576–1660* (1963), pp. 158–60.
13. Both men are the subjects of distinguished modern biographies: Claire Cross, *The Puritan Earl: The life of Henry Hastings, third Earl of Huntingdon, 1536–1595*, London: Macmillan, 1966; and Patrick Collinson, *Archbishop Grindal 1519–83: The struggle for a reformed church*, London: Jonathan Cape, 1979.
14. York: D. M. Palliser, *The Reformation in York 1534–1553*, York: St Anthony's Press, 1971, p. 27; Chester: R. M. Lumiansky and D. Mills, *The Chester Mystery*

Cycle: Essays and documents, Chapel Hill NC: University of North Carolina Press, 1983, pp. 38–40, 190–1; The Towneley Cycle: Cawley, *Wakefield Pageants*, pp. xii–xiii.

15. This point is made by Patrick Collinson, *From Iconoclasm to Iconophobia: The cultural impact of the second Reformation*, Reading: University of Reading, 1986, pp. 9–10.

16. Charles Phythian-Adams, 'Ceremony and the citizen: The communal year at Coventry 1450–1550', in P. Clark and P. Slack, eds, *Crisis and Order in English Towns 1500–1700*, London: Routledge & Kegan Paul, 1972, pp. 57–85; Mervyn James, 'Ritual, drama and social body in the late medieval English town', in *Society, Politics and Culture: Studies in early modern England*, Cambridge: Cambridge University Press, 1986, pp. 16–47.

17. Lumiansky and Mills, *Chester Mystery Cycle*, p. 224.

18. For the significance of this term, E. H. Kantorowicz, *The King's Two Bodies: A study in mediaeval political theology*, Princeton NJ: Princeton University Press, 1957, pp. 209, 305–11.

19. A very extensive controversy is usefully summarised in Alexandra F. Johnston, 'The York Corpus Christi play: A dramatic structure based on performance practice', in H. Braet, J. Nowé and G. Tournoy, eds, *The Theatre in the Middle Ages*, Leuven: Leuven University Press, 1985, pp. 362–73. Johnston, the co-editor of the volumes for York in the *Records of Early English Drama* series, Toronto: Toronto University Press, 1979, reasserts the theory of repeated staging in multiple locations. Those who retreat from the arithmetical extremes I have sketched usually do so by proposing that what scholars have is a list of all the plays, and all the stations, that were *ever* used, and that only a selection of each can have featured on any particular occasion. This opens up a broad field of speculation, sceptically surveyed (for instance), in Stanley J. Kahrl, *Traditions of Medieval English Drama*, London: Hutchinson, 1974, pp. 33–48. The significant point concerns the assumptions about dramatic practice which the arguments from 'practicality' bring into play.

20. A. C. Cawley, 'Staging', in A. C. Cawley, David Mills, P. F. McDonald and Marion Jones, *The Revels History of Drama in English*, vol. I: *Medieval Drama*, London, Methuen, 1983, p. 30.

21. D. M. Palliser, 'The trade gilds of Tudor York', in Clark and Slack, *Crisis and Order*, pp. 86–116 (87).

22. Richard Beadle and Pamela M. King, eds, *York Mystery Plays*, Oxford: Clarendon Press, 1984, p. 106. This reading is particularly persuasive because of the occasional attendance at Corpus Christi performances of actual monarchs. The plays, spectacular exhibitions of the prosperity and piety of the town, served as ceremonial acknowledgements of a royal visit – e.g. Elizabeth's to Coventry, as late as 1567 (R. W. Ingram, ed., *Records of Early English Drama: Coventry*, Manchester: Manchester University Press, 1981, p. 243).

23. Text in David Bevington, ed., *Medieval Drama*, London: Houghton Mifflin, 1975, pp. 479–535. Subsequent line references are to this edition.

24. See Lawrence M. Clopper, 'Lay and clerical impact on civic religious drama and ceremony', in Marianne G. Briscoe and John Coldewey, eds, *Contexts for Early English Drama*, Bloomington, IN: Indiana University Press, 1989, pp. 102–36.

25. Victor W. Turner, *The Ritual Process: Structure and anti-structure*, London: Routledge & Kegan Paul, 1969, p. 96.

26. That this purpose was more consciously theorised than a purely anthropological description suggests is argued, on the basis of the Prologue to the 1408 Ordinances of the York Corpus Christi guild, by Theresa Coletti, 'Reading REED: History and the records of early English drama', in Lee Patterson, ed., *Literary Practice and Social Change in Britain, 1380–1530*, Berkeley CA: University of California Press, 1990, pp. 248–84 (275–7).

27. 'Secunda Pastorum', in Cawley, *Wakefield Pageants*, pp. 43–63.

28. For example, in 'The Harrowing of Hell' and 'The Coronation of the Virgin', R. Beadle, ed., *The York Plays*, London: Edward Arnold, 1982, pp. 333–43, 400–4.

29. 'The Crucifixion', Beadle, *York Plays*, pp. 315–23.

30. See, for example, John Northbrooke, *A Treatise wherein Dicing, Dauncing, Vaine playes or Enterluds . . . are reproved*, ?1577, New York and London: Garland, 1974, p. 65; and *Phillip Stubbes's Anatomy of the Abuses in England in Shakspere's Youth A.D. 1583*, F. J. Furnivall, ed., New Shakspere Society, London, 1877–9, pp. 140–4. Both specifically reject religious drama as, if anything, even worse than secular drama, since, as Northbrooke says, 'to mingle scurrilitie with Divinitie . . . is, to eate meate with unwashed hands. . . . What fellowship hath righteousnesse with unrighteousnesse? what communion hath light with darknesse?'

31. Phythian-Adams, 'Ceremony and the citizen', p. 57.

32. Charles Phythian-Adams, *Desolation of a City: Coventry and the urban crisis of the late Middle Ages*, Cambridge: Cambridge University Press, 1979, p. 285.

33. R. B. Dobson, 'Urban decline in late medieval England', in R. Holt and G. Rosser, eds, *The Medieval Town 1200–1540*, Harlow: Longman, 1990, pp. 265–86.

34. See the editors' introduction in A. L. Beier and Roger Findlay, *London 1500–1700: The making of the metropolis*, Harlow: Longman, 1986, pp. 11–17.

35. A. G. R. Smith, *The Emergence of a Nation State: The commonwealth of England 1529–1660*, Harlow: Longman, 1984, pp. 175–80.

36. Christopher Hill, *Reformation to Industrial Revolution*, Harmondsworth: Penguin, 1969, pp. 25–8.

37. Mervyn James, 'The concept of order and the northern rising', in *Society, Politics and Culture*, pp. 270–307.

38. In this connection, it is interesting to note Coventry's late (1584) attempt to replace the cycle with a play about a single biblical episode – ironically, *The Destruction of Jerusalem*: Gardiner, *Mysteries' End*, p. 85.

39. Frances A. Yates, *Astraea: The imperial theme in the sixteenth century*, London: Routledge & Kegan Paul, 1975, p. 55; William Haller, *Foxe's Book of Martyrs and the Elect Nation*, London: Jonathan Cape, 1963, pp. 50–1.

40. A point made by Cornish rebels in 1549: see the list of their demands, reproduced in Julian Cornwall, *Revolt of the Peasantry 1549*, London: Routledge & Kegan Paul, 1977, p. 115.

41. Collinson, *Iconoclasm to Iconophobia*, p. 23.

42. The relevant Elizabethan political theory is outlined in Edward O. Smith,

Crown and Commonwealth: A study in the official Elizabethan doctrine of the prince, Transactions of the American Philosophical Society, NS Vol. 66, Part 8, 1976, pp. 30–43.

43. Patrick Collinson, *The Birthpangs of Protestant England: Religious and cultural change in the sixteenth and seventeenth centuries*, London: Macmillan, 1988, p. 55.
44. See Keith Thomas, *Religion and the Decline of Magic*, London: Weidenfeld & Nicolson, 1971, pp. 69–77.
45. Phythian-Adams, 'Ceremony and the citizen', pp. 79–80. The inescapable ambiguity of the idea of the public for Elizabethan Puritanism is analysed in Patrick Collinson, *The Religion of Protestants: The Church in English society 1559–1625*, Oxford: Oxford University Press, 1982, Chapter 5, 'Popular and unpopular religion'.
46. For a discussion of the likely date and occasion of the so-called 'Late Banns', see Lawrence M. Clopper, 'The history and development of the Chester cycle', *Modern Philology*, 75, 1978, 219–46 (236–40).
47. Text in Lumiansky and Mills, *Chester Mystery Cycle*, pp. 285–95.
48. 'The Traditional Community under Stress', Block II of Open University Course A322, *English Urban History 1500–1780*, Milton Keynes: Open University Press, 1977, p. 16.
49. Christopher Marlowe, Prologue to *The First Part of Tamburlaine the Great*, in *The Complete Plays*, ed. J. B. Steane, Harmondsworth: Penguin, 1969.
50. Chambers, *Elizabethan Stage*, Vol. II, p. 384.
51. Adapting Henry James's phrase about *Waverley*: 'the novel irresponsible', J. O. Hayden, ed., *Scott: The critical heritage*, London: Routledge & Kegan Paul, 1970, p. 429. For the more material view of this irresponsibility, see Terry Eagleton, *The Ideology of the Aesthetic*, Oxford: Basil Blackwell, 1990, p. 368.
52. The struggle is superbly presented in Chambers's sequence of Elizabethan 'Documents of Control', *Elizabethan Stage*, Vol. IV, pp. 262–335.
53. *Ibid.* Vol. II, pp. 87–8. Compare the analyses in Vol. I, pp. 281–3, and in Wickham, *Early English Stages*, Vol. II, part 1, pp. 158–60.
54. They are lucidly outlined by J. Leeds Barroll in Cawley *et al.*, *Revels History*, Vol. III: *1576–1613*, pp. 28–40.
55. The year 1593 was one of plague; in 1603 a less catastrophic outbreak was unluckily end-on to the period of mourning for Queen Elizabeth. See Leeds Barroll's table, Cawley *et al.*, *Revels History*, Vol. III, pp. 34–5.
56. Collinson, *Birthpangs*, pp. 112–14; Chambers, *Elizabethan Stage*, Vol. IV, pp. 197–228.
57. Perhaps the closest call, the Privy Council order of 1597 apparently requiring the theatres to be torn down, is discussed in Peter Thomson, *Shakespeare's Theatre*, London: Routledge, 1983, pp. 3–6.
58. James Burbage is vividly glimpsed playing this card in Chambers, *Elizabethan Stage*, Vol. IV, pp. 297–8.
59. For this argument in use, *ibid.*, Vol. IV, pp. 316, 325.
60. On the 1581 commission: *ibid.*, Vol. IV, pp. 286–7; 1589 extension: *ibid.*, Vol. IV, pp. 306–7; 1598 reinforcement: *ibid.*, Vol. I, pp. 299–301; 1606 regulations: Cawley *et al.*, *Revels History*, Vol. III, p. 43.

61. Beier and Finlay, *London 1500–1700*, pp. 12–13.
62. And, as Thomas Nashe shrewdly observed in *Pierce Penniless*, enough 'men that are their own masters' and are freed to amuse themselves on a weekday afternoon: *Works of Thomas Nashe*, ed. R. B. McKerrow, 5 vols, Oxford: Basil Blackwell, 1958, Vol. I, p. 212.
63. D. M. Palliser, *The Age of Elizabeth*, Harlow: Longman, 1983, p. 215.
64. Thomson, *Shakespeare's Theatre*, pp. 17–18.
65. William Shakespeare, *King John*, ed. E. A. J. Honigmann, London: Methuen, Arden Shakespeare, 1954, i, i, 134–7. Subsequent references in the text.
66. Geoffrey Bullough, ed., *Narrative and Dramatic Sources of Shakespeare*, London: Routledge, 1958–75, Vol. IV, 1962, p. 72. Bullough prints the entire play.
67. Lawrence Stone, *The Causes of the English Revolution 1529–1642*, London: Routledge & Kegan Paul, 1972, pp. 72–6;· and *The Crisis of the Aristocracy 1558–1641*, abridged edn, London: Oxford University Press, 1967, pp. 183–232, 258–60.
68. A. B. Grosart, ed., *The Nondramatic Works of Thomas Dekker*, repr., 5 vols, New York, NY: Russell & Russell, 1963, Vol. II, pp. 193–266 (247–51).
69. Chambers, *Elizabethan Stage*, Vol. IV, pp. 300, 317.
70. Andrew Gurr, *Playgoing in Shakespeare's London*, Cambridge: Cambridge University Press, 1987, pp. 59–79.
71. Jean-Christophe Agnew argues that attacks on the stage in these terms were essentially a *displacement* of anxiety about the social deracination of people and identities: the theatre served, so to speak, to locate dislocation. See *Worlds Apart: The market and the theater in Anglo-American thought, 1550–1750*, Cambridge: Cambridge University Press, 1986, Chapter 3.
72. Susan Brigden, 'Youth and the English Reformation', in P. Slack, ed., *Rebellion, Popular Protest and the Social Order in Early Modern England*, Cambridge: Cambridge University Press, 1984, pp. 77–107 (85). Reprinted from *Past and Present*, **95**, 1982.
73. The Inns: Wilfrid R. Prest, *The Inns of Court under Elizabeth I and the Early Stuarts 1590–1640*, Harlow: Longman, 1972, pp. 153–73; apprenticeship: S. R. Smith, 'The London apprentices as seventeenth-century adolescents', in Slack, *Rebellion*, pp. 219–31, from *Past and Present*, **61**, 1973; immigrants: Beier and Finlay, *London 1500–1700*, pp. 17–24, 40–54; Peter Burke, 'Popular culture in seventeenth-century London', in Barry Reay, ed., *Popular Culture in Seventeenth-Century England*, London: Croom Helm, 1985, pp. 31–58.
74. Burke, 'Popular culture', p. 53. See also R. B. Manning, *Village Revolts*, Oxford: Oxford University Press, 1988, pp. 191–3.
75. John Donne, *Satyres*, IV, ll.168–83, in *Poetical Works*, ed. H. J. C. Grierson, London: Oxford University Press, 1912.
76. The connection is casually noted in the Arden editor's note on these lines. Essex's entourage is anatomised in Mervyn James, 'At a crossroads of the political culture: The Essex revolt, 1601', *Society, Politics and Culture*, pp. 416–65 (424–38).
77. See E. A. J. Honigmann's Introduction to the Arden edition, pp. xxv–vi.
78. 'The Sixth Part of the Homily against Disobedience and willfull Rebellion', in *Certaine Sermons or Homilies Appoynted to be read in Churches* (1635 edition), pp. 313–19 (316).

79. *Troublesome Raigne*, ed. cit., i, xi.
80. Text in P. Happé, ed., *Four Morality Plays*, Harmondsworth: Penguin, 1979.
81. A. G. Dickens, *The English Reformation*, rev. edn, London: Fontana, 1967, p. 167.
82. Leslie P. Fairfield, *John Bale: Mythmaker for the English Reformation*, West Lafayette IN: Purdue University Press, 1976, p. 119.
83. The classic study of this meeting of sacred and national history is Haller's *Foxe's Book of Martyrs and the Elect Nation*. More recently, it has more than once been announced that Haller's thesis 'has been shown to be false': A. J. Fletcher, 'The origins of English protestantism and the growth of national identity', in S. Mews, ed., *Religion and National Identity*, Oxford: Basil Blackwell, 1982, p. 309. But it is not disputed that Foxe (and Bale) accorded the English people a role in God's metahistorical design. Haller is accused of exaggerating the uniqueness of that role, and of underestimating the intellectual and practical importance of Calvinist internationalism. These seem matters for re-emphasis rather than categorical denunciation.
84. Claire Cross, *Church and People 1450–1660: The triumph of the laity in the English Church*, London: Fontana, 1976, pp. 77–80.
85. E. S. Miller, 'The Roman rite in Bale's *King John*', *PMLA*, **64**, 1949, 802–22.
86. The word recurs around this part of the action: see iii, iii, 121, 182; iv, ii, 144; v, i, 11; ii, 27; vii, 18.
87. E. A. J. Honigmann, Arden Introduction, pp. lxiv–v.
88. Kantorowicz, *The King's Two Bodies*, p. 272.
89. Anderson, *Imagined Communities*, p. 25.
90. The inverted commas round 'natural' are there advisedly. The English Channel is genuinely natural, but the borders between England and the rest of Britain were historically produced, as was the state of affairs in which the English ruling class no longer spoke French. I mean what *seems* natural within the play.
91. W. A. Ringler Jr, 'The number of actors in Shakespeare's early plays', in G. E. Bentley, ed., *The Seventeenth-Century Stage*, Chicago IL: Chicago University Press, 1968.
92. Sidney, *New Arcadia*, p. 288.
93. Robert Weimann, *Shakespeare and the Popular Tradition in the Theater*, Baltimore MD: Johns Hopkins University Press, 1978, pp. 221–4.
94. Stephen Greenblatt, 'Murdering peasants: Status, genre, and the representation of rebellion', in S. Greenblatt, ed., *Representing the English Renaissance*, Berkeley CA: University of California Press, 1988, pp. 1–29 (24–5).
95. Perry Anderson, *Lineages of the Absolutist State*, London: New Left Books, 1974, pp. 38–9.
96. James, 'Ritual, drama and social body', p. 41.
97. David Cressy, *Bonfires and Bells: National memory and the Protestant calendar in Elizabethan and Stuart England*, London: Weidenfeld & Nicolson, 1989, esp. pp. 50–66.
98. Perry Anderson, *Lineages*, p. 39.
99. Donald W. Hanson, *From Kingdom to Commonwealth: The development of civic consciousness in English political thought*, Cambridge MA: Harvard University Press, 1970, p. 19.

100. S. L. Collins, *From Divine Cosmos to Sovereign State*, Oxford: Oxford University Press, 1989.
101. Yates, *Astraea*, p. 108.
102. The character of 'A common Player', in Chambers, *Elizabethan Stage*, Vol. IV, pp. 235–6.
103. John Pocock, 'England', in Orest Ranum, ed., *National Consciousness, History and Political Culture in Early-Modern Europe*, Baltimore MD: Johns Hopkins University Press, 1975, pp. 98–117 (99).
104. Nashe, *Works*, Vol. I, p. 212.

Medieval Women, Modern Women: Across the Great Divide

Judith M. Bennett

In our dominant vision of the past, a great chasm separates the medieval world from the world of early-modern Europe. This chasm partly reflects the genuine historical transitions of the fourteenth through seventeenth centuries: the development of humanism and reformed Christianity, the advance of capitalism and urbanisation, the rise of nationalism and national monarchies, the 'discovery' and exploration of 'New World' territories. Yet this breach in historical continuity has been deepened far beyond its natural contours by scholarly depictions of the great divide. As Lee Patterson has most recently argued, all of us collaborate in a master narrative that, in identifying our contemporary world with the changes of the early-modern era, perceives the Middle Ages as a sort of socio-cultural palindrome of modern life; medievalism functions in this narrative as an inversion of modernity, as a pre-modern society and culture utterly foreign to the modern world that succeeded it. This master narrative offers advantages to both early-modernists (for whom it privileges their period) and medievalists (to whom it offers segregated protection). It waxes strong in both literary and historical studies.[1]

This account of a great divide between medieval and early-modern life has never fully drowned out competing stories, but in recent years its pre-eminence as *the* interpretation of European history between the fourteenth and seventeenth centuries has been coming under particularly strong assault. Literary scholars have questioned some of the most basic assumptions of cultural difference between the two eras. Patterson, for example, has undermined one of the cornerstones of the master narrative: the supposed development of historical consciousness as a basic characteristic of modernity. He has shown that our understandings of the historical ideas of humanists not only have drawn too sharp a contrast with similar ideas among medieval intellectuals but also have wrongly privileged one particular form of historical consciousness (one which stresses discontinuity) over others.[2] David Aers has attacked a second cornerstone of the master narrative: the development of individual identity (or, in postmodern terms, the development of subjectivity) among humanists. This model contrasts a medieval world of organic social harmony (in which the self was absorbed into the community) against an early-modern world of competitive individualism. Yet as Aers has demonstrated, many late-medieval texts show a strong sense of selfhood, a strong individualism. He has concluded that 'it is thus time to put a self-denying ordinance on claims about the new "construction of the subject"' in the sixteenth century.[3]

Historians have also been vigorously questioning some of our basic assumptions about social and economic differences between the world of the Middle Ages and the world of early-modern Europe. The most vigorous questioner has been Alan Macfarlane, whose wide-ranging and polemical work has defined (and perhaps set back) recent discussions of continuities across the late-medieval and early-modern centuries. In 1978, Macfarlane argued, in a synthesis of historical work on English society between 1300 and 1700, that England underwent no fundamental structural changes in these centuries. To Macfarlane, England in 1300 was already a capitalist, market economy governed by a rampant individualism, an England very similar in its socio-economic structures to the England of 1700.[4] Macfarlane's argument has been rigorously and justly criticised from many quarters, but his critics have not yet proposed an alternative way of conceptualising social change (and continuity) over these centuries. Macfarlane, then, has succeeded on one front and failed on another; he has undermined the traditional master narrative according to which England experienced a dramatic socio-economic transformation in the sixteenth century, even though his own alternative narrative has not replaced it.

The notoriety of Macfarlane's thesis has perhaps discouraged other historians from undertaking similarly broad-ranging expeditions across the medieval/early-modern chasm. Yet, scholars working in specific areas of historical research have continued to challenge the notion of socio-economic discontinuity across these centuries. Family history provides a good example. In the last decade, medievalists have repeatedly attacked the model that posits, based largely on the arguments of Philippe Ariès and Lawrence Stone, an early-modern emergence of affective family relations. Studies by Barbara Hanawalt, Lorraine Attreed and others have demonstrated not only that medieval people recognised the special nature of childhood but also that medieval family relations could be quite warm, intimate and affectionate.[5] Similarly, medievalists have questioned the dominant demographic model of family formation which argues, based on the work of J. Hajnal, that people began in the sixteenth century to marry later in life (in their mid-twenties) or not at all (perhaps 10–15 per cent of the population never married). Analyses of social and demographic data for late-medieval England – by Richard Smith, P. J. P. Goldberg, and myself – suggest the very real possibility that this supposedly early-modern 'European Marriage Pattern' existed in England as early as the late fourteenth century.[6]

In this essay, I would like to extend these challenges to the master narrative into a new realm: the study of women. The assumption of a dramatic change in women's lives between 1300 and 1700 (and of a consequent definitive distinction between 'medieval women' and 'early-modern women') remains exceptionally strong. Both medievalists and early-modernists tend to agree – without trespassing much into each other's periods – not only that women's lives changed over these centuries but also about the nature of the change: things were better for women in the Middle Ages, and they worsened during the early-modern centuries. Social historians, such as Martha Howell and Merry Wiesner, argue that the early-modern economy severely limited and disadvantaged women workers.[7] Intellectual historians, such as Joan Kelly and Margaret King, argue that humanist ideas denigrated and marginalised women in new and nefarious ways.[8] Literary scholars, such as Linda Woodbridge, Catherine Belsey, Katharina Wilson and Elizabeth Makowski, trace in literary texts a new reduction of women's options and status.[9] And even modern-day philosophers, such as Ivan Illich, have built major theoretical models around the notion of a massive change for women between the medieval and early-modern centuries.[10]

This idea of a great transition in the history of women has been accepted for many reasons: because it rests upon authoritative works in the field of women's history (especially Alice Clark's study in 1919 of seventeenth-century Englishwomen's work and Joan Kelly's critical reassessment in 1977 of women in the Renaissance[11]); because it suits our presumptions about the problems and evils of our own society and our longings for another (in this case, pre-modern) world of a kinder and gentler variety; because it fits within the dominant historical tradition, neatly inverting Burckhardt's history in a feminist rereading of the past (yes, there was a Renaissance, but it was no Renaissance for women; because it accords well with Marxist historiography; and because women's history, revolutionary in its subject matter and marginal in its institutional status, simply cannot afford to question the master narrative.[12]

Although this assumption of a great and negative transition for women has not been entirely unchallenged, it nevertheless wields a strong and paradigmatic force over the field of women's history.[13] It might not strictly be a paradigm in the sense used by Thomas Kuhn in his ground-breaking studies of scientific thinking and research (as Kuhn himself has argued, scientific paradigms have particular characteristics that are not directly applicable to other scholarly fields).[14] Yet it is useful to think of this model of a great divide between medieval and early-modern women as a paradigm. It functions like a paradigm in many fundamental respects: it is based upon authoritative solutions to a problem; it fits within an accepted master narrative (what Kuhn would call a 'disciplinary matrix'); it provides a useful model for further problem-solving research. Most importantly, it functions like a paradigm in its ability to shape what Kuhn has called our 'ways of seeing', even our ways of seeing things far beyond our own research interests. Thus, Caroline Barron has concluded in her recent article on women in medieval London that 'In some senses women lost ground in the sixteenth century in the City of London which has still to be recovered.'[15] Thus, P. J. P. Goldberg has asserted in his recent dissertation that women in early-fifteenth-century York 'enjoyed a fuller economic role than at any subsequent period before the latter part of this present century'.[16] Barron and Goldberg, careful researchers and judicious historians, are driven to make these statements (which are entirely unwarranted according to their own standards of historical argumentation) by the force of the paradigm. Neither has compared medieval women with twentieth-century women (or, indeed, with sixteenth-century women), but both work within a paradigm that causes them to see a clear contrast across the centuries. And we – their readers – accept these statements (when we would normally demand rigorous comparisons) because we also work within the paradigm; Barron and Goldberg (and others) are merely telling us what we expect to hear.

It is time, however, to abandon this paradigm of dramatic change and to seek new theoretical schemes to guide our research into the history of women between 1300 and 1700. For the notion of a great and negative transition for women over these centuries is now faced with too many anomalies to be sustained. Its main authoritative works – the studies of Clark and Kelly – are valued today for their breadth of vision and theory, but generally acknowledged to be flawed in matters of detail and analysis.[17] And its usefulness is eroding under the onslaught of substantial evidence of continuity in women's experiences across the late-medieval and early-modern centuries, continuity that belies the paradigmatic assumption of a great transition. Let me illustrate these anomalies by examining in detail one specific aspect of women's history: the history of women's work in England between 1300 and 1700.

I have chosen women's work to illustrate the inaccuracies that plague the paradigm of great transition not only because of my own interest in the field but also because it provides exceptionally clear examples of both the paradigm and its anomalies. In examining women's work, I shall focus (as have most historians) upon women's productive work, setting to one side women's extensive labours in biological and social reproduction. The notion of a dramatic downturn in women's productive work, articulated authoritatively early in this century by Alice Clark, remains widely accepted among both medievalists and early-modernists. In the early part of this century, medievalists such as Annie Abram, Marian Dale and Eileen Power emphasised women's extensive role in the medieval economy, arguing, as Eileen Power put it, that medieval women enjoyed a 'rough and ready equality' with men.[18] Today, medievalists such as Caroline Barron, Peter Franklin, P. J. P. Goldberg, Barbara Hanawalt, Simon Penn and Kay Lacey have repeated and redrawn this positive assessment of the medieval economy, which they are even willing, at times, to label as a 'golden age' for working women.[19] Early-modernists like Susan Cahn, Roberta Hamilton, Bridget Hill, Keith Snell, Michael Roberts, W. Thwaites and Margaret George agree that women's options as workers declined after 1500, although some would date the decline later than others.[20] Objections to this paradigm have been raised, to be sure, but most historians of English-women's work during these centuries generally agree with some version of what Susan Cahn has called 'woman's descent from paradise'.[21]

Yet, the history of women's work provides exceptionally clear (and sometimes quantifiable) evidence not only of the low status of women's work in the Middle Ages (belying the notion of a lost golden age) but also of continuity between 1300 and 1700 (belying the notion of a medieval/early-modern great divide). Anomalies that plague the paradigm are particularly clear in four crucial aspects of women's work in late-medieval and early-modern England: the work of women within the family economy; the types of work undertaken by women; the involvement of women in guilds; and the wages paid to female workers.

In almost all histories of women's work, the 'family economy' – in which household and workplace were merged and in which family members worked interdependently in order to meet the needs of their household – is assumed to have provided women with a relatively egalitarian working relationship with men. To Alice Clark, most people until the seventeenth century laboured within such family-based work units in which all family members shared from the profits of their collective labour and in which, Clark believed, women's work was especially valued and respected because women's work was essential to family survival. When work moved outside the household and became more individualised (a change Clark located in late-seventeenth-century England), women's work declined in extent and value. In the time since Clark's book was published, her rosy view of the family economy has been repeated and elaborated by numerous scholars. Eileen Power has echoed Clark's views in her evocation of a 'rough and ready equality' in medieval households; Barbara Hanawalt has written about the economic 'partnership' of medieval husbands and wives; Louise Tilly and Joan Scott have argued that women's ability to work was 'strongly correlated' with the family economy; and Susan Cahn has attributed supposed changes in the family economy with the transformation of women's work in early-modern England.[22]

But how much of a true partnership was the family economy? If we look hard, I think we will find that it never really offered women anything close to equality with men. First, on the basis of theory alone, we should treat the family economy with much more caution. We know that households are not natural phenomena, we know that families are not natural organic units free from individual variance and conflict, and we know that women's work in social reproduction is not naturally ordained, but we nevertheless tend to treat the family economy as the best *natural* venue for women's work.[23] It might often have been the best accommodation that women could reach in their working lives, but it is not a natural accommodation. Instead, it was required by (among other social forces) marriage patterns, household structures, guild regulations, childrearing customs and the sexual division of labour. The family economy was a social phenomenon, and as such, it reflected the patriarchal authority of men in medieval society.

Second, it is quite clear that women were firmly subordinated to men in the productive functions of the medieval family economy. We should beware of assuming, as some historians have done, that evidence of women's extensive and essential work within the family economy suggests appreciation of women, for we have considerable evidence that women's work (although extensive and essential) was less valued than men's work.[24] Work within the medieval family economy was divided according to sex (as well as age and status), and women's work was generally less specialised, less skilled and less respected than men's work. In both countryside and town, the husband's work was usually the defining work of the family economy, which the work of wife and children supported and supplemented. His was primary; theirs was secondary. The centrality of the husband's work is reflected, for example, in fourteenth-century poll-tax lists which (in both rural and urban locales) usually detailed only the occupations of husbands, identifying others by household status (e.g. wife, son, daughter, servant) rather than occupational status.[25] Guild ordinances, which regularly assumed that masters were assisted in their workshops by wives and children, tell the same story. And patterns of women's work – which show wives working in occupations that supplemented those of their husbands (such as making candles from the tallow produced by their husbands' butchering) and women shifting occupations upon marriage or remarriage – report the same trend.[26] The labour of husbands within the family economy was the recognised and defining labour of the household.

Not surprisingly, women's work within the family economy was not only secondary but also less specialised. Men often worked at a single main task, recognised as a husbandman, artisan or merchant. Their wives worked at many tasks – their skill was the skill of juggling many responsibilities and many demands. The late-medieval 'Ballad of a Tyrannical Husband', for example, depicted a squabble between a husband and wife over who worked harder. The husband spent his day ploughing. The wife spent her day brewing, baking, caring for poultry and dairy animals, making butter and cheese, working wool and flax into cloth, as well as performing basic reproductive work by watching children, cleaning the house and preparing meals.[27] The multiple tasks of women received legislative sanction in 1363 when a statute restricted male artisans to only one trade, but permitted women to follow several.[28] We should not misinterpret this occupational eclecticism; women were, in the words of L. F. Salzman, 'eternal amateurs'.[29]

Third, the distribution of resources within the family economy was just as inequitable as its division of labour. We should beware of assuming that women controlled the value produced by their labour, for women clearly did not enjoy equal access to the collective resources of their family economies. Sons generally took more from their family economies than daughters. In most English medieval villages, inheritance laws favoured sons over daughters, and parental *inter vivos* gifts to children (which might have overriden the sexual bias inherent in *post mortem* distributions) similarly favoured sons. In towns, inheritance customs often dispersed goods equally to sons and daughters (at least in theory; no one has yet studied actual practice), but sons alone usually enjoyed the privileges of following their fathers' trades, gaining admittance to their fathers' guilds, and acquiring the freedom of their municipalities via patrimony. The effects of these legal and customary prescriptions were very real. In my studies of the rural community of Brigstock in the early fourteenth century, for example, I found that daughters were considerably less involved in land-holding than were sons – roughly one daughter traded or received land for every four sons that did so. This disproportionate control of land by men continued throughout the life-cycle, with women – whether daughters, wives or widows – controlling less than one-fifth of Brigstock's landed resources. Brigstock was typical in the economic disadvantages faced by its daughters; on most medieval manors, women controlled only a very small proportion of the available land.[30]

Marriage only exacerbated the economic inequality of women in the family economy. In both law and custom, a husband enjoyed extensive authority over all familial resources (including properties brought to the marriage by his wife or given explicitly by others to her). The condition of the married women, the *femme couverte* in common law, was a condition of virtual non-existence (especially in economic matters). As Glanvill succinctly

put it, 'since legally a woman is completely in the power of her husband
. . . her dower and all her other property are clearly deemed to be at his
disposal'.[31] A woman brought resources to the family economy created by
her marriage and she worked hard to support it, but *control* of the family
economy rested firmly in the hands of her husband. Any wife could find, as
did Quena ad Crucem of Brigstock in 1315, that she could not sell land
without her husband's involvement because, as the court put it, 'a wife's sale
is nothing in the absence of her husband'.[32]

Even in death and dissolution, the distribution of resources within the
family economy was inequitable. Widowers usually retained full control of
all household resources, for the death of a wife did not precipitate dissolution of the family economy. Widows, however, faced a much more
difficult situation, for the death of a husband effectively dissolved the family
economy (whose resources were then dispersed, at least in part, to the next
generation). Some widows could claim full control of household resources,
but many others were able to claim only one-half or one-third of family
property. Although rules varied widely, many widows faced not only
bereavement but also impoverishment.[33]

We might like to think that these laws and customs were mitigated in
actual practice, but we should posit such mitigation with extreme caution.
As John Stuart Mill advised in another context over a century ago, we must
judge the family economy not by the behaviour of good men (who often
ease the force of patriarchal institutions), but rather by the behaviour of bad
men (who often exploit such institutions to their fullest extent).[34] Hence, we
cannot ignore the fact that English laws and customs in the Middle Ages permitted husbands to deny their wives control over both their capital resources
and their labour. With a good husband and a happy marriage, a woman could
achieve a satisfying working life. But such voluntary egalitarianism – if it
existed – was shadowed by inequality. Even in sharing, the greater material
resources of the husband bespoke inequality. And even in sharing, the
husband's power remained merely suspended, not fully yielded. With an
indifferent husband or an abusive marriage, a woman could find herself a
sort of servant to her husband or even cast aside altogether. We can rarely
catch glimpses of such miseries in medieval sources, but ecclesiastical courts
– a recourse only for women of some wealth or power – offer a few. In such
courts, women, like Matilda Trippes of the Canterbury diocese in 1373, had
to seek court orders to force their husbands to provide them with the basic
necessities of life.[35] The experiences of women such as these underscore the
relative economic powerlessness of women within their family economies.

One escape hatch existed: the urban custom of *femme sole*.[36] In some
towns, married women were permitted, if formally registered as *femmes soles*,
to trade independently of their husbands. Although this custom potentially
mitigated the economic subservience of women within the family economy,

it did not alter the family economy per se; it offered women not equal control of the resources of the family economy, but rather the opportunity to work outside the family economy altogether. A wife who traded as a *femme sole*, therefore, had some independence, but very little support; she probably often found it difficult to compete effectively with either married men (who were supported by the labour of wives and children) or single women (who were relatively more free of family responsibilities). Moreover, the actual effects of this custom are hard to assess. It was confined only to urban areas and indeed, only to some urban areas; towns such as Shrewsbury and Salisbury apparently offered no such reprieve to married women.[37] It has been observed more as a rule than as an actual practice. In London, for example, we know about the theory of the *femme sole*, but we have very few records demonstrating its actual use, and some of these records show wives, designated as *femmes soles*, nevertheless acting in concert with their husbands (acting, in other words, as *femmes couvertes*).[38] And finally, it possibly evolved not as a means of liberating women from the legal coverage of marriage, but instead as a means of freeing husbands from the debts and obligations of their wives; the custom, in other words, might have primarily benefited men.

The family economy, then, was never a haven of rough and ready equality for women; instead, it was shot through with sexual inequality – from its basis as a social construction of a patriarchal society, to its sexual division of household labour, and to its distribution of control over material resources. Hence, although the medieval family economy has been repeatedly described by historians as a 'partnership' of husband and wife, this description masks practical inequality beneath an ideal of mutuality. The family economy might be idealised by historians as a mutual partnership, but this ideal was rarely approached in actual practice.[39] Daughters worked as hard as sons, but they took much less than their brothers from their family economies; wives worked as hard as their husbands, but their tasks were ancillary and their control over family wealth was strictly abrogated; widows also worked hard, but they often faced massive insecurity, as the resources of their family economies – deemed dissolved by the deaths of their husbands – were dispersed in part to the next generation. The medieval family economy was a very weak foundation for a working woman's 'golden age'; women worked within it, but its resources usually belonged in the final resort to men.[40]

Our second important index of women's work – the types of work undertaken by women (whether within a family economy or not) – demonstrates that women's work retained certain crucial characteristics across the late-medieval and early-modern centuries. In many respects, the actual occupations of women remained remarkably unchanged. Comparisons of women's occupations across the centuries are difficult to draw: extant sources vary widely (and are often incomparable), occupational designations shifted over time, and of course, economic contexts also changed. I have attempted, however, a rough comparison based upon occupations of unmarried women noted in the Southwark poll tax of 1381 and Peter Earle's tabulation of women's occupation in London (including the Southwark suburb) in *c*.1700. As shown in Table 5.1, I have matched as closely as possible the occupations of late-fourteenth-century women to the broad categories used by Earle for the seventeenth and eighteenth centuries.[41]

Table 5.1 Unmarried Women's Work in London and Vicinity 1381 vs. *c*.1700

Earle's occupational categories	Southwark women, 1381	London women, 1695–1725	Categorisation of occupations in 1381
Domestic service	38.0	39.8	Servants (62)
Making/ mending clothes	12.3	17.9	Dressmakers (11) Tailors (4) Cappers (2) Girdler (1) Lacemaker (1) Glover (1)
Nursing/medicine	1.2	8.4	Midwife (1) Barber (1)
Charring/laundry	3.7	7.0	Washerwomen (6)
Shopkeeping	1.8	7.8	Upholdsters (3)
Catering/victualling	8.0	5.9	Brewers (3) Cooks (2) Ostlers (2) Tapsters (2) Baker (1) Garlicmonger (1) Fisherman (1) Fruitier (1)
Hawking/carrying	13.5	4.5	Hucksters (21) Fishbearer (1)
Textile manufacture	17.2	3.6	Spinsters (24) Kempsters (2) Dyer (1) Fuller (1)
Misc. services	0.6	2.8	Gardiner (1)
Misc. manufacture	3.7	1.7	Skinners (3) Shoemaker (1) Saddler (1) Carpenter (1)
Hard labour/day work	0	0.6	

A comparison of this nature is fraught with difficulty: Are fourteenth-century servants fully comparable to domestic servants *c.*1700? Can a fourteenth-century suburb (and a poor suburb, at that) be fairly compared to a seventeenth-century metropolis? Should glovers and girdlers be re-grouped with manufacturers? Yet if we pass over these conundrums and look at *general patterns*, some striking similarities emerge. First, note the basic stability in the occupational structure. Some occupations attracted remarkably similar proportions of single female workers – especially domestic service, but also laundering, making clothes, and victualling. Others varied, but in ways that suggest either changing economic structures in the London area (e.g. the decline in textile manufacture) or problems of categorisation (e.g. shopkeeping vs. hawking and carrying). Second, consider that most unmarried women – in 1381 as well as 1700 – worked in either service or the textile and clothing trades. In both 1381 and 1700, two of every five singlewomen found employment in service and another found employment in textile or clothing manufacturing. Third, note the absence in both the fourteenth century and the seventeenth century of certain high-status and high-income occupations. In neither 1381 nor 1700 were singlewomen able to find employment in long-distance trade, in professional occupations, in civil service.[42]

These data, difficult as they are to compare across the centuries, present two further interpretive challenges. First, they only report upon the occupations of unmarried women – whether never married or widowed. The occupations of such women are, however, important measures of the occupational opportunities of *all* women, married as well as unmarried. When married women sought to supplement their family economies with paid labour, they found employment in these same occupations (with the important exception of domestic service, which often required residence at the place of employment).[43] For example, in late-fourteenth-century Howdenshire (where poll-tax assessors recorded the occupations of many wives), married women most frequently worked in victualling, especially brewing. For another example, in late-seventeenth-century London, Earle's figures show wives working most frequently in clothing manufacture, charring and laundering, victualling and nursing.[44]

Second, these data also only report upon the experiences of women in London and its suburbs, atypical locales in the fourteenth century as well as the seventeenth. Yet, data from other places – such as Oxford and Howdenshire in the late fourteenth century – suggest the same trends: more women worked in service than in any other sector of the economy; after service, textiles and clothing manufacturing attracted considerable numbers of women; very few women worked in high-status trades or occupations.[45] In this sense, it is quite misleading to state, as one medieval historian has recently done, that women's occupations constituted the 'medieval equivalent of the Yellow Pages'.[46] Singlewomen found work in very discrete sectors of the economy and were conspicuously absent from a large number of high-status occupations.

These continuities in the occupational patterns of working women are highly suggestive, but more important than occupations per se are continuities in the defining characteristics of women's work, no matter what their actual employment. Women's work throughout these centuries tended to be low-skilled; it usually yielded low remuneration in terms of either wages or profits; it was regarded with low esteem; it was work that combined easily with a wide variety of other remunerative tasks or schemes. These characteristics are repeated in an almost numbing echo throughout studies of women's work in medieval and early-modern England: in my study of early-fourteenth-century Brigstock; in Maryanne Kowaleski's study of late-fourteenth-century Exeter; in Diane Hutton's study of Shrewsbury in the same century; in P. J. P. Goldberg's study of fifteenth-century York; in Sue Wright's study of early-modern Salisbury; in Mary Prior's study of early-modern Oxford; in Carole Shammas's study of seventeenth-century Lancashire; in Peter Earle's study of London *c*.1700.[47] No matter what the actual occupations of women, they tended to work in low-skilled, low-status, low-paid jobs, and they also tended to be intermittent workers, jumping from job to job or juggling several tasks at once. This was true in 1300, and it remained true in 1700.

These basic characteristics are, to my mind, much more important in the history of women's work than any shifts in actual occupations pursued by women (and as we have seen, there were relatively few such shifts). Brewing provides a good example.[48] As Alice Clark noted in her study, brewing was once a female trade that had, by the seventeenth century, come under the increasing control of men. The shift from a feminised industry to a masculinised one occurred much earlier and was patchier than Clark suggested. It happened, for example, quite early in the London area (which explains the relatively few female brewers noted in the 1381 poll tax for Southwark), but much later in many isolated villages, especially in the west and north. Nevertheless, the transition identified by Clark was a genuine one. In 1300, many villages boasted numerous female brewers who supplemented their household's income by selling ale to friends and neighbours; in 1700, those same villages often hosted only a handful of male brewers.

The history of brewing, then, seems to fit the paradigm of a dramatic and negative transformation in women's work. Women ceased to brew commercially as frequently as they had done in the past, suggesting a substantial change for the worse in the history of women's work. Two perspectives, however, belie this interpretation. First, the change was not cataclysmic. Women were not, after all, forced out of a trade that had once yielded them high profits and high status; when women brewed, brewing yielded low profits and low esteem. Second, the substantial change occurred in brewing itself, not in women's work. In 1300, brewing was a localised, small-scale industry that required little capital investment and yielded small profits; it was, therefore, a classic sector of women's work, characterised by low status, low skill, and low remuneration, and suitable for intermittent work patterns.[49] By 1700, brewers often served regional, national or even international markets, and the successful pursuit of the trade required considerable capital investment and considerable technical skill.[50] Therefore, women, whose work continued to be concentrated in low-skilled, low-status, low-paid sectors, were no longer able to compete in brewing. They continued to brew in regions unaffected by the transformation of the trade, and they continued to find employment in less profitable sectors of brewing (for example, as petty retailers of ale and beer). In general, however, the brewing industry had developed beyond the realm of women's work. Although women ceased to brew for profit as frequently as in the past, their work did not really change, it was simply relocated – as brewing grew in prestige and profits – into other sectors of the economy that better suited women's low status as workers. In brewing, then, the real change was in the industry itself, not in women's work per se.

A third measure of women's work – women's access to guilds and guild-supervised work – has been a keystone of many arguments for a great transition. Two sources have suggested a decline in women's place within English guilds: apprenticeship records and guild ordinances. Both provide, I think, very ambivalent evidence of a real decline in the relationship between women and guilds. Although some scholars cite apparent declines in female apprenticeships in the sixteenth century, hard evidence for such a trend has yet to be adduced.[51] For late-medieval London, for example, we have data on female apprentices gathered from miscellaneous contracts and cases. These can provide us with examples and anecdotes, but little more.[52] For late sixteenth-century London, we have exactly the same thing – several dozen agreements involving female apprentices.[53] Guild ordinances provide equally weak evidence of a decline. It is tempting to cite guild restrictions on female work – such as the 1461 order of Bristol weavers that guild members were not to employ their wives, daughters or female servants in weaving – as indicating a progressive decline in female guild participation.[54] But such restrictions are very hard to interpret: they can be found in every century between 1300 and 1700; they probably reflect more prescription than actual practice; they especially proliferate in later centuries simply because more guild records are extant for later periods; and they often suggest short-term responses to economic crisis, not long-term declines in female work.[55]

In short, our evidence does not (as yet) show any clear transition in guild treatment of women workers over the late-medieval and early-modern centuries. Our evidence does, however, demonstrate one fact very clearly: women were never – even in the High Middle Ages – full members of guilds in England. Unlike some towns on the continent, no English towns boasted exclusively female guilds, and even the silkworkers of London failed to organise themselves into a guild until significant numbers of men had joined the trade.[56] As a result, English women, in so far as they participated in guilds at all, participated in guilds controlled by men; in these guilds, women's roles varied by town, by trade and by marital status, but women never participated as fully as men.

The most crucial variable in women's guild activity was probably marital status.[57] Unmarried girls in medieval English towns were sometimes apprenticed under guild aegis, but their numbers were extremely small compared with those of men, they tended to predominate in textile trades, and the end of their apprenticeships did not lead to guild or civic en-franchisement (as was the case for men). Apprenticeship – whether in medieval or early-modern towns – seldom entailed for women what it offered for men; it was rarely a route to recognised status as a skilled tradesperson. Wives were sometimes accepted as 'sisters' into their hus-bands' guilds, but they were clearly second-rank members, paying lower admission fees, prohibited from wearing guild livery, excluded from guild enfranchisement and office, and proscribed from the civic privileges that often accompanied guild membership. And even this minimal acceptance of wives into guild activity – an acceptance that reflected the family-based economy of urban workshops – was not recorded for all medieval English guilds.[58] Widows enjoyed the most extensive guild privileges of all women, for in the interest of maintaining the workshop of the deceased member, guilds often allowed widows to supervise workshops, employ apprentices and journeymen, and participate in selected religious and social activities. But widows were not enfranchised within guilds, they often did not par-ticipate fully in guild society and ceremony, they could sometimes lose their privileges via remarriage, and their numbers within guilds were always small.[59]

The history of women's relationship with guilds needs further examina-tion, but our evidence at hand suggests neither a great transition nor a medieval 'golden age'. The same is true of our final index of women's work – the history of women's wages between 1300 and 1700. Not all women worked for wages, to be sure, but sums paid to wage-earning women provide crucial measures of not only the perceived value of women's work but also women's earning power. Our very earliest records show clearly that women's work was very poorly valued. In the twelfth and thirteenth centuries, the *famuli* employed on an annual basis by manorial estates were mostly males. Tasks designated for females were very few, quite unskilled and relatively poorly paid. These patterns continued into the fourteenth century and beyond.[60]

Women's work performed on a day basis was also poorly remunerated. Before the plague, the day tasks most clearly designated as female tasks were planting beans and collecting stubble – both were generally paid at the rate of a penny (1*d.*) per day (occasionally three farthings – 3/4*d.*). Men hired for such tasks as digging were usually paid at least a penny-halfpenny (1½*d.*) and as much as tuppence-halfpenny (2½*d.*).[61] Indeed, the wage differential between 'women's work' and 'men's work' seems to have been remarkably stable, with women paid about two-thirds to one-half the wages of men: this was true of female labourers in the early fourteenth century; of female reapers and other workers in the seventeenth century; of female agricultural workers in the nineteenth century; and of women working in the modern wage market.[62] Medieval employers were apparently as well aware as modern employers of the possibilities of exploiting the sexual division of labour in order to cut costs. In the thirteenth century, the author of a treatise on estate management advised hiring a woman for certain tasks because she could be relied upon to work 'for much less money than a man would take'.[63]

Why, then, do some historians claim that, as William Beveridge put it in 1955, the 'principle of equal pay as between men and women for the same work was . . . accepted and put into practice more than 600 years [ago]'?[64] The answer is a straightforward one: on occasions when women found employment in tasks also undertaken by men, they were *sometimes* paid equally with men. Historians have made much of evidence – such as that for reapers at Pocklington in 1363 – that shows female workers doing the same jobs as men receiving the same wages. Equal pay for equal work was not – it must be emphasised – an invariable rule, and many examples can be proffered of women paid less than men for equal work. At Pocklington itself, only nine women were paid the same rate as men; the other twenty-one received only threepence (3*d.*) (to the fourpence – 4*d.* – paid to men).[65] Or, for another example, unskilled female labourers at Alton Barnes in 1404 were paid tuppence (2*d.*) per day, while unskilled males received fourpence (4*d.*).[66] Hence, we must treat evidence of equal pay for equal work with considerable caution. Since we know that equal work by women and men was oftentimes not remunerated with equal pay, we must ask: how common was it to pay men and women equally for equal tasks? Since we know that wages often distinguished persons by age as well as sex, we must ask: were the 'men' paid equally with women at places like Pocklington actually 'boys'? And since we know that most women continued to work in low-paid 'women's work', we must ask: how many women were able to benefit from working alongside men?[67] Until we can answer questions such as these, we simply cannot assess the importance of evidence showing women paid equally with men for the performance of equal tasks, nor can we assess how it changed over time. We must, on balance, remain very sceptical of claims about the earning potential of female wage-workers during the Middle Ages.

In the history of women's work between 1300 and 1700, then, these four measures – women's place within the family economy, the types of work pursued by women, women's roles within guilds and the wages paid to women – suggest that there was no great divide between a medieval 'golden age' and an early-modern age of growing inactivity and exploitation. Changes occurred, to be sure – the family economy lost its effectiveness in some economic sectors, women left some trades (such as brewing), guilds became generally more exclusive, female wage-earners competed more or less effectively for better wages. Yet, we must view these changes (and others) with a strong scepticism. First, many of the changes that occurred were of quite short duration. For example, it seems possible – from both extant evidence and economic theory – that the labour shortages of the decades that followed the Black Death improved the wage-earning potential of women. During the late fourteenth and early fifteenth centuries, wage differentials between unskilled and skilled labourers narrowed considerably, and since 'women's work' was generally unskilled work, its wages – together with wages for unskilled male labour – gained ground on skilled wages. At the same time, women might have been able to bargain more effectively not only for better pay but also for equal work paid at equal wages; most of our examples of equal pay for equal work come from these labour-short decades.[68] But these changes were a short-term phenomenon, confined to the peculiar circumstances of a population ravaged by disease. For another example, many guild ordinances against women's work seem to have been prompted by adverse economic conditions and seem to have applied (if they ever had real effect at all) only to years of hard times. Hence, such ordinances were very common in London during the difficult years of the 1540s; they are rare before and rare thereafter.[69] Changes such as these are very telling, for they indicate both the vulnerability of female workers and the economic usefulness of their occupational adaptability. We need to study these changes (and others) in more detail, but we also need to remember that they proved to be ephemeral. They were small and temporary shifts, not transformations.

Second, even the most positive shifts affected only a tiny minority of women. Most of our evidence for an improvement in the working opportunities of women after the plague, for example, involves wage-earning women or women in urban locales. Yet only a very small proportion of women would have been able to take advantage of these short-term changes. Relatively few people (and even fewer women than men) worked for wages in the later Middle Ages and relatively few people lived in towns.[70] Moreover, even in the best of times and places, most women were unable to take advantage of new opportunities that were potentially theirs; most wage-earning women still worked in lower-paid female jobs, as did most urban women. For example, P. J. P. Goldberg has argued that women found in early-fifteenth-century York an expanding and favourable economy, basing his argument on, among other things, a rise in female admissions to the freedom of the city (women admitted to York's freedom between 1414 and 1444 constituted 45 per cent of all women admitted in the century and a half after the plague). But very few women actually acquired civic enfranchisement between 1414 and 1444. Fifty-two women, to be precise, in a population of well over 10,000, and in a city in which literally thousands of men gained the freedom during the same decades.[71] Even genuine shifts, then, had quite limited effect.

Third, these changes – as ephemeral and as limited as they were – must also be placed within a context of enduring continuities in the circumstances, status and experiences of women workers. As I have demonstrated from four perspectives, most women – in 1300 as in 1700 – sought to support themselves (and their families) through a variety of low-skilled, low-status, low-paid occupations. In the world of pre-industrial England, all people – men as well as women – worked hard, long and in difficult circumstances, but the working status of women – compared with that of men – was consistently lower: they received less training, they worked at less desirable tasks, they enjoyed less occupational stability and a weaker work identity, they received lower wages.[72] This was as true in the best of times (as perhaps in some locales after the plague) as in the worst of times. We need to collect much more information about how women's work and women's wages shifted and altered within this framework of economic subordination, but the framework remained: there was no transformation.

In one sense, my argument with those who posit a great transition in women's work is a perceptual one. Scholars like Caroline Barron and Susan Cahn look at the 'glass' of women's economic activity in fifteenth-century England and see it as half full; I see the same 'glass' but I see it as half empty. My disagreement is, however, more substantial than merely a matter of perspective. For scholars who work within the paradigm of great transformation see women's work within an entirely different framework, a framework that best accommodates not small and temporary shifts but instead transformative and dramatic change. This framework suits well a liberal historiographic tradition, for it implies that a 'golden age' for women – part of the relatively recent past of the West – can be easily recovered in the future without major structural changes.[73] Within this framework, the Middle Ages – in which women worked within family economies that firmly subordinated their interests to those of their husbands, in which women's work was characteristically low-status, low-skilled, and low-paid, in which women attained at best only very restricted access to guild life, and in which women worked for wages usually far below the wages paid to men – becomes a 'golden age', a 'paradise' which early-modern women lost.

Women's work is, of course, just one aspect of the paradigmatic assumption of a great transition in women's history coinciding with the end of the Middle Ages and the rise of modern Europe. Yet it illustrates well first, how strongly the paradigm operates within a specific research area and second, how many anomalous findings now undercut the paradigm's efficacy. Women's work certainly changed over these centuries, but it was not transformed. If we look critically at other aspects of women's history across these centuries – family relations, patterns of marriage and fertility, political participation, religious life and so on – I think we will discern similar continuities across the centuries.[74] The paradigm of a great divide, quite simply, does not hold.

How then should we think about the history of women between 1300 and 1700?[75] I think that we should develop a 'way of seeing' women's history that better recognises continuity and that, indeed, takes continuity as its chief problematic. In the study of women's work, to continue with the central example of this essay, we should take as our central question not trans-formation (whether, when and why it occurred) but instead continuity. We should ask: why has women's work retained such dismal characteristics over so many centuries? We should ask: why did women leave brewing as it became profitable and capitalised? We should ask: why have wages for 'women's work' remained consistently lower than wages paid for work associated with men? We should ask, in short: why has women's work stood still in the midst of considerable economic change?

As I have argued elsewhere, I think that this emphasis on continuity demands an attention to the mechanisms and operations of patriarchy in the history of women.[76] In other words, I think that we need to pursue our historical study of women with a greater attention to the (varied and changing) patriarchal contexts of women's lives. We need to understand how patriarchy has worked in certain times and places, how it has been challenged, accepted and changed by women and men, and how it has adapted and adjusted to changing times. As used by feminist historians, a study of patriarchy would assume that the subordination of women is neither pre-ordained nor natural, but is instead a complex historical phenomenon. It offers a framework within which to pursue questions such as those posed above, without dictating what the answers must be. And it simply fits our historical evidence much better than the paradigm of great transition; the balance of continuity over change in such areas as women's work requires an approach that can better accommodate a history of small shifts, short-term changes and enduring continuities.

Furthermore, the challenge of understanding the history of patriarchy within this framework of continuity also promises to integrate much more effectively research into the socio-economic and legal-political history of women, on the one hand, and research into the literary history of women, on the other. Hence, it is a project particularly well-suited to the inter-disciplinary ventures of medieval studies. Patriarchies have changed historic-ally, but the institution of patriarchy has endured because of its complex and multi-faceted nature; patriarchy draws its strength from ideology, custom and affective relations as well as from politics, law, economy and society. This multi-faceted structure calls upon the attention of literary scholars as much as the attention of historians. Indeed, some of the standard causal forces of historical writing (such as economic and political forces) seem to have had little transformative power in women's history, suggesting the possibility of an exceptionally prominent place in women's history for the study of misogyny, popular culture, attitudes towards sexuality and other ideological matters.[77]

Finally, by refocusing our attention upon the problematic of continuity, we will re-place women's history in the avant garde of historical thinking on the late-medieval and early-modern centuries. The master narrative of a great transformation is under attack in many areas of research, yet remains curiously strong in the paradigmatic assumptions of women's history. This essay has suggested that this strength is unwarranted – that the paradigm of a great divide in women's history is undermined by many factual anomalies. Indeed, given the challenges that women's history poses to traditional history on so many fronts, support of this tradition of a great divide by historians of women is itself quite anomalous. Women's history should ally itself with those who are questioning the master narrative, not with those who would try to buttress its crumbling foundations.

Acknowledgements

I am grateful to the John Simon Guggenhein Memorial Foundation, from which I held a fellowship during the year in which this essay was written. I would also like to thank Cynthia Herrup, Maryanne Kowaleski and Lyndal Roper for their criticisms of a draft of this essay. An abbreviated version was presented at a conference on 'Medieval Women: Work, Spirituality, Literacy, and Patronage' at the University of York in September 1990.

Notes

1. Lee Patterson, 'On the margin: Postmodernism, ironic history, and medieval studies', *Speculum*, **65**, 1990, 87–108. Throughout this essay I shall use the

term 'early-modern' to denote the period that succeeded the Middle Ages. Some scholars (especially literary scholars) prefer 'Renaissance', but I have avoided this term because it over-emphasises aspects of cultural change.

2. Patterson, 'On the margin', esp. 93–5. See also Chapters 5 and 6 in his *Negotiating the Past: The historical understanding of medieval literature*, Madison WI: University of Wisconsin Press, 1987.

3. David Aers, *Community, Gender, and Individual Identity: English writing 1360–1430*, London: Routledge, 1988, quote from p. 17.

4. Alan Macfarlane, *The Origins of English Individualism: The family, property, and social transition*, Oxford: Basil Blackwell, 1978. For one critique, see Stephen White and Richard Vann, 'The invention of English individualism: Alan Macfarlane and the modernization of pre-modern England', *Social History*, **8**, 1983, 345–63.

5. The main authorities for the dominant model are: Philippe Ariès, *Centuries of Childhood: A social history of family life*, trans. Robert Baldick, New York NY: Vintage Books, 1962; and Lawrence Stone, *The Family, Sex and Marriage in England 1500–1800*, New York NY: Harper & Row, 1977. For critiques by medievalists, see Lorraine Attreed, 'From *Pearl* maiden to Tower princes: Towards a new history of medieval childhood', *Journal of Medieval History*, **9**, 1983, 43–58, and Barbara Hanawalt, 'Childrearing among the lower classes of late medieval England', *Journal of Interdisciplinary History*, **8**, 1977, 1–22. See also early-modern critiques, such as Linda A. Pollock, *Forgotten Children: Parent–child relations from 1500 to 1900*, Cambridge: Cambridge University Press, 1983.

6. For the model, see J. Hajnal, 'European marriage patterns in perspective', in *Population in History*, D. V. Glass and D. E. C. Eversley, eds, Chicago IL: Aldine, 1965, pp. 101–43. For evidence of medieval antecedents, see R. M. Smith, 'Some reflections on the evidence for the origins of the "European Marriage Pattern" in England', in *The Sociology of the Family*, Chris Harris, ed., Sociological Review Monograph 28, Keele: University of Keele, 1979, pp. 74–112; P. J. P Goldberg, 'Female labour, service and marriage in the late medieval urban North', *Northern History*, **22**, 1986, 18–38; and Judith M. Bennett, 'Medieval peasant marriage: an examination of marriage license fines in the *Liber Gersumarum*', in *Pathways to Medieval Peasants*, J. A. Raftis, ed., Toronto: Pontifical Institute of Mediaeval Studies, 1981, pp. 193–246. For the arguments of a medievalist who supports Hajnal's chronology, see Zvi Razi, *Marriage and Death in a Medieval Parish: Economy, society and demography in Halesowen 1270–1400*, Cambridge: Cambridge University Press, 1980.

7. Martha C. Howell, *Women, Production and Patriarchy in Late Medieval Cities*, Chicago IL: University of Chicago Press, 1986; Merry E. Wiesner, *Working Women in Renaissance Germany*, New Brunswick NJ: Rutgers University Press, 1986.

8. Joan Kelly, 'Did women have a Renaissance?', 1977 essay reprinted in her *Women, History and Theory*, Chicago IL: University of Chicago Press, 1984, pp. 19–51; Margaret King, 'Book-Lined Cells: Women and humanism in the early Italian Renaissance', in *Beyond Their Sex: Learned women of the European past*, Patricia H. Labalme, ed., New York NY: New York University Press,

1984, pp. 66–90, and (with Albert Rabil, Jr), eds, *Her Immaculate Hand*, Binghampton NY; Center for Medieval and Early Renaissance Studies, 1983.

9. Linda Woodbridge, *Women and the English Renaissance*, Urban IL; University of Illinois Press, 1984. Catherine Belsey, *The Subject of Tragedy*, London: Methuen, 1985; Katharina M. Wilson and Elizabeth M. Makowski, *Wykked Wyves and the Woes of Marriage*, Albany NY: State University of New York Press, 1990.

10. Ivan Illich, *Gender*, New York NY: Pantheon, 1982.

11. Alice Clark, *Working Life of Women in the Seventeenth Century*, 1919: rpt London: Routledge & Kegan Paul, 1982; Kelly, 'Did women have a Renaissance?'.

12. Curiously, popular perceptions of women's history across the great divide differ from the dominant professional interpretation. Women's status is popularly thought to have changed dramatically *for the better* with the advent of modernity. This popular narrative reflects two influences – first, the perception of the Middle Ages as a backward era (and hence, presumably, a terrible time for women) and second, the idea of history as a story of steady progress (in, among other things, the status of women). Hence, in the popular imagination, women's status from *c*.1300 to the present day could be depicted as a steadily ascending line. For historians, that history is best represented by a U-shaped or J-shaped curve, with women's status declining between the Middle Ages and the present day and women's current status either equalling (as in the U-shaped version) or exceeding (as in the J-shaped model) the status of medieval women.

13. See, for example, Chris Middleton, 'Women's labour and the transition to pre-industrial capitalism', in *Women and Work in Pre-Industrial England*, Lindsey Charles and Lorna Duffin, eds, London: Croom Helm, 1985, pp. 181–206; and his 'The familiar fate of the *famulae*: Gender divisions in the history of wage labour', in *On Work*, ed. R. E. Pahl, Oxford: Basil Blackwell, 1988, pp. 21–47; Judith M. Bennett, '"History that stands still": Women's work in the European past', *Feminist Studies*, **14**, 1988, 269–83.

14. Thomas S. Kuhn, *The Structure of Scientific Revolutions*, 2nd edn, Chicago IL: University of Chicago Press, 1970. See especially his comments on the applicability of his notion of paradigms to other fields on pp. 208–10.

15. Caroline Barron, 'The "golden age" of women in medieval London', in *Medieval Women in Southern England*, Reading: Reading Medieval Studies, 15, 1989, pp. 35–58, quote from p. 49.

16. P. J. P. Goldberg, 'Female labour, status, and marriage in late medieval York and other English towns', Dissertation, Cambridge University, 1987, quote from abstract.

17. For Clark, see criticisms of Miranda Chaytor and Jane Lewis in their introduction to the reissue of her book in 1982. For Kelly, see the criticisms of Judith Brown, 'A woman's place was in the home: Women's work in Renaissance Tuscany', in *Rewriting the Renaissance*, Margaret Ferguson *et al.*, eds, Chicago IL: University of Chicago Press, 1986, pp. 206–24. See also David Herlihy, 'Did women have a Renaissance? A reconsideration', *Medievalia et Humanistica*, n.s., **13**, 1985, 1–22.

18. Annie Abram, 'Women traders in medieval London', *Economic Journal*, **26**, 1916, 276–85; Marian K. Dale, 'The London silkwomen of the fifteenth

century', *Economic History Review*, **4**, 1933, 324–5; Eileen Power, *Medieval Women*, essays collected posthumously, Cambridge: Cambridge University Press, 1975, esp. pp. 57–75, quote from p. 34.

19. Barron, 'Golden age'; Peter Franklin, 'Peasant widows' "liberation" and re-marriage before the Black Death', *Economic History Review*, 2nd ser., **39**, 1986, 186–204; Goldberg, 'Female labour, status', and articles extending the conclusions of this dissertation, such as 'Female labour, service', and 'Women in fifteenth-century town life', in *Towns and Townspeople in the Fifteenth Century*, John A. F. Thomson, ed., Gloucester: Sutton, 1988, pp. 107–27; Barbara A. Hanawalt, 'Peasant women's contribution to the home economy in late medieval England', in *Women and Work in Preindustrial Europe*, B. A. Hanawalt, ed., Bloomington IN: University of Indiana Press, 1986, pp. 3–19; Simon A. C. Penn, 'Female wage-earners in late fourteenth-century England', *Agricultural History Review*, 37, 1987, 1–14; Kay. E. Lacey, 'Women and work in fourteenth and fifteenth century London', in *Women and Work*, Charles and Duffin, eds, pp. 24–82. Rodney Hilton has argued not for a medieval golden age, but for the relatively higher status of working women in the Middle Ages *vis-à-vis* women of other classes. See R. H. Hilton, 'Women in the village', in *The English Peasantry in the Later Middle Ages*, Oxford: Oxford University Press, 1975, pp. 95–110, and 'Women traders in medieval England', *Women's Studies*, 11, 1984, 139–55. In a recent study, David Herlihy has posited a similarly dramatic and negative transition, but has dated it much earlier (in the High Middle Ages); see *Opera Muliebria: Women and work in medieval Europe*, New York NY: McGraw Hill, 1990.

20. Susan Cahn, *Industry of Devotion: The transformation of women's work in England, 1500–1660*, New York NY: Columbia University Press, 1987; Roberta Hamilton, *The Liberation of Women: A study of patriarchy and capitalism*, London: George Allen & Unwin, 1978; Bridget Hill, *Women, Work, and Sexual Politics in Eighteenth-Century England*, Oxford: Basil Blackwell, 1989; Keith Snell, *Annals of the Labouring Poor*, Cambridge: Cambridge University Press, 1985, pp. 270–319; Michael Roberts, 'Sickles and Scythes: women's work and men's work at harvest time', *History Workshop Journal*, 7, 1979, 3–29; W. Thwaites, 'Women in the market place: Oxfordshire *c*.1690–1800', *Midland History*, **9**, 1984, 23–42; Margaret George, 'From "Goodwife" to "Mistress": The transformation of the female in bourgeois culture', *Science and Society*, **37**, 1973, 152–177. I shall not deal in this essay with women's work outside England, but the idea of a great transition also dominates continental work; see particularly the studies of Howell and Wiesner.

21. For explicit queries of the paradigm, see Middleton, 'Women's labour' and 'Familiar fate', and Bennett, 'History that stands still'. For examples of findings contrary to the paradigm, see Maryanne Kowaleski, 'Women's work in a market town: Exeter in the late fourteenth century', in *Woman and Work*, Hanawalt, ed., pp. 145–64, and Diane Hutton, 'Women in fourteenth century Shrewsbury', in *Women and Work*, Charles and Duffin, eds, pp. 83–99. For quote, see Cahn, *Industry of Devotion*, p. 9.

22. Power, *Medieval Women*, p. 34; Hanawalt, 'Peasant women's contribution'; Louise Tilly and Joan Scott, *Women, Work and Family*, New York NY: Holt, Rinehart Winston, 1978, p. 230; Cahn, *Industry of Devotion*.

23. Olivia Harris, 'Households as natural units', in *Of Marriage and the Market*, ed. Kate Young *et al.*, 2nd edn, London: Routlege & Kegan Paul, 1984, pp. 136–55; Rayna Rapp *et al.*, 'Examining family history', *Feminist Studies*, 5, 1979, 174–200.

24. Anthropological studies regularly demonstrate that women often labour longer and harder than men, but nevertheless fail to derive from their work either high status or economic power. See, for examples, Ernestine Friedl, *Women and Men*, New York NY: Holt, Rinehart & Winston, 1975; and Michelle Z. Rosaldo and Louise Lamphere, *Woman, Culture and Society*, Palo Alto CA: Stanford University Press, 1974. Alice Clark and her contemporaries in the early twentieth century were particularly concerned to demonstrate that medieval women had been active, contributing members of their households, not passive, idle ornaments. In this effort, they were right; medieval women did contribute in substantial ways to the economic well-being of their families. Yet they were wrong to assume that these contributions were highly appreciated: women's work was perceived as easy and unskilled; it was poorly paid; it was easily replaced. Women worked hard, but their labour was neither ipso facto valued nor ipso facto empowering.

Despite the considerable challenges of determining popular attitudes towards women's work in the Middle Ages, a few observations can be made. First, popular literature suggests (see discussion of the 'Ballad of the Tyrannical Husband' below) that medieval people did discuss the relative value of the work performed by women and men. Second, it is clear that women's work in medieval and early-modern Europe was sometimes avoided by men and considered to be less honourable. See, for examples, Herlihy, *Opera*, p. 34; and Jean H. Quataert, 'The shaping of women's work in manufacturing: Guilds, households, and the state in Central Europe, 1648–1870', *American Historical Review*, 90, 1985, 1122–48. Third, early-modern legal records show that women avoided service, suggesting a dislike of basic domestic labour. See Michael Roberts, '"Words they are women and deeds they are men": Images of work and gender in early modern England', in *Women and Work*, Charles and Duffin, eds, pp. 126 and 157–8; and Diane Willen, 'Women in the public sphere in early modern England: The case of the urban working poor', *Sixteenth Century Journal*, 19, 1988, p. 561. Fourth, women had a weak work identity, suggesting a low self-evaluation of their own labour. See especially: Natalie Z. Davis, 'Women in the crafts in sixteenth-century Lyons', in *Women and Work*, Hanawalt, ed., pp. 167–97; Kowaleski, 'Women's work'; and Roberts, 'Words they are women', pp. 138–9. Fifth, women's work was remunerated with lower wages than men's work (as discussed more fully below).

25. See, for example, the Southwark poll tax, Public Record Office, E179 184/30. To my knowledge, the only poll-tax return that regularly records the occupations of wives is the 1379 return for Howdenshire: see 'Assessment roll of the poll-tax for Howdenshire, etc. in the second year of the reign of King Richard II (1379)', *Yorkshire Archaeological and Topographical Journal*, 9, 1886, 129–61. (The omission of wives' occupations was not noted by Goldberg in his recent analysis of occupational structures in poll taxes; see his 'Urban identity and the poll taxes of 1377, 1379, and 1381', *Economic History Review*, 2nd ser., 43,

1990, 194–216, esp. 209–12.) The tendency to record only the occupations of husbands continues well into the modern era: see Peter H. Lindert, 'English occupations, 1670–1811', *Journal of Economic History*, **40**, 1980, 691–2.

26. See, for examples, Goldberg, 'Female labour, service', p. 30; and Davis, 'Women in the crafts'.

27. 'Ballad of a Tyrannical Husband', in *Reliquiae Antiquae*, vol. II, Thomas Wright and James O. Halliwell, eds, London: J. R. Smith, 1845, pp. 196–9.

28. *Statutes of the Realm, Vol. I*, London: Record Commission, 1810, pp. 379–80.

29. L. F. Salzman, *English Industries of the Middle Ages*, Oxford: Oxford University Press, 1923, pp. 328–9.

30. Judith M. Bennett, *Women in the Medieval English Countryside*, New York NY: Oxford University Press, 1987, p. 33 and n. 23, pp. 78–84.

31. *The Treatise on the Laws and Customs of the Realm of England commonly called Glanvill*, ed. G. D. G. Hall, London: Nelson, 1965, Book VI, no. 3, p. 60.

32. Northamptonshire Record Office, Montagu Collection, Box X364B, court for 20/3/1315. The jurors stated '*vendicio illa nulla est de uxore in absentia mariti sui*'.

33. For a fuller discussion of the circumstances faced by rural widows, see Chapter 6 of Bennett, *Women in the Medieval English Countryside*.

34. John Stuart Mill, *The Subjection of Women* (1869), esp. Chapter II.

35. R. H. Helmholz, *Marriage Litigation in Medieval England*, Cambridge: Cambridge University Press, 1974, p. 102. Goldberg concludes from the rarity of suits for divorce or legal separation that most marriages were stable and affectionate ('Female labour, service', pp. 27–8). But this conclusion ignores the inaccessibility of ecclesiastical courts for most people and the relative ease with which people could effect *de facto* divorces. See Michael M. Sheehan, 'The formation and stability of marriage in fourteenth-century England: Evidence of an Ely register', *Mediaeval Studies*, **33**, 1971, 228–63. As discussed in her excellent paper on 'Women and Trade in Eighteenth-Century England', at the Eighth Berkshire Conference on the History of Women, Margaret Hunt has uncovered some very interesting evidence of economic conflicts between husbands and wives in the eighteenth century (when the common law on marital property still remained unchanged in essentials). This information will be presented in her forthcoming book. For the later history of married women's property rights, see Lee Holcombe, *Wives and Property*, Toronto: University of Toronto Press, 1983.

36. Mary Bateson, ed., *Borough Customs*, 2 vols, Selden Society 18, London: B. Quaritch, 1904, esp. pp. 222–8; and 21, London: B. Quaritch, 1906, pp. c–cxv, 102–29. By the early-modern centuries, some women (especially elite women) were able to circumvent the disabilities of *couverture* through pre-marital property settlements that gave a wife a separate estate which could not be touched by her husband. See Amy Louise Erickson, 'The property ownership and financial decisions of ordinary women in early modern England', Dissertation, Cambridge University, 1989. As with the custom of *femme sole*, separate estates mitigated the wife's condition not by changing the husband's control of familial resources but rather by giving women some autonomy outside of the marital economy.

37. Diane Hutton, 'Women in fourteenth century Shrewsbury', in *Women and*

Work, Charles and Duffin, eds, p. 86: Sue Wright, '"Churmaids, huswyfes and hucksters": The employment of women in Tudor and Stuart Salisbury', in *Women and Work*, Charles and Duffin, eds, p. 107.

38. For discussion of *femmes soles* in London, see Lacey, 'Women and work', esp. pp. 41–5, and Barron, 'Golden age', esp. pp. 39–40. In the surviving Mayor Court Bills for London, several cases involved women, noted as trading as *femmes soles*, who were nevertheless impleaded with their husbands. See, for examples, Corporation of London Record Office, Mayor Court Bills 1/123, 3/210, 3/373, 3/377. I would like to thank Caroline Barron for directing me to this source. Mary Bateson notes that husbands joined their wives in such cases in London 'for conformity': see *Borough Customs*, Vol. 2, p. cxiv.

39. For examples of the evocation of the 'partnership' ideal, see Goldberg, 'Female labour, service', and Hanawalt, 'Peasant women's contribution'.

40. I have treated the family economy in a static fashion in order to demonstrate that it never offered an ideal situation for women – in either medieval or early-modern Europe. The full history of its development and evolution are beyond the purposes of this essay. Maxine Berg, however, has raised substantial doubts about the supposedly negative effects of the decline of the family economy on women's work. See 'Women's work, mechanization and the early phases of industrialization in England', in *On Work*, ed. Pahl, pp. 61–94.

41. Data for London 1695–1725 extracted from Table 10 of Peter Earle, 'The female labour market in London in the late seventeenth and early eighteenth centuries', *Economic History Review*, 2nd ser., **42**, 1989, 328–53. Earle breaks his data down by marital status; since the 1381 poll tax reports occupations only for unmarried women, I have used only Earle's data for spinsters and widows. Data for Southwark in 1381 from Public Record Office E179 184/30. I have excluded from my figures unmarried women whose occupations were unstated.

42. In the Southwark poll tax, for example, numerous skilled occupations were identified with men alone, including: spicer, vintner, goldsmith, marshal, armiger, weaver, cooper and smith. See also the occupations of males and females listed in Penn, 'Female wage-earners', p. 5 (Table I).

43. As suggested by the work of Tilly and Scott, married women might have worked in even more marginal occupations, because they were less able to compete with singlewomen in the labour market. See *Women, Work and Family*.

44. For Howdenshire, see 'Assessment roll'. For London, see Earle, 'Female labour market'.

45. For Oxford, see the transcription of the 1381 poll tax in J. E. Thorold Rogers, ed., *Oxford City Documents 1268–1665*, Oxford: Oxford University Press, 1891. I have tabulated the following occupations for unmarried women from this list: servants 152; dressmakers 11; tailor 1; laundresses 5; tapsters 12; brewers 5; butcher 1; alebearer 1; hucksters 3; spinsters 39; kempsters 2; ironmonger 1; stringer 1; smith 1; netmaker 1; saddler 1; chandler 1; labourers 2. For Howdenshire, see 'Assessment Roll'. Most singlewomen in these returns are noted as servants or labourers. For example, I tabulated the following figures for the town of Howden: servants 57; labourers 15; brewers 9; weaver 1; brazier 1; artificer 1; seamstress 1.

46. Goldberg, 'Female labour, service', p. 30.

47. Bennett, *Women*; Kowaleski, 'Women's work'; Hutton, 'Women'; Goldberg, 'Female labour, service'; Sue Wright, 'Churmaids'; Mary Prior, 'Women and the urban economy: Oxford 1500–1800', in *Women in English Society 1500–1800*, Mary Prior, ed., London: Methuen, 1985, pp. 93–117; Carole Shammas, 'The world women knew: Women workers in the North of England during the late seventeenth century', in *The World of William Penn*, R. Dunn, ed., Philadelphia PA: University of Pennsylvania Press, 1986, pp. 99–115; Earle, 'Female labour market'.

48. What follows is a summary of my ongoing work on women in the brewing industry over these centuries. Some of the material is presented in greater detail in my 'The village ale-wife: Women and brewing in fourteenth-century England', in Hanawalt, ed., *Women and Work*, pp. 20–38, and in 'Misogyny, popular culture, and women's work', *History Workshop Journal*, **31**, 1991, 166–88.

49. Bennett, 'The village ale-wife'.

50. Peter Mathias, *The Brewing Industry in England 1700–1830*, Cambridge: Cambridge University Press, 1959.

51. Barron, 'Golden age', p. 48.

52. See examples cited in Barron, 'Golden age', and Lacey, 'Women and work'.

53. Nancy Adamson found seventy-three agreements involving female apprentices in late-sixteenth-century London; see her dissertation, 'Urban families: The social context of the London elite, 1500–1603', Dissertation, University of Toronto, 1983, pp. 245–50. Barron in 'Golden age', p. 48, cites V. B. Elliott's finding of no agreements involving female apprentices between 1570 and 1640; I can only assume that Adamson's work covered companies not examined by Elliott.

54. Francis B. Bickley, ed., *The Little Red Book of Bristol*, II, Bristol: W. C. Hemmons, 1900, pp. 127–8.

55. For an example of a fourteenth-century restriction, see Adamson, 'Urban families', p. 238 (girdlers of London in 1344). For the short-term purposes of such ordinances, see Wright, 'Churmaids', p. 106 and Steve Rappaport, *Worlds within worlds: Structures of life in sixteenth-century London*, Cambridge: Cambridge University Press, 1989, pp. 38–9.

56. For the silkworkers of London, see Marian K. Dale, 'The London silkwomen of the fifteenth century', *Economic History Review*, **4**, 1933, 324–35, and Walter B. Stern, 'The trade, art or mistery of silk throwers of the City of London in the seventeenth century', *The Guildhall Miscellany*, vol. 1, no. 6, 1956, 25–30. The only suggestion of a female guild in England (and a weak one at that) is a set of ordinances enacted by Southampton for its female woolpackers in 1503. See typescript available from the Southampton City Archives of text found in the Second Book of Remembrance, SC2/1/4 f. 26v–8r.

57. For a fuller elaboration of many of the points made in this paragraph, see Maryanne Kowaleski and Judith M. Bennett, 'Crafts, gilds, and women in the Middle Ages: Fifty years after Marian K. Dale', *Signs*, **14**, 1989, 474–88.

58. For example, although some guild ordinances suggest the involvement of women in the use of the phrase 'brothers and sisters', the ordinances of other

guilds mention only 'brothers'. For examples, see the selected ordinances printed in Toulmin Smith, ed., *English Guilds*, Early English Text Society 40, London: Trübner, 1870. In Exeter, for example, the ordinances of the tailors mention only 'brothers'; those of the bakers mention 'brothers and sisters' (pp. 312–16, 334–7). Lucy Toulmin Smith interpreted the language of these ordinances with excessive optimism, noting in her introduction to the volume (p. xxx): 'Scarcely five out of five hundred were not formed equally of men and of women.'

59. Rappaport has found, for example, that women (mostly widows) constituted less than 2 per cent of those who engaged apprentices in sixteenth-century London, *Worlds*, p. 41. Widows constituted some 5 per cent of the membership of York's bakers' and weavers' guilds, *c.*1560–1700 (see Willen, 'Guilds-women', p. 218).

60. M. M. Postan, 'The famulus: The estate labourer in the XIIth and XIIIth centuries', *Economic History Review*, supplement 2, 1954; Middleton, 'Familiar fate'.

61. I extracted wages paid *specifically* to males or females from the data listed in James E. Thorold Rogers, *A History of Agriculture and Prices in England, Vol. II: 1259–1400*, Oxford: Oxford University Press, 1866, pp. 273–334. Between 1262 and 1350, women received three farthings (¾*d.*) to a penny (1*d.*) per day (usually for planting or gathering); men received a penny-halfpenny (1½*d.*) to tuppence-halfpenny (2½*d.*) per day (usually for digging). Between 1350 and 1400, women received a penny (1*d.*) to tuppence (2*d.*); men received tuppence (2*d.*) to threepence (3*d.*). On the continent, women were also paid roughly two-thirds of men's wages before the plague, and roughly three-fourths in the decades immediately after. See the work of G. d'Avenal as cited in Shulamith Shahar, *The Fourth Estate*, London: Methuen, 1983, pp. 198–9.

62. For the seventeenth century, see Roberts, 'Sickles', p. 19, and Shammas, 'Women workers', pp. 110–11. For the nineteenth century, see comment of Thorold Rogers in *A History, Vol. I*, p. 274 that wages paid female agricultural workers before the plague were 'relatively as good' as those paid nineteenth-century female farm workers. Wage differentials have, of course, waxed and waned over time. Arthur Young's wage rates for the eighteenth century show women paid only about one-third the rate paid to men (see Eric Richards, 'Women in the British economy since about 1700: An interpretation', *History*, 59, 1974, 341). Perhaps more important than the actual ratio of wages for 'women's work' to wages for 'men's work' is the simple fact of the ratio; since the High Middle Ages (and perhaps before), wages for 'women's work' have – with few exceptions – not equalled wages for 'men's work'.

63. Dorothea Oschinsky, ed., *Walter of Henley and Other Treatises on Estate Management and Accounting*, Oxford: Oxford University Press, 1971, p. 427.

64. Lord Beveridge, 'Westminster wages in the manorial era', *Economic History Review*, 2nd ser., 8, 1955, p. 34. See also Rodney Hilton, 'Women in the village', pp. 102–3; Hanawalt, 'Women's contribution', p. 11; Penn, 'Female wage-earners'.

65. Penn, 'Female wage-earners', p. 9. Penn's numbers for the Pocklington wages do not tally. He claims that wages paid to thirty-three reapers are listed, but his

breakdown – that two men were paid at fourpence (4*d.*), (plus board), that nine women were paid fourpence (4*d.*), (plus board), and that twenty-one women were paid threepence (3*d.*), (plus board) – totals to only thirty-two.

66. J. E. Thorold Rogers, *A History of Agriculture and Prices in England, Vol. III: 1401–1582*, Oxford: Oxford University Press, 1882, p. 585.

67. Even Beveridge notes, p. 34 of 'Westminster wages', that 'for the most part women were used for special kinds of work' (i.e. that most women worked at tasks designated specifically as 'women's work' that were paid at different wage rates). The poll-tax evidence discussed above suggests the same; most women worked in female occupations that were usually paid less than comparable male occupations.

68. Penn, 'Female wage-earners'.

69. Rappaport, *Worlds*, pp. 38–9. See also Sue Wright's observation that the 1461 Bristol weavers' order against the work of women was followed two years later by an ordinance urging women to work in support of their husbands, 'Churmaids', p. 106.

70. Our estimates about the numbers of wage-earning persons in the late-medieval population are expanding, but even our highest estimates indicate that only a minority of persons were so engaged; perhaps as much as one-third of the populace worked for wages at least occasionally. Only a minority of these wage-workers would have been women; perhaps one in every four wage-earners (or fewer). See Simon A. C. Penn and Christopher Dyer, 'Wages and earnings in late medieval England: Evidence from the enforcement of the labour laws', *Economic History Review*, 2nd ser., **43**, 1990, 356–76. Similarly, our estimates of the urban population, although also growing, still suggest a largely rural population; perhaps as many as one in six persons lived in towns. See Christopher Dyer, 'The past, the present and the future in medieval rural history', *Rural History*, **1**, 1990, 47. See also Paul Bairoch, 'Urbanization and the economy of preindustrial societies: The findings of two decades of research', *Journal of European Economic History*, **18**, 1989, 239–90.

71. Goldberg, 'Female labour, service', p. 35. Goldberg estimates that the population of York in 1377 was perhaps 12,000, and that sustained growth did not occur until the middle of the next century: 'Mortality', 49–50. Between 1400 and 1449, 4,870 persons were admitted to the freedom of York: see E. Miller, 'Medieval York', in *The Victoria History of the Counties of England: City of York*, P. M. Tillott, ed., London: Oxford University Press, 1961, p. 86.

72. Barron, in 'Golden age', n. 76, dismisses bleak assessments of women's work status by noting that 'working conditions were rarely golden for men in the middle ages'.

73. Two curiosities about the liberal feminism behind this interpretive framework are worth noting. First, the role of Marxist historiography in supporting the paradigm of a great transition is largely indirect. It motivated some early authoritative work in the field (especially the work of Clark and Kelly), but it does not lie behind the arguments of Barron, Goldberg, Hanawalt, *et al.* Second, although the political impact of this framework within women's history supports a liberal feminist perspective, it is, of course, part of a master narrative whose politics are much more conservative. See Patterson, 'On the

margin'. My own framework, which focuses on continuities that run across major economic shifts, suggests that women's condition can be improved only through major structural changes, indeed through changes of a revolutionary nature.

74. Although I cannot explore other areas of women's history in detail here, similar anomalies afflict the paradigm from other perspectives. Consider, for example, the continuities being sketched in the history of family life and family formation which I outlined at the beginning of this essay. For the history of women, these particular criticisms of the master narrative have special meaning. Continuities in familial relations suggest that affection within families – an absolutely central institution for women's lives – might have varied over time (as well as across classes and regions), but was not transformed between 1300 and 1700. And the possible existence of the 'European Marriage Pattern' as early as the fourteenth century suggests that women's experiences of celibacy, singleness and marriage were also not transformed over these centuries.

75. For the purposes of this essay, I have confined my observations to continuities across the medieval/early-modern divide. But we should certainly look harder at continuities that extend beyond the confines of these centuries – going back earlier than 1300 and extending beyond 1700. For example, Peter Earle noted of the occupations of women in London, *c.*1700 that they are 'very similar to that revealed by the 1851 census' (see 'Female labour market', pp. 341–2). For another example, Maxine Berg concluded her recent study of women's work in the early phases of industrialisation by noting that the notion of a 'great transition in women's working lives with the advent of industrialization' might be 'a chimera of simplistic linear notions', in 'Women's work', p. 91.

76. Judith M. Bennett, 'Feminism and history', *Gender and History*, 1, 1989, 251–72.

77. I have offered some preliminary thought about such a historical approach in my article on 'Misogyny, popular culture, and women's work'. See also my comments at a panel on 'What should women's history be doing?' at the Eighth Berkshire Conference on Women's History, printed in a forthcoming issue of the *Newsletter of the Coordinating Committee for Women in the Historical Profession*, 21 (5), 1990, 18–20.

A Whisper in the Ear of
Early Modernists; or,
Reflections on Literary
Critics Writing the
'History of the Subject'*

David Aers

Et inde admonitus redire ad memet ipsum, intravi in intima
mea, duce te, et potui, quoniam factus es adiutor meus.

And thence being admonished to return to my own self, I
entered into my innermost being, you being my leader; and
I could because you were become my helper.[1]

The key issue is not interiority, since inner repentance is essential in both public penance, which was introduced in the third
century, and private penance, which made its initial appearance
in the sixth. . . . From the twelfth century on codified penitentials appeared, and, in the thirteenth, case-books of conscience.[2]

The reflections offered here concern an influential 'history of the subject',
a history of what its writers variously call the 'humanist subject', 'the
liberal humanist subject', 'the essentialist humanist subject' or the 'bourgeois subject'. It is the history of how interiority and the subjectivity to
which that belongs emerged in Western culture, an emergence that can, so
its cultural historians maintain, be quite precisely located – the time of
Shakespeare. Indeed, for some of these writers, the decisive transitional

* An earlier and shorter version of this essay was published in *Literature and History*, **2**,
Autumn 1991.

moment can be adequately represented by *Hamlet*. The history in question is taken for granted in many articles, books and students' essays, with critics such as those I shall address being cited as authorities who have demonstrated its veracity. These authorities tend to present themselves as 'radical' critics, radical in terms of traditional literary studies (whether older historicisms or old formalisms) and radical in political sympathies. The kind of radicalism varies according to the particular mix of deconstruction, cultural anthropology, neo-Marxism, psychoanalysis and Foucault (especially prominent is *Discipline and Punish*), but all its varieties, on both sides of the Atlantic, are explicitly anti-humanist and devotedly anti-essentialist.[3]

My present reflections were prompted by observing a convergence between the story being told by current radical criticism and a familiar story that had once been told in a school of medieval studies which prided itself on its conservatism. The convergence between radical criticism and the extremely influential current of medievalism which called itself 'historical criticism', flourishing through the 1950s into the early 1970s, and still not quite extinct, seemed puzzling. After all, that phase of medieval criticism had proved especially inhospitable to the study of social power and its relations to medieval institutions and texts, both sacred and secular. It rejected attempts to explore the relevance of concepts and empirical material drawn from the study of economic history, politics, ideology-formation, psychoanalysis and studies in the cultural construction of gender and gender's relation to forms of power/knowledge. Characteristic of its position is the now classic formulation in D. W. Robertson's *Preface to Chaucer*:

> the medieval world was innocent of our profound concern for tension. . . . We project dynamic polarities on history as class struggles, balances of power, or as conflicts between economic realities and traditional ideals. . . . But the medieval world with its quiet hierarchies knew nothing of these things.[4]

Centuries of Christian traditions, an extraordinarily diversified, complex and profoundly adaptive culture of discourses and practices, was thus turned into a homogeneous, static and uncomplicated monolith. The key to this monolith and its literatures was the *Glossa ordinaria* and texts gathered in Migne's *Patrologia latina*. These themselves became decontextualised ghosts, conjured up from some strange and undifferentiated limbo. All medieval literature propagated 'o sentence' which was 'of course also the message of the Bible': such univocality and homogeneity, we were assured, was all 'the medieval reader' knew or expected.[5] This hardly seems likely company for contemporary radical critics. Nor would the historical motives, described by Derek Pearsall, seem at all compatible with these critics' stance:

> deeply disturbed by certain developments in modern society, particularly those that tended towards moral relativism, the proponents of the historical criticism

had no hesitation in setting up their interpretation of the Middle Ages not merely as historically correct, but as a model of a superior society and culture, suitable for the correction of a depraved age. Non-medievalists will often express their surprise that the historical criticism, which seems to them a naive form of homiletics at best, has exerted such a powerful influence in North America (it has had very little influence in England). The explanation must be in some such terms as those outlined above: the seeking of an expression in the Middle Ages of traditional American values of domestic and social hierarchy, prompted by shock at the threat to those values.[6]

The history of this school of criticism, including its institutional and political history, has been examined in Lee Patterson's *Negotiating the Past*.[7] While there is no need to go over ground he has covered so admirably, I do wish to outline certain features in this criticism which I have found particularly relevant to my reflections on its convergence with current radical histories of the subject.

These features can be gathered under the general term *amnesia*. It is something that concerned Frank Lentricchia in his study of tradition in *Criticism and Social Change*. During his discussion he considers a passage from *European Literature and the Latin Middle Ages* in which Curtius described Western literature as representing the best of which 'the European mind' has been capable, a beautiful reality above and beyond politics, economy and society. In a definition Lentricchia finds 'astounding' the great medievalist noted that 'Much must be forgotten if the essential is to be preserved.'[8] One sees why Lentricchia is perturbed, although we should understand Curtius as attempting to salvage what he valued in the face of the Nazi catastrophe. And Curtius acknowledged, however unsatisfactorily, the way his version of 'the European mind' and its production of 'beauty' actually depended on cultivating amnesia. Exegetical critics, however, made no such acknowledgement. Yet their 'historical criticism', which continued to influence medieval literary studies even when its allegorism had been abandoned, was the result of an amnesia systematic and institutionalised. Building a version of culture from prescriptive texts, not only did they reduce Christian traditions to a static monolith, as we noted, they repressed the sustained struggles of tenants and labourers against landlords and employers in late-medieval England together with the heterogeneity of experience and values in different late-medieval communities, languages and rituals. Repressed too, most significantly, were the 'systems of exchange and communication, equally effective in economic, social and cultural relations' developing from the early *twelfth* century, a development in which, Brian Stock notes, 'commodities with a monetary value emerged as the chief force for objectifying economic conditions'.[9] As I have argued elsewhere, these repressions have serious consequences for our understanding of late-medieval English writing. Their effects will be as misleading if they shape the version of the late Middle Ages in the works of those writing a history which claims to identify in the sixteenth century a new 'construction' of the subject and new socio-economic features which allegedly cause it. Indeed such serious repressions would tend to disqualify the whole claim to be writing history, whether described as 'Cultural Materialism' or 'New Historicism'. But before moving to the radical critics' Middle Ages I shall say a little more about the repressions at issue.[10]

We have available to us the fruits of a long tradition of research into the market in the commodities of international trade, their financing, production and exchange. This includes an impressively detailed literature on the extensive growth of markets and towns in the thirteenth century, on merchant oligarchies and their commodities – specialised studies, for example of English production and trade in such commodities as fur, wine, coal, iron, tin and building. This work shows decisively that by the end of the thirteenth century (thirteenth, not sixteenth), 'Communities of merchants, artisans, urban property owners and workers had become a powerful element in English society', forming a social network stimulating a self-interested, highly competitive and prudential outlook.[11] But commodity production was not confined to the few large medieval towns and the international markets in wool, wine, timber, grain and luxuries for the affluent. As Edward Miller and John Hatcher, among others, have shown, the thirteenth century witnessed 'the growth of a market economy' involving both a great intensification and a great extension of simple commodity production and exchange in rural England, a proliferation of those organised markets we know as small towns and villages, ones increasingly integrated in a national economy. Miller, Hatcher, Postan and other historians have shown how both gentry and peasant communities were drawn into the production of commodities for both local and international markets in the thirteenth century. There can be no good reason for literary critics to ignore this substantial work and its evidence, gathered, it should be noted, by historians of strikingly different ideological conviction. In this matter, the outstanding Marxist historian of the English peasantry, Rodney Hilton, is in accord with equally distinguished non-Marxist historians like Postan, Miller and Hatcher.[12] It seems to me important that literary scholars take note of the pre-capitalist market economy and explore what consequences it may have for their version of both the medieval period and the early-modern or, as many still say, 'Renaissance'. It is also high time we all assimilated the fact that there is no necessary incompatibility in medieval society between reliance on a family economy for subsistence and on the sale of surplus for cash – to buy commodities (manufactured goods, food, animals) and to pay money rents and taxes. Nor is there any necessary incompatibility between mercantile interests in the bigger towns and the interests of the magnates and gentry, the landed ruling classes of the later

Middle Ages. The basic estates ideology and its sustaining rituals were perfectly acceptable to the merchant classes of England and their public behaviour.[13] As Rodney Hilton has observed: 'No social problems for rich vintner's sons.'[14]

Turning away from issues of systematic amnesia concerning economic and social organisation, I wish now to consider an aspect of exegetical or 'historical' criticism which is also relevant to the convergence that has puzzled me, namely the way it was explicitly anti-humanist. This is perhaps hardly surprising. If a culture is spectacularly homogeneous, free from commodity production, free from economic instabilities, class conflicts, political struggles and free from any ideological contests, it is likely to be free as well from anything remotely resembling the versions of the individual and individual subjectivity taken for granted in later Western societies which were neither as homogeneous nor free from features such as those just mentioned. So it seemed reasonable for medievalists who accepted any version of this historical dichotomy to insist that 'realistic and motivational-psychological categories' are totally irrelevant to our understanding of all medieval literature and its cultures. Even in *Troilus and Criseyde*, rather unusual in many ways, there could be no good reason for talking about Chaucer's interest in 'individual psychologies'. To find *any* such interest in Chaucer, or Petrarch, or Hoccleve, or *Sir Gawain and the Green Knight*, or any other medieval writer, was merely to show one's benighted 'humanism', one's incorrigible 'anachronism'. For in that unified medieval world, so it was maintained, *all* figures were actually illustrations, types of universally shared moral and philosophic patterns. All writing was a version of the simplest homiletic *exemplum* in its representations of human beings. So Chaucer's Criseyde could in no way demonstrate any interest in individual subjectivity and inwardness, in a 'consciousness set over against that which it experiences'. No, she is in fact an emblem for the terms in a unified ideology universally and unproblematically assented to – for example, 'a way of saying something about . . . vanity', or about mutability . . . or incorrigible female carnality, in a work which figures forth the unambiguous message appropriate to a unitary culture free from anything remotely resembling the subjectivity invented by the products of that famous fall called the 'dissociation of sensibility' which set in during the seventeenth century.[15]

However, in a recent essay on postmodernism, history and medieval studies, Lee Patterson explicitly challenges this version of medieval writing, arguing that 'the dialectic between an inward subjectivity and an external world that alienates it from both itself and its divine source provides the fundamental economy of the medieval idea of the selfhood'. He points to this 'dialectic at work in a wide variety of texts and contexts', ranging through courtly romances, courtly lyrics, hagiographic writing, the use of penitential discourse in Langland and Gower, Petrarch's 'confessional

Augustinianism', Lollard confessions, Chaucer's *Troilus and Criseyde* and
his *Canterbury Tales*, concluding that 'To write the history of the medieval
subject is in effect to write the history of medieval culture.'[16]

This conclusion will probably seem sound to most medievalists not under
the vestigial influence of exegetical criticism. But I wish to take up Patterson's passing invocation of Petrarch's 'confessional Augustinianism'. I do so
because it points towards one of the most monumental pieces of amnesia in
the radical histories of the subject that initially prompted these reflections.
Perhaps this particular loss of memory is bound up with a general lack of
interest in specifically religious traditions that seems characteristic of both
'cultural materialism' and 'new historicism'; but whatever the explanation,
this will certainly be a decisive impediment in the attempt to compose a
history of the Western subject. As A. C. Spearing wrote about the *twelfth*
century, there then emerged 'a new focus on the inner landscape or subjectivity of the human being – new at least since St. Augustine's *Confessions*'
– and that 'knowing the inner core of human nature within oneself is an
explicit theme and preoccupation in literature of the period'. Spearing goes
on to comment: 'The sense of self was doubtless sharpened and pressed
towards articulation by the increasing possibility of choice among the
models, roles or groups to which people might attach themselves.'[17] It is
over this domain that I wish to pause before considering some examples of
the radical critics' history of the subject. It seems worth pausing here to
recall, however briefly, some of the resources within medieval Christian
traditions which should be particularly relevant to those writing this history
and the alleged rupture that occurs in the late sixteenth century. That this
reminder is needed will become clear when we consider the version of the
Middle Ages current in this influential criticism.

The place to which anyone seeking to write a history of interiority and the
subject must return is St Augustine's *Confessions*. Here passages of extra-
overt subject as for the very *lack* that it seems, on the surface, an attempt to re-
medy. Or the account in Book Four of his feelings at the death of his closest
friend, his tracing of their increasing bemusement as 'I became a great
riddle [*magna quaestio*] to myself', a riddle for whom the very recognition of
loss and inner fragmentation was the path to a saving self-knowledge.
Or analysis in Book Nine of the inward grief at his mother's death, the
description of how those to whom he spoke thought, judging as they did by
outward signs, that he was without sorrow even as he was feeling, and he
alone knew, a great agony in his heart. Or his analysis in Book Ten of his
description of how those to whom he spoke thought, judging as they did by
outward signs, that he was without sorrow even as he was feeling, and he
alone knew, a great agony in his heart. Or his analysis in Book Ten of his
erotic dreams after he becomes a priest and the way this analysis led to
questions about the basis of self-identity: 'Am I not myself [*ego non sum*] at

that time?' Or take the gripping account in Book Eight of his divided will laying waste to his soul, the sense of inner struggle in which he sought to break the bonds of custom, feeling bound not with external chains but an inner compulsion of the will.[18] But central to the *Confessions* is an approach that remains basic throughout the Augustinian tradition – in the Middle Ages as in the early-modern period. Namely, that the journey to God demands a move from the outer person to the inner, while in the very activity of an introspective search for self-knowledge we may hope to encounter God. The *Confessions* is replete with calls such as these: 'Turn again to your own heart. . . .'; 'Let them be turned back; and behold, thou art there in their heart, in the heart. . . .'; 'being hence admonished to return to myself, I entered even into mine own inwards [*intravi in intima mea*] thou being my Leader: . . . Into myself I went, and with the eyes of my soul (such as it was) I discovered . . . the unchangeable light of the Lord'. God, he writes, 'is both the light and the voice . . . of my inner man'.[19] The depths of our heart and memory remain mysterious, an abyss: yet there is, accord-ing to Augustine, a way, with grace and faith, in this abyss to the source of the self which will be discovered acting *in* our introspective exploration, the Trinity mirrored in the very structure of the soul, as the *De Trinitate* articulates at length.[20] As Charles Taylor observes in his magnificent study of the making of modern identity, it was Augustine 'who introduced the in-wardness of radical reflexivity and bequeathed it to the Western tradition'.[21]

Let us briefly recall the pervasive presence of this bequeathment in the fourteenth century. We have already noted Patterson's invocation of Petrarch: in his *Secretum* he chose St Augustine and the *Confessions* as the exemplar of his own experience of inner and wandering search, of his own emphasis on the role of the Will in this quest.[22] But Augustinian theology of inwardness also shapes the mystical tradition so powerfully articulated by Chaucer's contemporary Walter Hilton. Characteristic of *The Scale of Perfection* is a constant invitation to self-examination and an inward path in search of God: 'there is a work which is needful and speedful for to travail in. . . . And that is a man to enter into himself, for to know his own soul and the mights thereof, the fairness and the foulness of it.' In this 'inward beholding' Hilton expects people to find their fallen condition and 'a desire with great longing' to recover the image of God. In this inward movement, 'Thee behoveth for to delve deep in thine heart, for there He is hid. . . .' Hilton applies the parable of the woman and the lost coin (Luke 15.8–9) to his Augustinian version of quest: the coin is Jesus, the light is God's word and the search is an inward one. As he observes wryly, 'It needeth not run to Rome nor to Jerusalem for to seek Him there. But turn thy thought in thine own soul, where He is hid.'[23] This expresses very clearly the basic inner/ outer language, the inside/outside dichotomy of this tradition.[24] Certainly it points us to those areas of *Piers Plowman* which belong to the same tradition and make this dialectic between inner quest and search for external 'Rome or Jerusalem' absolutely central. For Langland the search for God is certainly bound up with the search for a just community and a reformed Church, a search constantly engaging with specific contemporary problems and conflicts. Yet *Piers Plowman* includes an exploration of the divided will and the need to turn inward if the sources of salvation are to be encountered. In his first instructions to the lost pilgrims Piers's outline of ethical and penitential forms of life culminates in the assurance that:

> if grace graunte thee to go in this wise
> Thow shalt see in thiselve truthe sitte in thyn herte
> In a cheyne of charite as thow a child were. . . .[25]

This is the corrective to his audience who, deeply moved by confession, cry out for 'grace to go to truthe' but searching for an external path, for a pilgrimage to Rome or Bethlehem, could find no way and 'blustreden forth as beestes' (V.506–36). The vision Piers offers fades and seems lost, but it re-emerges during Will's recovery from a stage in which he yielded up moral questions in despair, turning to hedonistic egotism:

> Clerkes kenne me that crist is in alle places
> Ac I saw hym nevere soothly but as myself in a Mirour.
>   (XV.161–2)

It is through the long confrontation with the divided subject that Will reaches the great visions of Charity, the Incarnation and salvation history, the visions which alone can sustain the *viator* in the face of a community and Church whose final representation is as bleak as the image of history with which Milton closes *Paradise Lost*.[26] A different, but related, attempt to develop responses to a Church deemed to be lost can be found in heretical movements, groups of individuals who made a *choice* (heresy) based on an individual decision to pursue a way of life which would usually challenge bonds of authority, lordship, kinship and community. As the early-fifteenth-century Norfolk Lollard Thomas Moneof Loddon declared, he and others 'ofte tymes have kept, holde, and continued scoles of heresie yn prive chambres and places of myne, yn the whiche scoles Y have herd, conceyved, lerned and reported the errours and heresies. . . .'[27] His wife, Hawisia, confirms this picture of individually chosen and risky meetings, 'yn prive chambres and prive places of oures'.[28] These choices could lead to a deep split between an *outward* conformity to the norms of Church and community and an *inward* dissent. For example, 'I feyned with myn hondys to honour it [the 'blessed sacrament'] . . . but my mynd and entent was nothyng therto'.[29] Such splits and such secrecy clash with certain widespread assumptions about the Middle Ages in early-modern criticism, as we shall illustrate.

There is no space here to draw any further attention to the many relevant works of the Middle Ages in either the Augustinian traditions of inwardness or in the various dissenting movements from the twelfth century onwards. I shall close this brief memorial excursus by turning to Chaucer. But instead of the poet who makes the dazzling exploration of subjectivity in *Troilus and Criseyde* or in many stages of *The Canterbury Tales*, I select a passage from the *Parson's Tale*. This is, as scholars have shown us, Chaucer's translation of thirteenth-century penitential manuals, and represents standard teaching developed in response to the immensely influential Fourth Lateran Council of 1215.[30] Why I mention this here is again to remind those seeking to describe what is 'new' in the late sixteenth century that it is necessary not only to engage seriously with medieval Augustinian traditions but to give as serious attention to one of the basic forms of 'personal religious formation' in the Middle Ages – private confession.[31] The importance of the version of self and inwardness it offered can hardly be over-emphasised, for as John Van Engen recently observed, 'Confession and penance shaped Christian faith and practice in all spheres of life, from the more overtly "spiritual" to matters of business (usury) and sexuality.'[32] The *Parson's Tale* stresses that contrition demands that a person search out (and show sorrow for) not only sinful actions but 'alle his synnes that he hath doon in delit of his thought'; it encourages careful self-scrutiny concerning the nature of the inward 'consentynges' given in such movements of individual consciousness. The teacher carefully emphasises that attention to external actions, to 'outward' deeds, is not remotely adequate. He warns that self-scrutiny, confession and repentance must address the most intimate movements of thought, con- trition leading to a 'wonder sorweful and angwissous' response. But this should certainly not be an occasional activity. The focus on the individual's inner life, affections and thoughts needs to be a *continual* process integrated in the individual's very self-identity: 'contricioun moste be continueel'.[33] Plainly enough, the whole medieval penitential tradition involves a funda- mental and perfectly explicit distinction between *inner* and *outer*, between that which is within and passes show and that which is without, the external act. Furthermore, this material was basic Christian instruction in the later Middle Ages: it is the opposite to esoteric. I do stress this because it will be well to keep it in mind as we consider certain current claims about Shakespeare and his moment which I shall be exemplifying.

What I have been pointing towards in medieval Christian tradition can be endlessly demonstrated in devotional, mystical and instructional works as well as in more exploratory religious poetry such as *Piers Plowman*: it can also be paralleled in the equally characteristic dramatisations of subjectivity, inward examination and soliloquy in courtly romances and lyrics, as Lee

Patterson has observed and others have shown.[34] There is no reason to think
that languages and experiences of inwardness, of interiority, of divided selves,
of splits between outer realities and inner forms of being, were unknown
before the seventeenth century, before capitalism, before the 'bourgeoisie',
before Descartes, before the disciplinary regimes addressed in Foucault's
Discipline and Punish. This is certainly not to deny that decisive changes
occurrred in Western societies between the seventeenth and nineteenth
centuries: capitalism, the Industrial Revolution, the Enlightenment, the
mechanisation of Nature from which the 'ontic logos' was expelled.[35] All
these, in so many different ways, worked to transform our planet, our self-
understanding and our societies. But any account that tells us stories of
transformations, whether in the 'construction of the subject' or in production for markets, will have to describe with great care, let me say it again,
precisely that against which it is being alleged the changes are identifiable as
decisive changes and ruptures. This is an elementary demand. How this
basic logical and historical demand is being met by the radical historians of
the subject I shall now consider.

Let us return to the convergence between idealist mythologies concerning medieval cultures, propagated by the conservative school of exegetical
or 'historical' criticism, and the version of the Middle Ages assumed by
radical critics writing about early-modern England and the history of the
subject. Claims that are characteristic of those I have in mind are found in
Francis Barker's *The Tremulous Private Body*.[36] He argues that in the 'pre-
bourgeois' political order the individualised 'subject' was utterly unknown.
For Barker subjectivity begins to emerge only in and around Shakespeare,
in his 'transitional and contradictory *oeuvre*'. In late-medieval culture, so he
asserts, there was simply no 'interiorized self-recognition'. This alleged fact
is not surprisingly unsubstantiated by analysis of any of the medieval
writings mentioned in this essay, by, say, Margery Kempe's Book, or
Chaucer's work (say, *Troilus and Criseyde*, *Canterbury Tales* or *Book of the
Duchess*), or *Piers Plowman*, or Petrarch's *Secretum*. Instead it is explained by
another alleged fact, namely, that in medieval culture individual identity
simply did not involve individual self-consciousness since that polity did
not produce or need to produce such individuated subjects. Because claims
such as Barker's have gained such currency in 'Renaissance' criticism it is
worth exemplifying them at some length:

> Pre-bourgeois subjection does not properly involve subjectivity at all, but a
> condition of dependent membership in which place and articulation are defined
> not by an interiorized self-recognition – complete or partial, percipient or un-
> knowing, efficient or rebellious – (of none the less socially constituted subject-
> positions), but by incorporation in the body politic which is the king's body in its
> social form. With a clarity now hard to recapture, the social plenum *is* [Barker's
> italics] the body of the king and membership of this anatomy is the deep
> structural form of all being in the secular realm.

With a clarity hard to recapture, indeed! Hard or not, having 'recaptured' this vision it is plain that only those who read the medieval past to fit an utterly anachronistic 'bourgeois' or 'humanist' version of subjectivity and the individual will find anything that can be acknowledged as 'subjectivity', as 'interiorized self-recognition' before around 1600. Before that time, if only we join Barker in laying aside our post-Cartesian, humanist and bourgeois blinkers, our 'modern subjectivity', we will see that human beings were totally 'incorporated' in the 'body politic', incorporated in the 'social plenum', which '*is*', Barker stresses, 'the body of the king' structurally determining 'all' social existence. There could not be any 'interiorized self-recognition' in this totalised and homogeneous culture.

Between this version of pre-Shakespearean, pre-Cartesian, pre-humanist culture and that propagated by the exegetical critics discussed above many continuities are clear. Although now in Foucauldian costume, the basic picture is still of a static homogeneous collective in which there simply could not be any self-conscious concern with individual identity or subjectivity because these could simply not exist in that society. Much less could there be any problematisation of individual identity and mobility, any exploration of different forms of order in voluntary associations, or any conflicts concerning authority and rights in social and ecclesiastical institutions.

In fact, Barker's 'clarity' is 'recaptured' at the cost of all we now know about late-medieval societies, cultures and polities (both ecclesiastical and secular), but it is necessary to stay with his history of the subject a little longer. He claims that only when we reach the second scene of *Hamlet* do we even begin to glimpse what he calls 'a separation . . . between the inner reality of the subject' and an 'exterior'. The decisive indicator of this world-historically significant moment, enacted at the Globe around 1600, is when the play-acting Hamlet reminds his mother that he has 'that within that passeth show'. Here, claims the radical critic, 'an interior subject begins to speak'. But only begins. Barker emphasises that this is a crucial beginning, that this moment in *Hamlet* is historically 'premature': true enough, subjectivity has entered the world but 'emergent only in promissory form'. For those who study the range of medieval materials invoked above, it will be surprising to see such a big deal made of Hamlet observing he has 'that within that passeth show'. Such a reader will wonder just what Barker, and those who reproduce similar views, have actually studied with any real attention before Shakespeare.[37] Suffice it here just to recall an English poem written well over two hundred years before *Hamlet*, Chaucer's *Troilus and Criseyde*. In that long poem the last two books display a man whose sense of 'separation', to use the radical critic's terms, between his 'inner reality' and what he feels as 'exterior' leads him to immense pain, chronic melancholy and the proposal to abandon his historical community. The same tension is explored in the treatment of Criseyde in Book Five. We would do well to recall, indeed, how so often in that poem Troilus and Criseyde are *alone* . . .

are soliloquising . . . are aware of a sense of tension, of 'separation', between their 'inner reality' and the norms, forms and commitments of the class and community in terms of which, of course, they have individual identity. *If* there is any reason for trying to write a linear 'history of the subject', it certainly cannot be done on Barker's lines, with his materials, or with his periodisation of English culture, a periodisation determined by ideological factors he never addresses.

In the same year as *The Tremulous Private Body* entered the scene, another radical critic, Jonathan Dollimore, published a stimulating book on 'the drama of Shakespeare and his contemporaries' (now republished in a second edition). This influential book celebrates the forthcoming and final death of the humanist subject and of 'essentialist humanism', now at the end of a historical existence which began in the seventeenth century and will be superseded by 'decentred subjectivity', the 'declared objective' of the author's anti-humanism. This 'anti-humanism' and its rather obscure social and political teleology is part of a project which, according to Dollimore, involves a 'materialist conception of subjectivity', a 'challenge' to all 'the residual categories of . . . idealist culture' – one that will deliver past literature from the misrepresentations of 'essentialist humanism'.[38] For him too the time of Shakespeare is a distinct period of major cultural 'transition' in English history. This crucial transition is between the Middle Ages, described as the period of 'Christian essentialism' and the mid-seventeenth century onwards, described as the period of 'essentialist humanism' of which conventional literary criticism is the 'idealist' product. In the preface added to the 1989 edition of his book he elaborates this theme, writing of the Renaissance as the 'displacement of the metaphysical (divine/natural law) by the social. The contradictions of history flood the space vacated by metaphysics. Correspondingly, the metaphysically constituted subject suddenly becomes a decentred, contradictory subjectivity.'[39] It seems a little odd to find a self-styled 'cultural materialist' defining a historical period, marked by dynamic changes and conflicts in its economic, social, ecclesiastic and philosophic dimensions, in such distinctly *non*-materialist categories as 'Christian essentialism' and as a culture where the 'social' is completely dissolved into the 'metaphysical'. It is just this kind of categorisation that has been a basic part of the conservative critical ideology that shaped the deeply idealist version of the Middle Ages dominating exegetical criticism through the 1950s into the 1970s – as we observed. But, leaving aside the strange political twists in this convergence, what are the hallmarks of the medieval era, of this undifferentiated 'Christian essentialism'? *Radical Tragedy* gives an answer with which Robertson's or Barker's readers will be familiar: in that period 'what mattered was . . . not the individual but society, the corpus of all individuals', one in which the 'conception of identity' can apparently be satisfactorily described 'as hierarchical location'.[40] Once again we encounter a peculiarly dematerialising and idealist version of medieval culture and society against which supposedly major cultural changes in Shakespeare's England can be identified and understood. So undifferentiated is this culture that it and its versions of subjectivity can apparently be adequately represented by two morality plays.[41]

A year after *Radical Tragedy* Catherine Belsey published a book whose 'main aims' were headed by the wish 'to contribute to the construction of a history of the subject in the sixteenth and seventeenth centuries'. In this history the central figure is 'liberal humanism' which, so she maintains, is 'the consensual orthodoxy of the west', one running back from the worlds of F. A. Hayek and Margaret Thatcher to . . . the great bard himself. The 'emergence of the individual', bound up with the emergence of 'a market economy' and 'liberal humanism', can be confidently located in the seventeenth century. As in Francis Barker's study, Shakespeare once more turns out to be the crucial transitional figure, and, within his works, 'The classic case is, of course, Hamlet.'[42] Explicitly following *The Tremulous Private Body*, Belsey too finds Act One, scene two of *Hamlet* the perfect illustration of the new subject and the new 'interiority' just emerging in world history. It is manifested in 'Hamlet's assertion of an authentic inner reality defined by its difference from an inauthentic exterior'. So new is this 'interiority', she claims, that it cannot be sustained for the whole play. In Act Five, 'Hamlet utters no soliloquies, makes no further efforts to define the nobler course, ceases to struggle with and between reason and revenge, readily surrenders to providence (v, ii, 212–13) and the "divinity that shapes our ends" (v, ii, 10)'.

From this shift in the dramatic fiction Belsey assumes it is legitimate to read off a historically and culturally significant message of great range: 'This Hamlet [the one of Act Five] is an inhabitant of a much older cosmos, no more than the consenting instrument of God, received into heaven at his death by flights of angels.'[43] He is, of course, now the inhabitant of that homogeneous Age of Faith, that world without individual subjectivities, without soliloquisings, without 'interiorities' and without 'the individual'. Now this kind of move is familiar in the versions of cultural history habitually produced by those trained as literary critics: from a moment in a particular fiction the critic moves to wide generalisations about the history of Europe supposedly displayed in the fictive moment. In the particular case of Hamlet's performance in Act Five at least two points need making. First, there are good and sufficient reasons to give for Hamlet's abstention from soliloquy which are totally independent of the supposed cultural history Belsey invokes – Peter Erickson, for example, has given some of these in his important study of Shakespeare's drama.[44] Second, and this cannot be over-emphasised, soliloquies and concern with inward states of being are abundant in courtly literature from Chrétien to *Sir Gawain and the Green Knight* or Chaucer's *Troilus and Criseyde*; and, to repeat, such concerns were a fundamental aspect of mysticism and the literature of self-examination and self-fashioning in late-medieval culture.

Nevertheless, Belsey maintains that any sense of division between 'individual and society, private and public, family and state' is entirely and exclusively the product of the 'liberal humanist' ideology that emerged in the seventeenth century and has reigned ever since in the West.[45] Culture, society and human subjectivity before then can be satisfactorily represented, apparently, by two fifteenth-century morality plays – surprisingly enough, precisely the same two morality plays that stand in for the Middle Ages in *Radical Tragedy*.[46] These two plays allegedly justify the global claims so familiar in literary criticism's 'history of the subject': 'In the fifteenth century the representative human being has no unifying essence . . . no single subjectivity . . . is not a subject' – subjects and subjectivity were the invention of the seventeenth century.[47] Why the historian of the subject should select two morality plays to represent 'the representative human being' before the seventeenth century is never explained, nor is the startling absence of *comparison* with other genres of medieval writing to test out the broad scope of the claims being made. Belsey's justification for this absence (although the issue is not articulated) seems to be the fact that 'any single contribution to the history of the subject has to start somewhere'.[48] While this claim is uncontestable, it does not entail the absence of any comparison of representations of the subject in other genres and contexts. Yet it is on the dangerously narrow base of two texts from one genre that Belsey builds her 'history' of change through the transitional Shakespearean play into the 'Classic realist theatre' of the Restoration where for the first time in Western history one finds 'unified subjects'. They, we are told, reflect the 'imaginary unity' of the new bourgeois subject.[49] The Middle Ages, she insists, certainly knew absolutely nothing of the 'unified subjects' who stepped on to the world-historical stage in the seventeenth century. Indeed, the cultural historian can apparently date their birth with great precision. The bourgeois subject, the new unified subject of 'liberal humanism', is the 'effect of the revolution'. By this she means the seventeenth-century civil war and within that war a particular event in 1649 – the execution of the king whose widely unpopular ecclesiastic, political, fiscal and legal choices had pushed large sectors of the ruling elites into opposition and, reluctantly, war. The execution of Charles, Belsey says, is 'the moment when the bourgeoisie is installed as the ruling class'. From here alone do we find a version of the human being with 'interiority', a being who is now defined through 'consciousness'. Here 'the history of the subject' is read off or tied to the most schematic Marxist chronology of the transition from feudalism to capitalism, the transition from a supposedly feudal ruling class to a supposedly bourgeois ruling class 'installed' in 1649.[50] This is a very simple view of sixteenth- and seventeenth-century political, religious, economic and social history, one to which no practising seventeenth-century historian could subscribe. What is relevant here, however, is the way that, once more, a radical history of the subject reproduces a version of the pre-seventeenth-century past propagated by an exceptionally idealist and conservative sector of literary studies. It is a sign of how entrenched her account has become that her recent book on John Milton makes just the same claims about the history of the subject, a version of 'history' which is used to locate Milton's work – and one which is content to cite her own book on *The Subject of Tragedy* as the authority that has established its validity.[51]

Here I wish to mention the tendency in current literary criticism known as the New Historicism. The literature analysing the theoretical and political premises of this project is now substantial and includes much astute and stimulating commentary.[52] All that need concern us now, however, is its relationship to the present argument. And here, despite other major theoretical and political differences, there is little significant disagreement. It is undoubtedly true that New Historicism or Cultural Poetics lacks the interests of Cultural Materialism in diachrony and prefers to treat the objects of its attention as elements in a synchronic system of, to use Greenblatt's favoured images, circulating and negotiating energies.[53] Despite this, its practitioners conceive what they habitually call the Renaissance as, in Jean Howard's words, 'a boundary or liminal space between two or more monolithic periods'.[54] It is in relation to the medieval monolith that the allegedly new subjectivity of 'Renaissance self-fashioning' is to be defined. Only in the sixteenth century do we begin to meet self-conscious self-fashioning subjects concerned with an interiority simultaneously 'constituted' (in Foucauldian ideology) by the power of the Tudor state.[55] It is appropriate enough that the most influential book yet produced in this critical tendency should open its eloquent pages with this statement: 'My subject is *self-fashioning* from More to Shakespeare; my starting point is quite simply that in sixteenth-century England there were both selves and a sense that they could be fashioned.' A nod in the direction of Chaucer's 'subtle and wry manipulations of *persona*' is followed by the claim that in the sixteenth century we find 'a change in the intellectual, social, psychological and aesthetic structures that govern the generation of identities', at least an 'increased self-consciousness about the fashioning of human identity as a manipulable, artful process'. This the author finds antithetical to 'Christianity' and Augustine.[56] To meet the elementary demand entailed by such claims about 'change', the critic, Stephen Greenblatt, would need to offer some serious engagement with the state of affairs in relation to which the sixteenth century involves a major 'change'. Yet, as Lee Patterson has observed, this is never even attempted: 'the book – and, so far as I can tell, all of Greenblatt's writing – is innocent of any discussion of any writer prior to Sir Thomas More'.[57] As in Cultural Materialism, New Historicism turns the Middle Ages into a homogeneous and mythical field which is defined in terms of the scholars' needs for a figure against which 'Renaissance' concerns with inwardness and the fashioning of identities can be defined as new. (And at the leading edge of ever-revolutionary consumerism, what that does not represent 'change' and the new could deserve our attention?) It is not, of course, the first time that medieval culture has been used in these ways, used as a figure against which to affirm an identity. As Brian Stock writes in *Listening for the Text*:

> The Renaissance invented the Middle Ages in order to define itself: the Enlighten-ment perpetuated them in order to admire itself; and the Romantics revived them in order to escape from themselves. In their widest ramifications 'the Middle Ages' thus constitute one of the most prevalent cultural myths of the modern world.[58]

So the 'history of the subject' produced by Cultural Materialists and New Historicists seems committed to reproducing aspects of the ideology which gave us the term 'Renaissance'.[59] This is hardly a satisfactory way to go about writing the history of what is allegedly a major transformation in Western mentalities and societies.

I shall now round off my brief illustration of current radical histories of the subject and the representations of the late Middle Ages in England to which this account is committed. Without some version of the pre-seventeenth-century past there could plainly not be a 'history', and the diachronic pretensions of such criticism would have to be completely abandoned. They are certainly not abandoned in the work to which I now refer, work done by Britain's most distinguished writer of literary theory. The book is a reading of Shakespeare by Terry Eagleton, published in 1986. It concludes with an account of the late-medieval world against which we are to set Shakespeare and his epoch. The move seems a retrospective one designed to give us some historical explanation of just how the post-structuralist understanding of language and meaning which Eagleton finds in Shakespeare's plays should have appeared in a group of works written around 1600. It turns out that the historical process which made Shakespeare and his time so significantly transitional is the answer. It is the uncertainties of the transition between different socio-economic formations that prompted Shakespeare to see, for example, that 'perception is itself a text'; to see 'Reality itself' as a 'kind of blank'; a 'nothing', one which 'can be abolished only by the supplementary benefit of language' – although 'language itself can be a sort of nothing'. As in the accounts of other radical critics mentioned in this essay, 'Hamlet is a radically transitional figure'. He is 'strung out between a traditional social order . . . and a future epoch made of achieved bourgeois individualism'. Indeed, 'Hamlet signifies the beginnings of the dissolution of the old feudalist subject who is as yet, however, unable to name himself affirmatively in any other way'. Typical of such cultural history, it remains extremely unclear who 'the old feudalist subject' actually is, who it is represented by and just how she or he should still exist in the England of 1600, by no stretch of even *that* protean term a 'feudal' society. Nor is it only *Hamlet* that displays the great transition from 'the old feudalist subject' to 'bourgeois subject'. Other plays and figures do so too: for example, Lady Macbeth turns out to be 'a bourgeois individualist' allegedly pursuing 'private ends' peculiar to the bourgeoisie, while Coriolanus, to this reader's surprise, is 'perhaps Shakespeare's most developed study of a bourgeois individualist'.[60] (One of the many commonplace but quite mistaken assumptions in such assertions is that competitive assertiveness and competitive forms of individualism were alien to pre-seventeenth-century culture and to those whose class position could not be classified as 'bourgeois': the specific relations, motivations, ethos and politics of 'honourmen' seem quite hidden from such 'Renaissance' critics.)[61] Terry Eagleton concludes by spelling out the premises on which such claims about Shakespeare and the great transition depend. The pre-Shakespearean 'traditional feudal social order', he maintains,

> is founded on ties of physical kinship, the sacredness of the king's physical presence, and forms of labour and social relations which are less 'abstract' than those of capitalist production. The typical economic product of feudalism, for example, is less abstract than that of capitalism because it is not a commodity on the market.

In this 'traditional' world production is for 'actual use value' and *not* for 'exchange value'.[62] Once more we encounter a model of late-medieval culture and society that converges perfectly with the idealist and grossly misleading model propagated by the literary medievalists considered earlier. No commodity production, no production for exchange value, no contractualism, no market relations, no voluntary religious associations, no political, ideological and cultural heterogeneity or conflict and, it would seem, no nuclear families. In this context certainly no individual subjectivities, no puzzled selves conscious of tensions between self and received norms, roles and expectations in changing communities. No Langland, no Petrarch, no Chaucer, no Margery Kempe, no Walter Hilton, no William Thorpe . . . and no need to bother with the work of such medieval historians as those mentioned earlier in this essay or with those engaged in studies of the social relations and conflicts around commodity production in specific communities.[63]

Indeed, as one reads the history of the subject propagated in such works it becomes striking that the Middle Ages is constructed with the odd quote from Kantorowicz or Ullmann but without mention of, let alone assimilation of, the work done by Hilton, Postan, Hatcher, Miller, Bolton, Razi, Dobson, MacIntosh, Hanawalt, Judith Bennett and the Toronto school . . . work done, that is, by those engaged with writing the histories of the economy, society and particular communities, classes and, increasingly, of specifically gendered experience in late-medieval England. Quite as remarkable is the lack of attention to the specificities and diversities of religious practices and writings. Lacking too is acknowledgement of the recent and relevant work of intellectual historians such as Tierney. Such omission is itself an indicator of the fundamental idealism in the methods of these ambitious cultural historians. It may also, perhaps, be an indication of a certain lack of scrupulousness in its treatment of both medieval culture and of religious experience in general, but in the current state of literary studies this seems to be no impediment to the acceptance of their basic historical thesis. Be this as it may, it seems worth stressing that Richard Levin's attack on these radical critics is wide of the mark when he treats them as exemplars of peculiarly Marxist methods of analysis.[64] Even Terry Eagleton's comments on modes of production and exchange seem no more than a dim memory of Marxist rhetoric since the terms he invokes have not guided his research into the history he writes or the texts he exegises. As I have pointed out, the cultural history in the 'history of the subject' we have been considering is grounded in an idealism which hardly seems the most distinguishing feature of a peculiarly Marxist historiography. Perhaps the puzzling facts of its continuities with myths about the Middle Ages fostered by conservative medievalists point rather to some common antecedents. Could Lee Patterson's passing suggestion about the role of Jacob Burckhardt be a fruitful line of enquiry into the possible role of such antecedents? He recalls Burckhardt's well-known argument that in the Middle Ages, unlike the Renaissance, 'man was conscious of himself only as a member of a race, people, party, family or corporation – only through some general category'. He sees Burckhardt's views as shaping modern thinking about 'individualism' even among those critics who think they 'demolish Burckhardtian humanism'.[65] Certainly radical critics and New Historicists all reject Burckhardt's celebration of the Renaissance as giving 'the highest development to individuality' and bringing out 'the full, whole nature of man' in an individual who, at last, 'recognised himself as such'. They all, in their different ways, subscribe to the contemporary academic truism that the individual is constituted by no more than linguistic and cultural systems, that s/he is never the free, autonomous spirit of romantic individualism, or 'liberal humanism' or 'essentialist humanism'. Yet whatever the challenge to Burckhardt's idealist account of 'Renaissance' subjectivity, his depiction of that against which he seeks to define the specificity of the Renaissance has been silently, unselfconsciously and uncritically assimilated.[66] For in all the radical writers we have been considering the Burckhardtian Middle Ages is an essential part of their version of our history: 'man was conscious of himself only as a member of a race, people, party, family or corporation', a sentence that would fit as cosily into the books by Eagleton, Barker, Belsey, Dollimore or Greenblatt as into the anti-humanist conservative medievalism with which this essay began. These are only preliminary reflections to a history of a history that is yet to be written. Nevertheless it seems significant that Burckhardt's humanist master narrative, as Lee Patterson observed, is reproduced by the critics I have been discussing. And this master narrative, it is worth reiterating, was constructed by early-modern humanists, inventing a 'Middle' or 'Dark Ages' against which, and in terms of which, they could define and legitimise their own commitments.[67]

I will conclude by putting a couple of questions about the strange story I have been recounting, and by offering some very tentative answers – this essay is, as its title conveys, no more than reflections that are in the process of an elaboration which involves its own counter-history of 'the subject'. Certainly the answers I shall offer here are pretty simple-minded, but then truth does not always lie at the bottom of a deep well.

First question: Why should self-styled radical and materialist critics write such idealist accounts of English culture, at least up to the seventeenth century? My first answer, embarrassingly lacking in theoretical or political grandeur, is that they do so because they received their decisive training as literary critics in traditional English Literature departments. This training tends to encourage concentration on a narrow range of certain kinds of text, canonised 'literary' texts, and a readiness to construct large-scale cultural generalisations on the basis of a few prescriptive texts. Perhaps the roles of the 'canon', of Arnold, Eliot and Leavis, of the institutions that produced the radical critics, are more important than these critics have noticed, guiding their projects at a level other than that of overt political stance and rhetoric. My second answer is that writing such a version of criticism and cultural history is far less laborious than attempting a version which would commit itself to exploring the relations between different versions of the self, different genres, different communities, different ideologies, different class and gender experiences in the later Middle Ages – an essential task *if* someone wishes to write a '*history* of the subject' in which it is claimed and shown just how the Shakespearean moment and its texts represent a major cultural transition in this domain. (After all, nobody is obliged to write, or claim to write, 'history' – the critics could just write about 'the subject' in *Hamlet* . . . or in any other texts. They could, easily, jettison all diachronic claims: why don't they?) My third answer is less obvious: I suggest that these critics display a marked lack of interest in Christian traditions, Christian practices and Christian institutions, and that in response to medieval and early-modern culture the thoroughly secular commitments of their approach have, ironically, contributed to the idealism that marks their treatment of the Middle Ages. One simply cannot write the history of the subject in a culture where Christian beliefs and practices are pervasive without taking Christianity extremely seriously.

Second question: Why should these radical critics choose this particular version of the English Middle Ages against which to set their account of Shakespeare and the development of 'the bourgeois subject' and Western subjectivity? My first answer here is that they are driven by the pressures in their choice of narrative. If someone wants, for whatever reason, to tell a linear, developmental story it is pleasurable to have a clear beginning. If someone wants to tell a linear story about the development of the 'subject' ('liberal', 'humanist', 'bourgeois' or whatever) it will seem necessary to begin with a transition from the 'other', the totally alien or different in which this entity definitely did not exist, indeed against which the entity in question can be defined. My second answer is even more simple. It is the suggestion that these radical literary critics are the victims of an institutionally fostered ignorance. Trained as Literary Critics, they have been trained and mostly work in departments which still compartmentalise our discipline, whatever the claims to subvert received boundaries and canons: this means that a specialist in Shakespeare and early-modern English literature simply does not read the texts of fourteenth- and fifteenth-century England – the 'literary' texts, the texts around the institution of penance and confession, the mystical texts, the political texts – let alone study them in relation to recent social, economic and political work being done on the period. So deeply ingrained is this compartmentalisation that even when literary critics specialising in the early-modern period and in literary theory want to tell a story that *depends* on claims about the period 1300–1600 they cannot erode its effects. One of the effects of this ignorance is to facilitate the belief that 'everything suddenly changed' during the period of one's own specialisation.[68] The 'history of the subject' written by the radical critics in Britain and the New Historicists in the USA may be more crudely determined by inadequacies in 'the history of the subject' we call English Literary Criticism than the critics have noticed. The problem now is how to write a history of the subject which is conscious of the distorting limitations of our training and is able to utilise whatever strengths it may have (in the face of a certain vulgar positivism and treatment of texts as transparent which is still not uncommon in historical studies). Writing this history will certainly need such self-consciousness if it is to struggle against the limitations of our training and current compartmentalisations. My own view, at the moment, however, is that the enterprise in its present form may be misconceived. It seems to be driven by an *a priori* commitment to a simple linear master narrative which, in its conventional literary critical forms, is unwarranted. We need to write a 'history' which does not know, before the exploratory work has been done, that there was a totally new and far greater sense of 'interiority' in 1600 than in 1380 or 1400 . . . we need to suspend the master narrative of Dark Ages to Renaissance or of feudalism to capitalism. What if subjectivity is more bound into a microhistory that is less linear than the master narrative determining the story told by Burckhardt, Robertson, Barker, Belsey, Dollimore, Greenblatt and Eagleton and, it must be acknowledged, suggested too by Foucault? What if, in England, there is a greater preoccupation with 'interiority', and with the divided self in the 1380s than in 1415–20? If this turned out to be so, why? How would the discovery have been established and with what consequences for our understanding of the different 'levels' in a social formation and its institutions as they effect 'subjects'? We cannot even begin to address such basic questions until we question, put in suspension, the master narratives shaping the claims of the critics considered in this essay and until we commit ourselves to the kind of detailed historical and cross-generic work which radical literary critics have, so far, been rather reluctant to undertake. I hope that the present book will encourage such commitment. In conclusion, I should observe that bracketing the current master narratives I have mentioned does not entail any sympathy with those who conflate arguments for writing smaller, less linear narratives with the abandonment of all traditional attempts to distinguish truth from falsity, historical reality from fiction, justice from injustice and good from evil, abandonments that Terry Eagleton himself has recently criticised with admirable clarity.[69]

Notes

1. St Augustine, *Confessions*, with the English translation by W. Watts, ed. W. H. D. Rouse, 2 vols, Cambridge MA: Harvard University Press, 1989, VII. 10.

2. Brian Stock, *Listening for the Text: On the uses of the past*, Baltimore MD: Johns Hopkins University Press, 1990.

3. The main 'radical' works I shall address directly in this essay are as follows: F. Barker, *The Tremulous Private Body: Essays on subjection*, London: Methuen, 1984; C. Belsey, *The Subject of Tragedy*, London: Methuen, 1985; J. Dollimore, *Radical Tragedy*, Brighton: Harvester, 1984 – a second edition with a new preface appeared in 1989: see pp. xxvii–lvii; T. Eagleton, *Shakespeare*, Oxford: Basil Blackwell, 1986; S. Greenblatt, *Renaissance Self-Fashioning*, Chicago IL: Chicago University Press, 1980 and *Shakespearean Negotiations*, Los Angeles: California University Press, 1988. There has been some very impressive reflection on New Historicism: I have found the following especially helpful and they all include relevant bibliographies: Jean Howard, 'The new historicism in Renaissance studies', *English Literary Renaissance* , **16**, 1986, 13–43; the

essays by Walter Cohen and Don Wayne in Jean Howard and Marion O'Connor, eds, *Shakespeare Reproduced*, London: Methuen, 1987; Lee Patterson, *Negotiating the Past*, Madison WI: Wisconsin University Press, 1987, pp. 57–74; Carol Neely, 'Constructing the subject', *ELR*, **18**, 1988, 5–18; and the collection of essays edited by H. A. Veeser, *The New Historicism*, London: Routledge, 1989. The canonisation of the history of the subject I address makes dismissals such as those by Richard Levin less than satisfactory: 'incredible . . . it should be obvious that this . . . [history] is an absurd fiction'. It is obviously not obvious! See 'Bashing the bourgeois subject', *Textual Practice*, **3**, 1989, 76–86, here p. 78. Catherine Belsey's 'Reply' follows. See too the rehearsal of this debate in *New Literary History*, **21**, 1990, in essays by Levin (433–47), Belsey (449–56), Goldberg (457–62) and Levin again (463–70).

4. D. W. Robertson, A *Preface to Chaucer*, Princeton NJ: Princeton University Press, 1962, p. 51; see too his *Essays in Medieval Culture*, Princeton NJ: Princeton University Press, 1980. A recent example of this school's work is P. Olson, *The Canterbury Tales and the Good Society*, Princeton NJ: Princeton University Press, 1986.

5. Robertson, *Preface*, pp. 265, 501–2.

6. D. Pearsall, 'Chaucer's poetry and its modern commentators', Chapter 7 in *Medieval Literature*, ed. D. Aers, Hassocks: Harvester, 1986, pp. 138–9.

7. L. Patterson, *Negotiating the Past*, Madison WI: Wisconsin University Press, 1876, Chapter 1.

8. F. Lentricchia, *Criticism and Social Change*, Chicago IL: Chicago University Press, 1983, p. 128.

9. B. Stock, *The Implications of Literacy*, Princeton NJ: Princeton University Press, 1983, p. 85.

10. I have addressed this, in chapters I draw on here; *Community, Gender and Individual Identity . . . 1360–1430*, London: Routledge, 1988, Introduction, Chapters 1 and 2: I identified some of the radical critics addressed here on pp. 17, 184.

11. The quotation is from J. L. Bolton, *The Medieval English Economy 1150–1500*, London: Dent, 1980, p. 137; see n. 35 and 37 on p. 183 in Aers, *Community*.

12. E. Miller and J. Hatcher, *Medieval England: Rural society and economic change, 1086–1348*, Harlow: Longman, 1978; M. M. Postan, *Medieval Economy and Society*, Harmondsworth: Pelican, 1986 and his *Essays on Medieval Agriculture*, Cambridge: Cambridge University Press, 1973; R. Hilton, *The English Peasantry in the Later Middle Ages*, Oxford: Oxford University Press, 1975, Chapter 3 and his *Class Conflict and the Crisis of Feudalism*, London: Hambledon, 1985, Chapter 15; C. Dyer, *Standards of Living in the Later Middle Ages*, Cambridge: Cambridge University Press, 1989, a major and wide-ranging study – which its title rather conceals.

13. On this, see especially Sylvia Thrupp, *The Merchant Class of Medieval London*, Chicago IL: Chicago University Press, 1948; also C. Phythian-Adams, *Desolation of a City: Coventry and the urban crisis of the late Middle Ages*, Cambridge: Cambridge University Press, 1979.

14. Letter to author, 1986; see too Aers, *Chaucer*, Hassocks: Harvester, 1986, Chapter 2.

15. For the utterly conventional approach in a massive critical output gestured at in this paragraph see Robertson, *Preface, passim,* and Patterson's comments in *Negotiations,* pp. 33–4 (quoting from p. 33 in this para.); on *Troilus and Criseyde,* for example, R. O. Payne, *The Key of Remembrance,* New Haven CT: Yale University Press, 1963, pp. 81, 181–3, 221–2, 226, 233; A. Mizener, 'Character and action in the case of Criseyde', *PMLA,* **54,** 1939, 65–79; R. M. Jordan, *Chaucer and the Shape of Creation,* Cambridge MA: Harvard University Press, 1967, pp. 99–100; D. W. Robertson, 'Chaucerian Tragedy', *English Literary History,* **19,** 1952, 1–37; Criseyde as 'Nature', A. David, *The Strumpet Muse,* Bloomington IN: Indiana University Press, 1976, pp. 34–5. For a recent restatement of Eliot's position, see R. Wellek, 'The new critics', *Critical Inquiry,* **4,** 1978, 616; and for a recent version of the Middle Ages as a virtually homogeneous 'status society', J. B. Allen, *The Ethical Poetic of the Middle Ages,* Toronto: Toronto University Press, 1982, p. 305; similarly p. 4.
16. Patterson, 'On the margin: Postmodernism, ironic history and medieval studies', *Speculum,* **65,** 1990, 87–108, here 99–100.
17. A. C. Spearing, *Readings in Medieval Poetry,* Cambridge: Cambridge University Press, 1987, p. 12 (quoting Caroline Bynum's *Jesus as Mother*): see, too, *Readings,* pp. 21–3, 31, 47, 65, 80–2, 94, 96, 98–102, 121, 203.
18. St Augustine, *Confessions,* see, *seriatim,* III.1; IV.4 (see too IV.6 and 10); IX.12; X.30; VIII.5.
19. *Ibid., seriatim*: IV.12; V.2; VII.10 (tr. slightly adjusted); X.6.
20. Especially helpful here has been P. Courcelle, *Connais-toi toi-même,* Paris: Etudes Augustiniennes, 1974, especially pp. 149–62.
21. Charles Taylor, *Sources of the Self: The making of the modern identity,* Cambridge: Cambridge University Press, 1989, p. 131. This is a book that anyone concerned with the issues addressed in this essay will need to study. And despite its Burckhardtian assumptions, an awareness of the two-volume work of Georg Misch on autobiography up to St Augustine and Boethius would be helpful to many of those criticised in the present essay: *Geschichte der Autobiographie,* 1907, translated by E. W. Dickes and G. Misch, *A History of Autobiography in Antiquity,* 1949 and 1950, 2 vols, reprinted Westport CT: Greenwood Press, 1973.
22. Helpful commentary in C. Trinkaus, *In Our Image and Likeness,* 2 vols, London: Constable 1970, Volume I, Chapter 1; and on Salutati, Chapter 2.
23. Walter Hilton, *The Scale of Perfection,* ed. E. Underhill, London: Watkins, 1923, *seriatim,* I.42, 47, 48, 49. Relevant here is J. P. H. Clark, 'Augustine, Anselm and Walter Hilton', pp. 102–26 in *The Mystical Tradition in England,* ed. M. Glasscoe, Exeter: Exeter University Press, 1982.
24. On the way this dichotomy is a distinct invention of St Augustine, see Taylor, *Sources of the Self,* Chapters 5–7. Perhaps Taylor slightly distorts the story he tells by not considering St Paul's contribution?
25. *Piers Plowman: The B version,* ed. G. Kane and E. Donaldson, London: Athlone, 1988, V.605–7, modernising the letters: references hereafter in text. On this image see Elizabeth Salter, *Piers Plowman,* Oxford: Basil Blackwell, 1962, p. 32 and especially her earlier 'Piers Plowman and the pilgrimage to truth', *Essays and Studies,* **11,** 1958, 1–16, which makes the links with Hilton.

26. For a serious attempt to engage with Langland's treatment of the subject, see David Lawton's essay in *The Yearbook of Langland Studies*, 1, 1987, 1–30. This should prove a fruitful study.

27. *Heresy Trials in the Diocese of Norwich 1428–31*, ed. N. P. Tanner, Camden Series, Vol. 20, London, 1977, p. 179. See too A. Hudson, *The Premature Reformation*, Oxford: Oxford University Press, 1988, pp. 450–1 and, on the twelfth century, B. Stock, *Implications of Literacy*, Princeton NJ: Princeton University Press, 1983, pp. 88–151.

28. Tanner, *Norwich Heresy Trials*, p. 140.

29. Quote in Hudson, *Reformation*, p. 149 (a 1499 case).

30. See especially, on *Parson's Tale*, S. Wenzel, 'The sources of Chaucer's seven deadly sins', *Traditio*, 30, 1974, 351–78; and L. Patterson, 'The Parson's Tale and the setting of *The Canterbury Tales*', *Traditio*, 34, 1978, 331–80; S. Knight, *Chaucer*, Oxford: Basil Blackwell, 1986, pp. 153–6; Derek Pearsall, *The Canterbury Tales*, London: Allen & Unwin, 1985, pp. 228–93; and on the tradition, indispensable is T. N. Tentler, *Sin and Confession on the Eve of the Reformation*, Princeton NJ: Princeton University Press, 1977, here especially Part One. For some aspects of earlier penitentials, P. J. Payer, *Sex and the Penitentials: The development of a sexual code 550–1150*, Toronto: Toronto University Press, 1984.

31. The phrase comes from J. Van Engen, 'The Christian Middle Ages as a historical problem', *American Historical Review*, 91, 1986, 519–52, here p. 543. See too Tentler's work in the previous footnote.

32. Van Engen, 'Christian Middle Ages', n. 29, p. 544. Compare M. Foucault, *The History of Sexuality* (*La Volonté de savoir*), tr. R. Hurley, Harmondsworth: Penguin, 1981, pp. 18, 58–67.

33. *Parson's Tale*, 291–315, in *The Works of Geoffrey Chaucer*, ed. F. N. Robinson, second edn, Oxford: Oxford University Press, 1957.

34. Patterson, 'On the margin'; for a few relevant recent studies of this topic in medieval writings, see M. Zink, *La subjectivité littéraire*, Paris: Presses Universitaires de France 1985; K. Brownlee, *Poetic Identity in Guillaume de Machant*, Madison WI: Wisconsin University Press, 1984; Sarah Kay, *Subjectivity in Troubadour Poetry*, Cambridge: Cambridge University Press, 1990; M. Leicester, *The Disenchanted Self*, Berkeley CA: California University Press, 1990.

35. On the expulsion of the 'ontic logos' in relation to the subject of this essay, see Taylor, *Sources of the Self*.

36. Francis Barker, *The Tremulous Private Body*, London: Methuen, 1984; quotations from this book in the following discussion come from *seriatim*, pp. 41, 15, 31, 36, 35, 36 ('begins to speak' – see similar assertions on pp. 35, 36, 41). On Barker, see too Patterson, 'On the margin', 97–8 and Levin, 'Bashing', 79–80.

37. One may well wonder what such critics think medieval traditions made of characteristic New Testament directions to inward reflection in texts such as Luke 11.39; Luke 17.20–1; Matthew 9.3–4; Matthew 15.8, 18–20; not to mention the pervasive dialectic of inner and outer, of letter and spirit and of the divided will in St Paul's writings.

38. Jonathan Dollimore, *Radical Tragedy*, Hassocks: Harvester, 1984, Chapter 16 and Chapter 10. Dollimore is, of course, a self-styled 'cultural materialist': see

Political Shakespeare, ed. Dollimore and Sinfield, Manchester: Manchester University Press, 1985.

39. Dollimore, *Radical Tragedy*, pp. 153, 155–6; second edn, Hassocks: Harvester, 1989, p. xxxi.
40. *Ibid.*, pp. 155–6: the first phrase is from Ullmann's *Individual and Society*.
41. Levy, 'Bashing', 77, also notes and criticises this, as does Patterson, 'On the margin', 96.
42. C. Belsey, *The Subject of Tragedy*, London: Methuen, 1985, pp. ix, 7–8, 41.
43. *Ibid.*, p. 42: it is rather bizarre to transform the stoic Horatio's pious wishes into an event; as it is to assert that the belief in God's control of history and judgement of human life could be taken as a vestige of an 'older cosmos': this seriously misrepresents the religion of seventeenth-century Protestants, including the religion of those who made the seventeenth-century 'revolutions' (p. 8).
44. Peter Erickson, *Patriarchal Structures in Shakespeare's Drama*, Berkeley CA: California University Press, 1985, p. 70, explicitly and pp. 69–80 *passim*.
45. Belsey, *The Subject*, pp. 199, 8.
46. *Ibid.*, pp. 14–16, 19–23.
47. *Ibid.*, p. 18. Of course, as Richard Levin has observed, Belsey's account of the pre-seventeenth-century human being is not the same as Barker's: 'Bashing', 76–7.
48. *Ibid.*, p. 9.
49. *Ibid.*, pp. 23, 26.
50. *Ibid.*, pp. 33–4, 35.
51. C. Belsey, *John Milton*, Oxford: Basil Blackwell, 1988, pp. 85–6: see Lee Patterson, 'On the margin', 96.
52. See works cited in n. 3 and especially the collection edited by Veeser, *The New Historicism*.
53. On this see H. Felperin, *The Uses of the Canon*, Oxford: Oxford University Press, 1990, pp. 154–5: the whole chapter is relevant here.
54. Howard, 'The New Historicism', *English Literary Renaissance*, 16, 1986, 13–43, here 16.
55. See both Greenblatt's *Renaissance Self-Fashioning*, Chicago IL: Chicago University Press, 1980, and his still more explicitly Foucauldian reading of power in 'Invisible bullets', pp. 18–47 in *Political Shakespeare*, ed. J. Dollimore and A. Sinfield, Manchester: Manchester University Press, 1985. The use of Foucault by New Historicists seems to have been extremely uncritical: compare the characteristically sympathetic but profoundly critical analysis by Charles Taylor, 'Foucault on freedom and truth', Chapter 6 in his *Philosophy and the Human Sciences*, Cambridge: Cambridge University Press, 1985, and Lentricchia's very different critique, 'Foucault's a New Historicism?', Chapter 16 in *The New Historicism*, ed. H. A. Veeser, London: Routledge, 1989. For a cultural materialist studying an Elizabethan text and including arguments against the New Historicist's Foucault: A. Sinfield, 'Power and ideology . . . *Arcadia*', *English Literary History*, 52, 1986, 259–77.
56. Greenblatt, *Self-Fashioning*, pp. 1–2. It is striking that in the next moment he invokes Spenser in support of his claim without considering the role of St Augustine in the formation of Spenser's Protestantism.

57. Patterson, 'On the margin', 99. I have noticed a passing allusion to 'mysteries and moralities' in *Shakespearian Negotiations*, Berkeley CA: California University Press, 1988, p. 133, but Patterson's observation seems right.

58. Stock, *Listening for the Text*, p. 68.

59. See the reflections in A. C. Spearing, *Medieval to Renaissance in English Poetry*, Cambridge: Cambridge University Press, 1985, pp. 1–22.

60. T. Eagleton, *Shakespeare*, Oxford: Basil Blackwell, 1986, *seriatim*, pp. 65–6, 74–5, 4, 73.

61. The essential work here remains Mervyn James, *English Politics and the Concept of Honour*, Past and Present Society, 1978: for example, of its relevance to the study of medieval writings see Aers, *Community*, Chapter 4 and S. Knight, *Chaucer*, p. 34.

62. Eagleton, *Shakespeare*, p. 98; see too p. 100.

63. For example, M. C. Howell, *Women, Production and Patriarchy in Late Medieval Cities*, Chicago IL: Chicago University Press, 1986; M. K. McIntosh, *Autonomy and Community: The royal manor of Havering*, Cambridge: Cambridge University Press, 1986, pp. 136, 138, 152–66; S. Thrupp, *The Merchant Class of Medieval London*, Chicago IL: Chicago University Press, 1948; R. Bird, *The Turbulent London of Richard II*, London: Longman, 1949. It seems to me, however, that Eagleton's more recent work, *The Ideology of the Aesthetic*, Oxford: Basil Blackwell, 1990, implies criticism of some of the assimilation of post-structuralism in his own reading of Shakespeare and early-modern culture – see the admirable final chapter, 'From the *polis* to postmodernism'.

64. Levin, 'Bashing', 82–4.

65. Patterson, 'On the margin', 95; see J. Burckhardt, *The Civilization of the Renaissance in Italy*, London: Phaidon, 1965, p. 81.

66. Burckhardt quoted and challenged in Dollimore, *Radical Tragedy*, p. 175; see too S. Greenblatt, *Renaissance Self-Fashioning*, Chicago: Chicago University Press, 1980, pp. 1–2, 161–2, and in *Reconstructing Individualism*, ed. T. C. Heller *et al.*, Stanford CA: Stanford University Press, 1986, pp. 34–5.

67. See references in n. 58 and 59 above; also Patterson, 'On the margin'.

68. A. Macfarlane, *The Culture of Capitalism*, Oxford: Basil Blackwell, 1987, pp. 158–9: this chapter is extremely relevant here.

69. *The Ideology of the Aesthetic*, pp. 411–12; see pp. 394–401.

Notes on Contributors

David Aers is a Professor of English Literature at the University of East Anglia. His most recent book is *Community, Gender, and Individual Identity . . . 1360–1430*, London: Routledge, 1988. He is currently writing on literature, Christianity and history, 1360–1600.

Sarah Beckwith is Assistant Professor in the Department of English at Duke University. She has just completed a book entitled *Christ's Body: Symbol and social vision in late medieval English culture*, London: Routledge, 1992, and is currently working on late-medieval drama.

Judith M. Bennett is a Professor of History at the University of North Carolina. She is the author of *Women in the Medieval English Countryside*, Oxford: Oxford University Press, 1987, and is currently completing a study of women in the English brewing industry, 1200–1700.

Lee Patterson is a Professor of English at Duke University. He is the author of *Negotiating the Past: The historical understanding of medieval literature*, Madison WI: University of Wisconsin Press, 1987 and *Chaucer and the Subject of History*, Madison WI: University of Wisconsin Press, 1991. He is currently working on the idea of the modern in the late Middle Ages.

Miri Rubin is a Tutor in History at Pembroke College, Oxford. Her most recent book is *Corpus Christi: The eucharist in late medieval culture*, Cambridge: Cambridge University Press, 1991. She is currently writing a book on the emergence of the myth of host desecration.

Peter Womack is a Lecturer in English at the University of East Anglia. His most recent book is *Improvement and Romance: Constructing the myth of the Highlands*, London: Macmillan, 1989. He is now writing a book on the cultural history of English drama.

Index

Abram, Annie, 151
absolutism, 23, 28–9, 138
Actes and Monuments (Foxe), 105, 116
Act of Uniformity, 105
actors
  in Chorus, 91–2, 95–6, 127
  commercial theatre, 108, 110, 115
  commons, 134–5
  dialogic drama, 80–1
  stage devils, 101, 131–4
  and urban community, 99–100, 103
Aers, David, 148
Agincourt, 94, 95
agitational theatre, 4, 116–26
allegory, 14, 179
alliteration, 19–20, 68–9
Alnwick, Bishop, 72
Amalarius of Metz, 76
amnesia, 179–81, 182
Anderson, Benedict, 93–4
Anelida and Arcite (Chaucer), 15
animal-adoration, 56–7
anti-humanism, 178, 181–2, 188, 195
anti-populism, 130–1
anti-sacramentarianism, 67
anti-Semitism, 73, 75
anti-theatricalism, 77
apprenticeships (women's), 159, 160
Aquinas, St Thomas, 1
Arcadia (Sidney), 130–1

Ariès, Philippe, 148
Aristotle, 1, 46
army (representation of), 94
Art de dictier (Deschamps), 14
Artorius (merchant), 68–72
Attreed, Lorraine, 148
audience
  anti-populism, 130–1
  of commercial theatre, 108–9, 113–14
  crowds, 93, 99, 103, 109
  imaginary puissance, 91–6
  urban, 99–100, 103
Augustine of Hippo, St, 81, 182–3
Augustinian tradition, 45, 182–6

Bailly, Harry, 24
Bakhtin, Mikhail, 66, 80
Bale, John, 4, 97, 116–19, 121, 137
Balow, William, 67
banns, 107
Barker, Francis, 186–9, 195, 197
Barron, Caroline, 150–1, 163
Beauchamp, John, 16–17
Belle dame sans merci, La, 13, 27
Belsey, Catherine, 149, 189–90, 195, 197
Bennett, Judith, M., 149, 158, 194
Berengar of Tours, 45–6
Beveridge, William, 161
Bible, 104, 117, 178, 183